TOTAL BASIC SKILLS
Grade 3

Chameleon Press

Rainforest Recipes

Rainforest Recipes

D1224101

School Specialty
Children's Publishing

Copyright © 2004 by School Specialty Children's Publishing. Published by American Education Publishing, an imprint of School Specialty Children's Publishing, a member of the School Specialty Family.

Send all inquiries to:
School Specialty Children's Publishing
8720 Orion Place
Columbus, OH 43240-2111

ISBN 0-7696-3643-8

1 2 3 4 5 6 7 8 9 10 VHJ 09 08 07 06 05 04

Table of Contents

READING

Crocodile
Tears
& other
stories

Phonics

Some words are more difficult to read because they have one or more silent letters. Many words you already know are like this.

Examples: wrong and **night**.

Directions: Circle the silent letters in each word. The first one is done for you.

(w)rong	answer	autumn	whole
knife	hour	wrap	comb
sigh	straight	knee	known
lamb	taught	scent	daughter
whistle	wrote	knew	crumb

Directions: Draw a line between the rhyming words. The first one is done for you.

knew	try
sees	bowl
taut	stone
wrote	true
comb	song
straight	trees
sigh	home
known	great
wrong	caught
whole	boat

Phonics

Sometimes letters make sounds you don't expect. Two consonants can work together to make the sound of one consonant. The **f** sound can be made by **ph**, as in the word **elephant**. The consonants **gh** are most often silent, as in the words **night** and **though**. But they also can make the **f** sound as in the word **laugh**.

Directions: Circle the letters that make the **f** sound. Write the correct word from the box to complete each sentence.

ele(ph)ant	cough	laugh	telephone	phonics
dolphins	enough	tough	alphabet	rough

1. The **dolphins** were playing in the sea.

2. Did you have _____ time to do your homework?

3. A cold can make you _____ and sneeze.

4. The _____ ate peanuts with his trunk.

5. The road to my school is _____ and bumpy.

6. You had a _____ call this morning.

7. The _____ meat was hard to chew.

8. Studying _____ will help you read better.

9. The _____ has 26 letters in it.

10. We began to _____ when the clowns came in.

Phonics

There are several consonants that make the **k** sound: **c** when followed by a, o or u as in **cow** or **cup**; the letter **k** as in **milk**; the letters **ch** as in **Christmas** and **ck** as in **black**.

Directions: Read the following words. Circle the letters that make the **k** sound. The first one is done for you.

a(ch)e	school	market	comb
camera	deck	darkness	Christmas
necklace	doctor	stomach	crack
nickel	skin	thick	escape

Directions: Use your own words to finish the following sentences. Use words with the **k** sound.

1. If I had a nickel, I would _____.

2. My doctor is very _____.

3. We bought ripe, juicy tomatoes at the _____.

4. If I had a camera now,
   I would take a picture of _____.

5. When my stomach aches, _____.

Phonics

In some word "families," the vowels have a long sound when you would expect them to have a short sound. For example, the **i** has a short sound in **chill**, but a long sound in **child**. The **o** has a short sound in **cost**, but a long sound in **most**.

Directions: Read the words in the word box below. Write the words that have a long vowel sound under the word **LONG**, and the words that have a short vowel sound under the word **SHORT**. (Remember, a long vowel says its name—like **a** in **ate**.)

old	odd	gosh	gold	sold	soft	toast	frost	lost	most
doll	roll	bone	done	kin	mill	mild	wild	blink	blind

LONG

bone _____ _____

_____ _____

_____ _____

_____ _____

SHORT

doll _____ _____

_____ _____

_____ _____

_____ _____

Syllables

All words can be divided into **syllables**. Syllables are word parts which have one vowel sound in each part.

Directions: Draw a line between the syllable part and write the word on the correct line below. The first one is done for you.

lit|tle	bumblebee	pillow
truck	dazzle	dog
pencil	flag	angelic
rejoicing	ant	telephone

1 SYLLABLE

2 SYLLABLES

3 SYLLABLES

little

_____   _____   _____

_____   _____   _____

_____   _____   _____

_____   _____   _____

Syllables

When the letters **le** come at the end of a word, they sometimes have the sound of **ul**, as in raffle.

Directions: Draw a line to match the syllables so they make words. The first one is done for you.

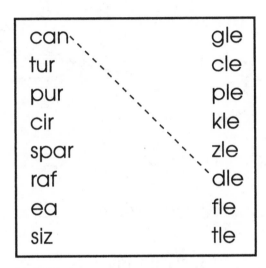

can	gle
tur	cle
pur	ple
cir	kle
spar	zle
raf	dle
ea	fle
siz	tle

Directions: Use the words you made to complete the sentences. One is done for you.

1. Will you buy a ticket for our school raffle?

2. The _____ pulled his head into his shell.

3. We could hear the bacon _____ in the pan.

4. The baby had one _____ on her birthday cake.

5. My favorite color is _____.

6. Look at that diamond _____!

7. The bald _____ is our national bird.

8. Draw a _____ around the correct answer.

Compound Words

A compound word is two small words put together to make one new word. Compound words are usually divided into syllables between the two words.

Directions: Read the words. Then divide them into syllables. The first one is done for you.

1. playground   play   ground
2. sailboat _____
3. doghouse _____
4. dishpan _____
5. pigpen _____
6. outdoors _____
7. beehive _____
8. airplane _____
9. cardboard _____
10. nickname _____

11. hilltop _____
12. broomstick _____
13. sunburn _____
14. oatmeal _____
15. campfire _____
16. somewhere _____
17. starfish _____
18. birthday _____
19. sidewalk _____
20. seashore _____

Compound Words

Directions: Read the compound words in the word box. Then use them to answer the questions. The first one is done for you.

sailboat	blueberry	bookcase	tablecloth	beehive
dishpan	pigpen	classroom	playground	bedtime
broomstick	treetop	fireplace	newspaper	sunburn

Which compound word means . . .

1. a case for books?   _____bookcase_____

2. a berry that is blue?

3. a hive for bees?

4. a place for fires?

5. a pen for pigs?

6. a room for a class?

7. a pan for dishes?

8. a boat to sail?

9. a paper for news?

10. a burn from the sun?

11. the top of a tree?

12. a stick for a broom?

13. the time to go to bed?

14. a cloth for the table?

15. ground to play on?

Name _____

Transportation Vocabulary

Directions: Unscramble the words to spell the names of kinds of transportation. The first one is done for you.

behelwworar   wheel <u>b</u> <u>a</u> <u>r</u> <u>r</u> <u>o</u> w

anirt   t __ __ __ n

moobattor   moto __ __ __ __ t

crattor   t __ __ c __ __ __ __

ceicbly   b __ __ __ __ __ e

tocker   r __ __ __ __ t

etobimuloa   aut __ __ __ __ __ __ e

rilanape   a __ __ p __ __ __ e

Directions: Use a word from above to complete each sentence.

1. My mother uses a _____ to move dirt to her garden.

2. The _____ blasted the spaceship off the launching pad.

3. We flew on an _____ to visit my aunt in Florida.

4. My grandfather drives a very old _____.

5. We borrowed Fred's _____ to go water skiing.

6. You should always look both ways when crossing a

   _____ track.

7. I hope I get a new _____ for my birthday.

Name _____

Space Vocabulary

Directions: Unscramble each word. Use the numbers below the letters to tell you what order they belong in. Write the word by its definition.

i r t b o
4 2 5 3 1

u t o n c w d n o
3 5 7 9 1 8 6 4 2

u l e f
2 4 3 1

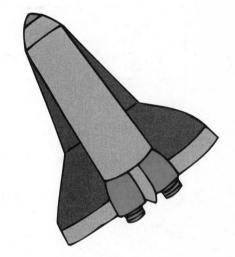

a t s r a t n o u
7 9 2 4 1 3 6 5 8

t e h t s u l
5 7 2 4 1 3 6

A member of the team that flies a spaceship. _____

A rocket-powered spaceship that travels between Earth and space. _____

The material, such as gas, used for power. _____

The seconds just before take-off. _____

The path of a spaceship as it goes around Earth. _____

Name _____

Weather Vocabulary

Directions: Use the weather words in the box to complete the sentences.

sunny	temperature	foggy	puddles	rainy
windy	rainbow	cloudy	lightning	snowy

1. My friends and I love _____ days, because we can have snowball fights!

2. On _____ days, we like to stay indoors and play board games.

3. Today was hot and _____ , so we went to the beach.

4. We didn't see the sun at all yesterday. It was _____ all day.

5. _____ weather is perfect for flying kites.

6. It was so _____ , Mom had to use the headlights in the car so we wouldn't get lost.

7. While it was still raining, the sun began to shine and created a beautiful _____ .

8. We like to jump in the _____ after it rains.

9. _____ flashed across the sky during the thunderstorm.

10. The _____ outside was so low, we needed to wear hats, mittens and scarves.

Name _____

Vocabulary Word Lists

Directions: Complete the vocabulary word lists. Be creative!

Drinks
chocolate milk

Lights
flashlight

Pets
dogs

School Supplies
paper

What other things can you think of to list?

_____

Name _____

Sequencing

Directions: Fill in the blank spaces with what comes next in the series. The first one is done for you.

year	Wednesday	day	sixth	large
twenty	February	night	seventeen	mile
paragraph	winter	ocean		

1. Sunday, Monday, Tuesday, _____ <u>Wednesday</u> _____

2. third, fourth, fifth, _____

3. November, December, January, _____

4. tiny, small, medium, _____

5. fourteen, fifteen, sixteen, _____

6. morning, afternoon, evening, _____

7. inch, foot, yard, _____

8. day, week, month, _____

9. spring, summer, autumn, _____

10. five, ten, fifteen, _____

11. letter, word, sentence, _____

12. second, minute, hour, _____

13. stream, lake, river, _____

Sequencing

When words are in a certain order, they are in sequence.

Directions: Complete each sequence using a word from the box. There are extra words in the box. The first one has been done for you.

below	three	fifteen	December	twenty	above
after	go	third	hour	March	yard

1. January, February, __March__

2. before, during, _____

3. over, on, _____

4. come, stay, _____

5. second, minute, _____

6. first, second, _____

7. five, ten, _____

8. inch, foot, _____

Sequencing

Directions: Read each story. Circle the phrase that tells what happened before.

1. Beth is very happy now that she has someone to play with. She hopes that her new sister will grow up quickly!

   A few days ago . . .

   Beth was sick.

   Beth's mother had a baby.

   Beth got a new puppy.

2. Sara tried to mend the tear. She used a needle and thread to sew up the hole.

   While playing, Sara had . . .

   broken her bicycle.

   lost her watch.

   torn her shirt.

3. The movers took John's bike off the truck and put it in the garage. Next, they moved his bed into his new bedroom.

   John's family . . .

   bought a new house.

   went on vacation.

   bought a new truck.

4. Katie picked out a book about dinosaurs. Jim, who likes sports, chose two books about baseball.

   Katie and Jim . . .

   went to the library.

   went to the playground.

   went to the grocery.

Name _____

Sequencing

Directions: Number these sentences from 1 to 5 to show the correct order of the story.

Building a Treehouse

_____ They had a beautiful treehouse!

_____ They got wood and nails.

__1__ Jay and Lisa planned to build a treehouse.

_____ Now, they like to eat lunch in their treehouse.

_____ Lisa and Jay worked in the backyard for three days building the treehouse.

A School Play

_____ Everyone clapped when the curtain closed.

_____ The girl who played Snow White came onto the stage.

_____ All the other school children went to the gym to see the play.

_____ The stage curtain opened.

__1__ The third grade was going to put on a play about Snow White.

Name _____

Following Directions

Directions: Learning to follow directions is very important. Use the map to find your way to different houses.

1. Color the start house yellow.
2. Go north 2 houses, and east two houses.
3. Go north 2 houses, and west 4 houses.
4. Color the house green.

5. Start at the yellow house.
6. Go east 1 house, and north 3 houses.
7. Go west 3 houses, and south 3 houses.
8. Color the house blue.

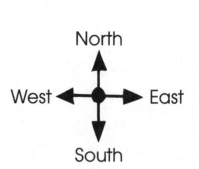

Following Directions

Directions: Read each sentence and do what it says to do.

1. Count the syllables in each word. Write the number on the line by the word.
2. Draw a line between the two words in each compound word.
3. Draw a circle around each name of a month.
4. Draw a box around each food word.
5. Draw an **X** on each noise word.
6. Draw a line under each day of the week.
7. Write the three words from the list you did not use. Draw a picture of each of those words.

_____ April	_____ vegetable	_____ tablecloth
_____ bang	_____ June	_____ meat
_____ sidewalk	_____ Saturday	_____ crash
_____ astronaut	_____ March	_____ jingle
_____ moon	_____ cardboard	_____ rocket
_____ Friday	_____ fruit	_____ Monday

_____   _____   _____

Name _____

Following Directions: A Recipe

Following directions means doing what the directions say to do. Following directions is an important skill to know. When you are trying to find a new place, build a model airplane or use a recipe, you should follow the directions given.

Directions: Read the following recipe. Then answer the questions on page 25.

Fruit Salad

1 fresh pineapple	2 oranges
1 cantaloupe	1 pear
2 bananas	1 cup seedless grapes
1 cup strawberries	lemon juice

- Cut the pineapple into chunks.

- Use a small metal scoop to make balls of the cantaloupe.

- Slice the pear, bananas and strawberries.

- Peel the oranges and divide them into sections. Cut each section into bite-sized pieces.

- Dip each piece of fruit in lemon juice, then combine them in a large bowl.

- Cover and chill.

- Pour a fruit dressing of your choice over the chilled fruit, blend well and serve cold.

  Makes 4 large servings.

Following Directions: A Recipe

Directions: Using the recipe on page 24, answer the questions below.

1. How many bananas does the recipe require? _____

2. Does the recipe explain why you must dip the fruit in lemon juice? _____

   Why would it be important to do this? _____

   _____

3. Would your fruit salad be as good if you did not cut the pineapple or section

   the oranges? Why or why not? _____

   _____

4. Which do you do first?

   (Check one.)

   ____ Pour dressing over the fruit.

   ____ Slice the pear.

   ____ Serve the fruit salad.

5. Which three fruits do you slice?

   _____

   _____

   _____

Name _____

Main Idea

Directions: Read about spiders. Then answer the questions.

Many people think spiders are insects, but they are not. Spiders are the same size as insects, and they look like insects in some ways. But there are three ways to tell a spider from an insect. Insects have six legs, and spiders have eight legs. Insects have antennae, but spiders do not. An insect's body is divided into three parts; a spider's body is divided into only two parts.

1. The main idea of this story is:

Spiders are like insects.
Spiders are like insects in some ways, but they are not insects.

2. What are three ways to tell a spider from an insect?

   1) _____

   2) _____

   3) _____

Circle the correct answer.

3. Spiders are the same size as insects.   True   False

Name _____

Main Idea

Directions: Read about the giant panda. Then answer the questions.

Giant pandas are among the world's favorite animals. They look like big, cuddly stuffed toys. There are not very many pandas left in the world. You may have to travel a long way to see one.

The only place on Earth where pandas live in the wild is in the bamboo forests of the mountains of China. It is hard to see pandas in the forest because they are very shy. They hide among the many bamboo trees. It also is hard to see pandas because there are so few of them. Scientists think there may be less than 1,000 pandas living in the mountains of China.

1. Write a sentence that tells the main idea of this story:

   _____

   _____

2. What are two reasons that it is hard to see pandas in the wild?

   1)_____

   2)_____

3. How many pandas are believed to be living in the mountains of China?

   _____

Main Idea

Directions: Read the story. Then answer the questions.

Because bamboo is very important to pandas, they have special body features that help them eat it. The panda's front foot is like a hand. But, instead of four fingers and a thumb, the panda has five fingers and an extra-long wrist bone. With its special front foot, the panda can easily pick up the stalks of bamboo. It also can hold the bamboo more tightly than it could with a hand like ours.

Bamboo stalks are very tough. The panda uses its big heavy head, large jaws and big back teeth to chew. Pandas eat the bamboo first by peeling the outside of the stalk. They do this by moving their front feet from side to side while holding the stalk in their teeth. Then they bite off a piece of the bamboo and chew it with their strong jaws.

1. Write a sentence that tells the main idea of this story.

_____

2. Instead of four fingers and a thumb, the panda has

_____

3. Bamboo is very tender.   True   False

Main Idea

The **main idea** of a paragraph is the most important point. Often, the first sentence in a paragraph tells the main idea. Most of the other sentences are details that support the main idea. One of the sentences in each paragraph below does not belong in the story.

Directions: Circle the sentence that does not support the main idea.

My family and I went to the zoo last Saturday. It was a beautiful day. The tigers napped in the sun. I guess they liked the warm sunshine as much as we did! Mom and Dad laughed at the baby monkeys. They said the monkeys reminded them of how we act. My sister said the bald eagle reminded her of Dad! I know I'll remember that trip to the zoo for a long time. My cousin is coming to visit the weekend before school starts.

Thanksgiving was a special holiday in our classroom. Each child dressed up as either a Pilgrim or a Native American. My baby sister learned to walk last week. We prepared food for our "feast" on the last day of school before the holiday. We all helped shake the jar full of cream to make real butter. Our teacher cooked applesauce. It smelled delicious!

Name _____

Main Idea: Inventing the Bicycle

Directions: Read about the bicycle. Then answer the questions.

One of the first bicycles was made out of wood. It  bicycle had no pedals. It looked like a horse on wheels. The person who rode the bicycle had to push it with his/her legs. Pedals weren't invented until nearly 50 years later.

Bikes became quite popular in the United States during the 1890s. Streets and parks were filled with people riding them. But those bicycles were still different from the bikes we ride today. They had heavier tires, and the brakes and lights weren't very good. Bicycling is still very popular in the United States. It is a great form of exercise and a handy means of transportation.

1. Who invented the bicycle? _____

2. What did it look like? _____
   _____

3. When did bikes become popular in the United States? _____

4. Where did people ride bikes? _____

5. How is biking good for you? _____

6. How many years have bikes been popular in the United States? _____

Main Idea: Chewing Gum

Directions: Read about chewing gum. Then answer the questions.

Thomas Adams was an American inventor. In 1870, he was looking for a substitute for rubber. He was working with chicle (chick-ul), a substance that comes from a certain kind of tree in Mexico. Years ago, Mexicans chewed chicle. Thomas Adams decided to try it for himself. He liked it so much he started selling it. Twenty years later, he owned a large factory that produced chewing gum.

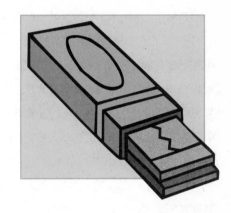

1. Who was the American inventor who started selling chewing gum? _____

2. What was he hoping to invent? _____

3. When did he invent chewing gum? _____

4. Where does the chicle come from? _____

5. Why did Thomas Adams start selling chewing gum? _____

6. How long was it until Adams owned a large factory that produced chewing gum? _____

Name _____

Main Idea: The Peaceful Pueblos

Directions: Read about the Pueblo Native Americans. Then answer the questions.

The Pueblo (pooh-eb-low) Native Americans live in the southwestern United States in New Mexico and Arizona. They have lived there for hundreds of years. The Pueblos have always been peaceful Native Americans. They never started wars. They only fought if attacked first.

The Pueblos love to dance. Even their dances are peaceful. They dance to ask the gods for rain or sunshine. They dance for other reasons, too. Sometimes the Pueblos wear masks when they dance.

1. The main idea is: (Circle one.)

   Pueblos are peaceful Native Americans who still live in parts of the United States.

   Pueblo Native Americans never started wars.

2. Do Pueblos like to fight? _____

3. What do the Pueblos like to do? _____

Main Idea: Clay Homes

Directions: Read about adobe houses. Then answer the questions.

Pueblo Native Americans live in houses made of clay. They are called adobe (ah-doe-bee) houses. Adobe is a yellow-colored clay that comes from the ground. The hot sun in New Mexico and Arizona helps dry the clay to make strong bricks. The Pueblos have used adobe to build their homes for many years.

Pueblos use adobe for other purposes, too. The women in the tribes make beautiful pottery out of adobe. While the clay is still damp, they form it into shapes. After they have made the bowls and other containers, they paint them with lovely designs.

1. What is the subject of this story? _____

2. Who uses clay to make their houses? _____

3. How long have they been building adobe houses? _____

4. Why do adobe bricks need to be dried? _____

5. How do the Pueblos make pottery from adobe? _____

Noting Details

Directions: Read the story. Then answer the questions.

   Thomas Edison was one of America's greatest inventors. An **inventor** thinks up new machines and new ways of doing things. Edison was born in Milan, Ohio in 1847. He went to school for only three months. His teacher thought he was not very smart because he asked so many questions.

   Edison liked to experiment. He had many wonderful ideas. He invented the light bulb and the phonograph (record player).

   Thomas Edison died in 1931, but we still use many of his inventions today.

1. What is an inventor?

_____

2. Where was Thomas Edison born?

_____

3. How long did he go to school?

_____

4. What are two of Edison's inventions?

_____

Name _____

Noting Details

Directions: Read the story. Then answer the questions.

The giant panda is much smaller than a brown bear or a polar bear. In fact, a horse weighs about four times as much as a giant panda. So why is it called "giant"? It is giant next to another kind of panda called the red panda.

The red panda also lives in China. The red panda is about the size of a fox. It has a long, fluffy, striped tail and beautiful reddish fur. It looks very much like a raccoon.

Many people think the giant pandas are bears. They look like bears. Even the word panda is Chinese for "white bear." But because of its relationship to the red panda, many scientists now believe that the panda is really more like a raccoon!

1. Why is the giant panda called "giant"?

   _____

2. Where does the red panda live?

   _____

3. How big is the red panda?

   _____

4. What animal does the red panda look like?

   _____

5. What does the word panda mean?

   _____

Inference

Inference is using logic to figure out what is not directly told.

Directions: Read the story. Then answer the questions.

In the past, many thousands of people went to the National Zoo each year to see Hsing-Hsing, the panda. Sometimes, there were as many as 1,000 visitors in one hour! Like all pandas, Hsing-Hsing spent most of his time sleeping. Because pandas are so rare, most people think it is exciting to see even a sleeping panda!

1. Popular means well-liked. Do you think giant pandas are popular?

_____

2. What clue do you have that pandas are popular?

_____

3. What did most visitors see Hsing-Hsing doing?

_____

Name _____

Inference

Directions: Read the messages on the memo board. Then answer the questions.

1. What kind of lesson does Katie have? _____

2. What time is Amy's birthday party? _____

3. What kind of appointment does Jeff have on September 3rd? _____

4. Who goes to choir practice? _____

5. Where is Dad's meeting? _____

6. What time does Jeff go to the doctor? _____

Name _____

Reading for Information

Directions: Read the story. List the four steps or changes a caterpillar goes through as it becomes a butterfly. Draw the stages in the boxes at the bottom of the page.

The Life Cycle of the Butterfly

One of the most magical changes in nature is the metamorphosis of a caterpillar. There are four stages in the transformation. The first stage is the embryonic stage. This is the stage in which tiny eggs are deposited on a leaf. The second stage is the larvae stage. We usually think of caterpillars at this stage. Many people like to capture the caterpillars hoping that while they have the caterpillar, it will turn into pupa. Another name for the pupa stage is the cocoon stage. Many changes happen inside the cocoon that we cannot see. Inside the cocoon, the caterpillar is changing into an adult. The adult breaks out of the cocoon as a beautiful butterfly!

1. _____

2. _____

3. _____

4. _____

Life Cycle of the Butterfly

Reading for Information

Telephone books contain information about people's addresses and phone numbers. They also list business addresses and phone numbers. The information in a telephone book is listed in alphabetical order.

Directions: Use your telephone book to find the following places in your area. Ask your mom or dad for help if you need it.

Can you find . . .

	Name	Phone number
. . . a pizza place?	_____	_____
. . . a bicycle store?	_____	_____
. . . a pet shop?	_____	_____
. . . a toy store?	_____	_____
. . . a water park?	_____	_____

What other telephone numbers would you like to have?

_____

Name _____

Analogies

Analogies compare how things are related to each other.

Directions: Complete the other analogies.

Example: Finger is to **hand** as **toe** is to **foot**.

1. Apple is to tree   as   flower is to _____ .

2. Tire is to car   as   wheel is to _____ .

3. Foot is to leg   as   hand is to _____ .

Analogies

Directions: Complete each analogy using a word from the box. The first one has been done for you.

week	bottom	month	tiny	sentence	lake	out	eye

1. **Up** is to **down**   as   **in** is to ____out____ .

2. **Minute** is to **hour**   as   **day** is to _____ .

3. **Month** is to **year**   as   **week** is to _____ .

4. **Over** is to **under**   as   **top** is to _____ .

5. **Big** is to **little**   as   **giant** is to _____ .

6. **Sound** is to **ear**   as   **sight** is to _____ .

7. **Page** is to **book**   as   **word** is to _____ .

8. **Wood** is to **tree**   as   **water** is to _____ .

Name _____

Classifying: Seasons

Directions: Each word in the box can be grouped by seasons. Complete the pyramids for each season with a word from the box.

July 4	hot	football	bike rides
kite	froze	sled ride	swimming
snowman	bunnies	ice	jack-o-lantern
windy	baseball	leaves	Thanksgiving

1. Spring

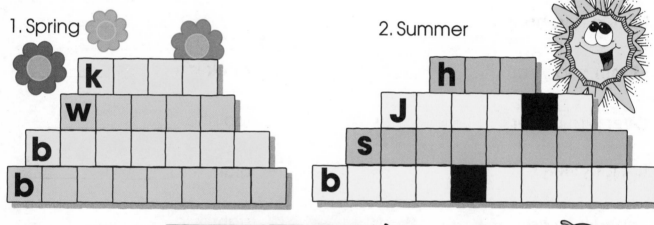

2. Summer

3. Fall

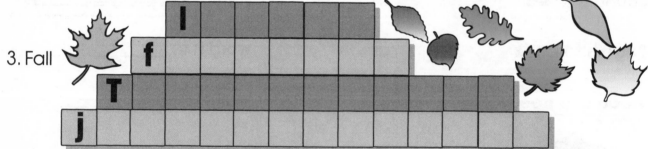

4. Winter

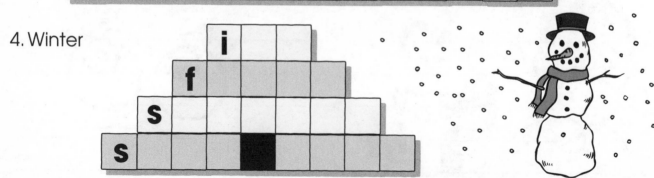

Classifying

Directions: Look at the three words in each box and add one more that is like the others.

cars	trucks	cows	pigs
airplanes	_____	chickens	_____
bread	bagels	pens	pencils
muffins	_____	paints	_____
square	triangle	violets	tulips
rectangle	_____	iris	_____
milk	yogurt	mom	dad
cheese	_____	sister	_____
merry-go-round	swings	snowpants	boots
sandbox	_____	jacket	_____

Challenge: Can you list the theme of each group?

_____   _____

_____   _____

_____   _____

_____   _____

Classifying

Directions: Write a word from the word box to complete each sentence. If the word you write names an article of clothing, write **1** on the line. If it names food, write **2** on the line. If it names an animal, write **3** on the line. If the word names furniture, write **4** on the line.

jacket	chair	shirt	owl	mice
bed	cheese	dress	bread	chocolate

__1__ 1. Danny tucked his _____ into his pants.

_____ 2. _____ is my favorite kind of candy.

_____ 3. The wise old _____ sat in the tree and said, "Who-o-o."

_____ 4. We can't sit on the _____ because it has a broken leg.

_____ 5. Don't forget to wear your _____ because it is chilly today.

_____ 6. Will you please buy a loaf of _____ at the store?

_____ 7. She wore a very pretty _____ to the dance.

_____ 8. The cat chased the _____ in the barn.

_____ 9. I was so sleepy that I went to _____ early.

_____ 10. We put _____ in the mouse trap to help catch the mice.

Classifying: Comparisons

Directions: Compare the people of Wackyville to each other. Read the sentences and answer the questions. The first one has been done for you.

1. Wanda cooks fast. Joe cooks faster than Wanda. Who cooks faster?

   _____ Joe _____

2. Mr. Green plants many flowers. Mrs. Posy plants fewer flowers than Mr. Green. Who plants more flowers?

   _____

3. Hugo weighs a lot. Edward weighs less. Who weighs more?

   _____

4. Sheila has 3 cats. Billy has 2 cats, 1 dog and 1 bird. Who has more pets?

   _____

5. Ms. Brown has many trees. Mr. Smith has fewer trees than Ms. Brown. Who has more trees?

   _____

6. An elephant moves slowly. A snail moves even slower. Which animal moves quicker?

   _____

Webs

Webs are another way to classify information. Look at the groups below. Add more words in each group.

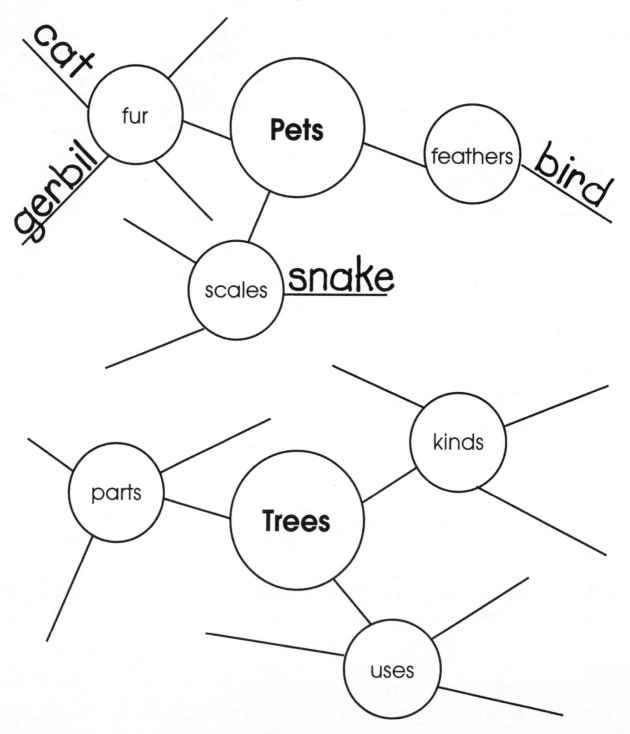

Name _____

Story Webs

All short stories have a plot, characters, setting and a theme.

The **plot** is what the story is about.

The **characters** are the people or animals in the story.

The **setting** is where and when the story occurs.

The **theme** is the message or idea of the story.

Directions: Use the story *Snow White* to complete this story web.

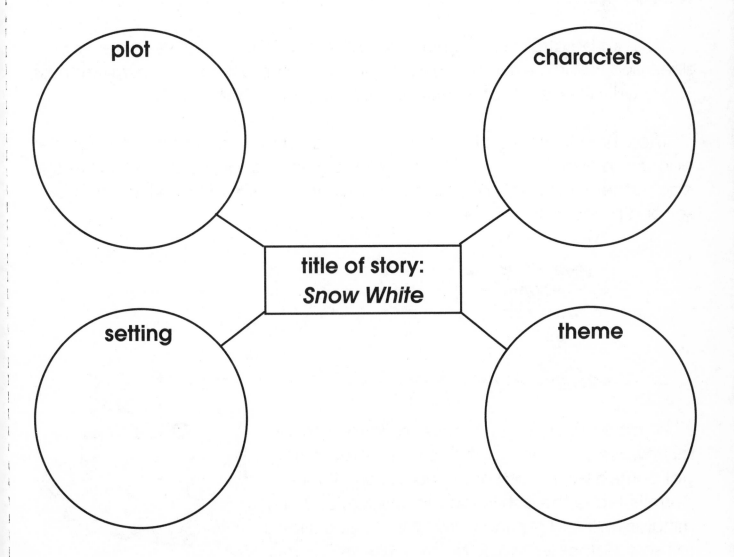

Fiction and Nonfiction

Fiction writing is a story that has been invented. The story might be about things that could really happen (realistic) or about things that couldn't possibly happen (fantasy). **Nonfiction** writing is based on facts. It usually gives information about people, places or things. A person can often tell while reading whether a story or book is fiction or nonfiction.

Directions: Read the paragraphs below and on page 49. Determine whether each paragraph is fiction or nonfiction. Circle the letter **F** for fiction or the letter **N** for nonfiction.

"Do not be afraid, little flowers," said the oak. "Close your yellow eyes in sleep and trust in me. You have made me glad many a time with your sweetness. Now I will take care that the winter shall do you no harm." **F N**

The whole team watched as the ball soared over the outfield fence. The game was over! It was hard to walk off the field and face parents, friends and each other. It had been a long season. Now, they would have to settle for second place. **F N**

Be careful when you remove the dish from the microwave. It will be very hot, so take care not to get burned by the dish or the hot steam. If time permits, leave the dish in the microwave for 2 or 3 minutes to avoid getting burned. It is a good idea to use a potholder, too. **F N**

Fiction and Nonfiction

Megan and Mariah skipped out to the playground. They enjoyed playing together at recess. Today, it was Mariah's turn to choose what they would do first. To Megan's surprise, Mariah asked, "What do you want to do, Megan? I'm going to let you pick since it's your birthday!" **F N**

It is easy to tell an insect from a spider. An insect has three body parts and six legs. A spider has eight legs and no wings. Of course, if you see the creature spinning a web, you will know what it is. An insect wouldn't want to get too close to the web or it would be stuck. It might become dinner! **F N**

My name is Lee Chang, and I live in a country that you call China. My home is on the other side of the world from yours. When the sun is rising in my country, it is setting in yours. When it is day at your home, it is night at mine. **F N**

Henry washed the dog's foot in cold water from the brook. The dog lay very still, for he knew that the boy was trying to help him. **F N**

Name _____

Compare and Contrast

To **compare** means to discuss how things are similar. To **contrast** means to discuss how things are different.

Directions: Compare and contrast how people grow gardens. Write at least two answers for each question.

Many people in the country have large gardens. They have a lot of space, so they can plant many kinds of vegetables and flowers. Since the gardens are usually quite large, they use a wheelbarrow to carry the tools they need. Sometimes they even have to carry water or use a garden hose.

People who live in the city do not always have enough room for a garden. Many people in big cities live in apartment buildings. They can put in a window box or use part of their balcony space to grow things. Most of the time, the only garden tools they need are a hand trowel to loosen the dirt and a watering can to make sure the plant gets enough water.

1. Compare gardening in the country with gardening in the city.

   _____

   _____

2. Contrast gardening in the country with gardening in the city.

   _____

   _____

Compare and Contrast

Directions: Look for similarities and differences in the following paragraphs. Then answer the questions.

Phong and Chris both live in the city. They live in the same apartment building and go to the same school. Phong and Chris sometimes walk to school together. If it is raining or storming, Phong's dad drives them to school on his way to work. In the summer, they spend a lot of time at the park across the street from their building.

Phong lives in Apartment 12-A with his little sister and mom and dad. He has a collection of model race cars that he put together with his dad's help. He even has a bookshelf full of books about race cars and race car drivers.

Chris has a big family. He has two older brothers and one older sister. When Chris has time to do anything he wants, he gets out his butterfly collection. He notes the place he found each specimen and the day he found it. He also likes to play with puzzles.

1. Compare Phong and Chris. List at least three similarities.

_____

_____

_____

2. Contrast Phong and Chris. List two differences.

_____

_____

_____

Name _____

Compare and Contrast: Venn Diagram

Directions: List the similarities and differences you find below on a chart called a **Venn diagram**. This kind of chart shows comparisons and contrasts.

Butterflies and moths belong to the same group of insects. They both have two pairs of wings. Their wings are covered with tiny scales. Both butterflies and moths undergo metamorphosis, or a change, in their lives. They begin their lives as caterpillars.

Butterflies and moths are different in some ways. Butterflies usually fly during the day, but moths generally fly at night. Most butterflies have slender, hairless bodies; most moths have plump, furry bodies. When butterflies land, they hold their wings together straight over their bodies. When moths land, they spread their wings out flat.

1. List three ways that butterflies and moths are alike.

_____

_____

_____

2. List three ways that butterflies and moths are different.

_____

_____

_____

3. Combine your answers from questions 1 and 2 into a Venn diagram. Write the differences in the circle labeled for each insect. Write the similarities in the intersecting part.

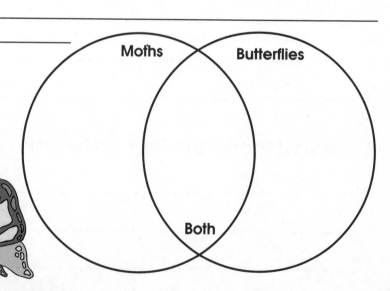

Moths   Butterflies

Both

Cause and Effect

A **cause** is the reason for an event. An **effect** is what happens as a result of a cause.

Directions: Circle the cause and underline the effect in each sentence. They may be in any order. The first one has been done for you.

1. (The truck hit an icy patch) and <u>skidded off the road</u>.

2. When the door slammed shut, the baby woke up crying.

3. Our soccer game was cancelled when it began to storm.

4. Dad and Mom are adding a room onto the house since our family is growing.

5. Our car ran out of gas on the way to town, so we had to walk.

6. The home run in the ninth inning helped our team win the game.

7. We had to climb the stairs because the elevator was broken.

8. We were late to school because the bus had a flat tire.

Name _____

Cause and Effect

Directions: Draw a line to match each phrase to form a logical cause and effect sentence.

1. Dad gets paid today, so   because she is sick.

2. When the electricity went out,   we're going out for dinner.

3. Courtney can't spend the night   so she bought a new sweater.

4. Our front window shattered   we grabbed the flashlights.

5. Sophie got $10.00 for her birthday,   when the baseball hit it.

Directions: Read each sentence beginning. Choose an ending from the box that makes sense. Write the correct letter on the line.

1. Her arm was in a cast, because ____

2. They are building a new house on our street, so ____

3. Since I'd always wanted a puppy, ____

4. I had to renew my library book, ____

5. My parents' anniversary is tomorrow, ____

> A. we all went down to watch.
> B. so my sister and I bought them some flowers.
> C. since I hadn't finished it.
> D. she fell when she was skating.
> E. Mom gave me one for my birthday.

Name _____

Causes

Directions: Complete each sentence by writing a possible cause.

1. I bought my best friend this book _____

_____.

2. Dad's back was really sore because _____

_____.

3. Our school bus was late this morning since _____

_____.

4. We don't have any homework this weekend so _____

_____.

Write two sentences that show a cause-and-effect relationship.

1. _____

_____.

2. _____

_____

_____

_____.

Name _____

Effects

Directions: Complete each sentence by writing a possible effect.

1. The front door was locked, so _____

_____.

2. Because of the heavy rains last night, _____

_____.

3. Since I spent all my money, _____

_____.

4. When my alarm clock did not wake me this morning, _____

_____.

READING COMPREHENSION

Main Idea: Iguanodon

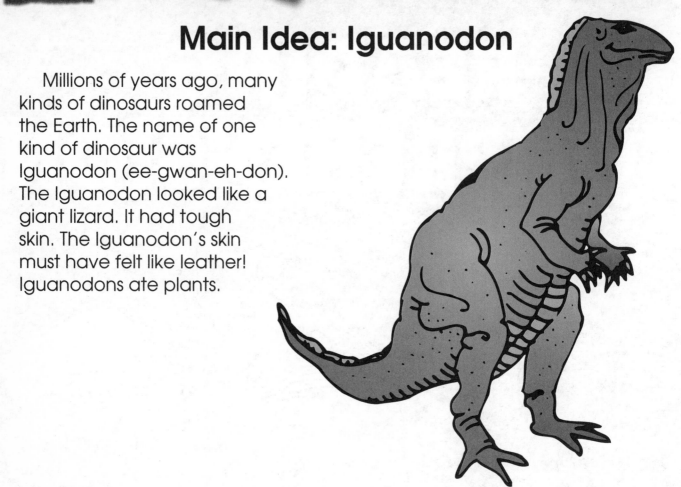

Millions of years ago, many kinds of dinosaurs roamed the Earth. The name of one kind of dinosaur was Iguanodon (ee-gwan-eh-don). The Iguanodon looked like a giant lizard. It had tough skin. The Iguanodon's skin must have felt like leather! Iguanodons ate plants.

Directions: Answer these questions about Iguanodons.

1. Circle the main idea:

    The Iguanodon's skin was like leather.

    The Iguanodon was a plant-eating dinosaur with tough skin.

2. What kind of food did Iguanodons eat?

    _____

3. What animal living today did the Iguanodon look like?

    _____

Name _____

Comprehension: Tyrannosaurus Rex

One of the biggest dinosaurs was Tyrannosaurus Rex (ty-ran-oh-saur-us recks). This dinosaur walked on its two big back legs. It had two small, short front legs. From the top of its head to the tip of its tail, Tyrannosaurus Rex measured 50 feet long. Its head was 4 feet long! Are you taller than this dinosaur's head? Tyrannosaurus was a meat eater. It had many small, sharp teeth. Its favorite meal was a smaller dinosaur that had a bill like a duck. This smaller dinosaur lived near water.

Directions: Answer these questions about Tyrannosaurus Rex.

1. What is the story about?

_____

2. What size was this dinosaur?

_____

_____

3. When this dinosaur was hungry, what did it eat?

_____

_____

4. Where did this dinosaur find its favorite meal?

_____

_____

5. Why did this dinosaur need many sharp teeth?

_____

_____

Comprehension: Cold-Blooded Animals

Like snakes, dinosaurs were cold-blooded. Cold-blooded animals cannot keep themselves warm. Because of this, dinosaurs were not very active when it was cold. In the early morning they did not move much. When the sun grew warm, the dinosaurs became active. When the sun went down in the evening, they slowed down again for the night. The sun warmed the dinosaurs and gave them the energy they needed to move about.

Directions: Answer these questions about dinosaurs.

1. Why were dinosaurs inactive when it was cold?

   _____

   _____

2. What time of day were the dinosaurs active?

   _____

   _____

3. What times of day were the dinosaurs not active?

   _____

   _____

4. Why did dinosaurs need the sun?

   _____

   _____

Main Idea: Dinosaur Models

Some people can build models of dinosaurs. The models are fakes, of course. But they are life-size and they look real! The people who build them must know the dinosaur inside and out. First, they build a skeleton. Then they cover it with fake "skin." Then they paint it. Some models have motors in them. The motors can make the dinosaur's head or tail move. Have you ever seen a life-size model of a dinosaur?

Directions: Answer these questions about dinosaur models.

1. Circle the main idea:

   Some models of dinosaurs have motors in them.

   Some people can build life-size models of dinosaurs that look real.

2. What do the motors in model dinosaurs do?

   _____

   _____

3. What is the first step in making a model dinosaur?

   _____

   _____

4. Why do dinosaur models look real?

   _____

   _____

Comprehension: Kareem Abdul-Jabbar

Have you heard of a basketball star named Kareem Abdul-Jabbar? When he was born, Kareem's name was Lew Alcindor. He was named after his father. When he was in college, Kareem changed his religion from Christianity to Islam. That was when he took the Muslim name of Kareem Abdul-Jabbar.

Directions: Answer these questions about Kareem Abdul-Jabbar.

1. What was Kareem Abdul-Jabbar's name when he was born?

   _____

2. Who was Kareem named after?

   _____

3. When did Kareem become a Muslim?

   _____

4. When did he change his name to Kareem Abdul-Jabbar?

   _____

Name _____

Comprehension: Michael Jordan

Michael Jordan was born February 17, 1963, in Brooklyn, New York. His family moved to North Carolina when he was just a baby. As a young boy, his favorite sport was baseball, but he soon found that he could play basketball as well. At age 17, he began to show people just how talented he really was.

Throughout his basketball career, Michael Jordan has won many scoring titles. Many boys and girls look up to Michael Jordan as their hero. Did you know he had a hero, too, when he was growing up? He looked up to his older brother, Larry.

Michael Jordan, a basketball superstar, is not just a star on the basketball court. He also works hard to raise money for many children's charities. He encourages children to develop their talents by practice, practice, practice!

Directions: Answer these questions about Michael Jordan.

1. Michael says children can develop their talents by lots of _____.

2. Who was Michael's hero when he was growing up?

_____

3. Where was Michael Jordan born?

_____

4. At first, he played _____ instead of basketball.

Name _____

Recalling Details: The Home Run Race

The summer of 1998 was exciting for the sport of baseball. Even if you were not a big fan of this sport, you couldn't help but hear about two great sluggers—Mark McGwire and Sammy Sosa. By mid-summer, many baseball fans realized that several men were getting close to the home run record. The record of 61 home runs in a single season had been set by Roger Maris 37 years before!

On Tuesday, September 8, 1998, that record was broken. Mark McGwire, who plays for the St. Louis Cardinals, hit his 62nd home run in a game with the Chicago Cubs.

To make the home run race more interesting, a player for the Chicago Cubs, Sammy Sosa, was also close to breaking the 61 home run record. On Sunday, September 13, Sammy Sosa also hit his 62nd home run.

Directions: Write the letter of the correct answer in the blanks.

A. Sept. 13   B. McGwire   C. 37   D. Maris   E. Chicago Cubs

1. Had the home run record _____

2. First to hit 62 home runs _____

3. Sosa broke the home run record _____

4. Years record had stood _____

5. Sosa's team _____

64

Name _____

Comprehension: Christopher Columbus

What do you know about Christopher Columbus? He was a famous sailor and explorer. Columbus was 41 years old when he sailed from southern Spain on August 3, 1492, with three ships. On them was a crew of 90 men. Thirty-three days later, he landed on Watling Island in the Bahamas. The Bahamas are islands located in the West Indies. The West Indies are a large group of islands between North America and South America.

Directions: Answer these questions about Christopher Columbus.

1. How old was Columbus when he set sail from southern Spain?

   _____

2. How many ships did he take?

   _____

3. How many men were with him?

   _____

4. How long did it take him to reach land?

   _____

5. Where did Columbus land?

   _____

6. What are the West Indies?

   _____

Name _____

Comprehension: Lewis and Clark

In 1801, President Thomas Jefferson chose an army officer named Meriwether Lewis to lead an expedition through our country's "new frontier." He knew Lewis would not be able to make the journey by himself, so he chose William Clark to travel with him. The two men had known each other in the army. They decided to be co-leaders of the expedition.

The two men and a group of about 45 others made the trip from the state of Missouri, across the Rocky Mountains all the way to the Pacific Coast. They were careful in choosing the men who would travel with them. They wanted men who were strong and knew a lot about the wilderness. It was also important that they knew some of the Native American languages.

Directions: Answer these questions about Lewis and Clark.

1. Which president wanted an expedition through the "new frontier"?

   _____

2. Look at a United States map or a globe. In what direction did Lewis and Clark travel? (Circle one.)

   north   south   east   west

3. About how many people made up the entire expedition, including Lewis and Clark?

   _____

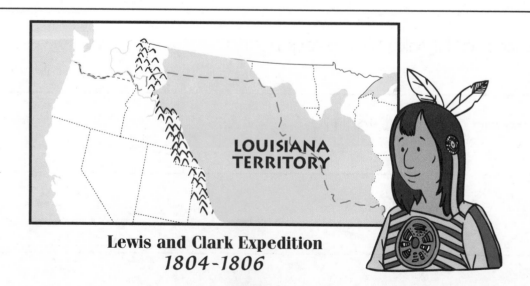

Lewis and Clark Expedition
1804-1806

Comprehension: George Washington

George Washington was the first president of the United States. He was born in Wakefield, Virginia, on February 22, 1732. His father was a wealthy Virginia planter. As he grew up, George Washington became interested in surveying and farming. When George was only 11 years old, his father died. George moved in with his older brother, Lawrence.

Even if he had not become the country's first president, he would have been well known because of his strong military leadership. Washington was a good leader because of his patience and his ability to survive hardships.

George Washington became president in 1789. At that time there were only 11 states in the United States. He served two terms (4 years each) as our first president. After his second term, he returned to a former home at Mt. Vernon. He died there in 1799 after catching a cold while riding around his farm in the wind and snow.

Directions: Answer these questions about George Washington.

1. In what year did George Washington become president? _____

2. Besides being our country's first president, how else did he serve our country?

   _____

   _____

3. Where was he born?

   _____

Name _____

Comprehension: Benjamin Franklin

Benjamin Franklin was born in Boston, Massachusetts, on January 17, 1706. Even though he only attended school to age 10, he worked hard to improve his mind and character. He taught himself several foreign languages and learned many skills that would later be a great help to him.

Ben Franklin played a very important part in our history. One of his many accomplishments was as a printer. He was a helper (apprentice) to his half-brother, James, and later moved to the city of Philadelphia where he worked in another print shop.

Another skill that he developed was writing. He wrote and published *Poor Richard's Almanac* in December 1732. Franklin was also a diplomat. He served our country in many ways, both in the United States and in Europe. As an inventor he experimented with electricity. Have you heard about the kite and key experiment? Benjamin Franklin was able to prove that lightning has an electrical discharge.

Directions: Answer these questions about Benjamin Franklin.

1. Circle the main idea:

   Benjamin Franklin was a very important part of our history.

   Benjamin Franklin wrote *Poor Richard's Almanac.*

   He flew a kite with a key on the string.

2. How old was Ben Franklin when he left school? _____

3. Write three of Ben Franklin's accomplishments.

   1) _____

   2) _____

   3) _____

Main Idea: Unusual Plants

Do you have a cat? Do you have catnip growing around your home? If you don't know, your cat probably does. Cats love the catnip plant and can be seen rolling around in it. Some cat toys have catnip inside them because cats love it so much.

People can enjoy catnip, too. Some people make catnip tea with the leaves of the plant. It is like the mint with which people make tea.

Another refreshing drink can be made with the berries of the sumac bush or tree. Native Americans would pick the red berries, crush them and add water to make a thirst-quenching drink. The berries were sour, but they must have believed that the cool, tart drink was refreshing. Does this remind you of lemonade?

Directions: Answer these questions about unusual plants.

1. What is the main idea of the first two paragraphs above?

   _____

   _____

2. Write two ways cats show that they love catnip.

   1) _____

   2) _____

3. How can people use catnip?

   _____

   _____

Name _____

Comprehension: Rainforests

The soil in rainforests is very dark and rich. The trees and plants that grow there are very green. People who have seen one say a rainforest is "the greenest place on Earth." Why? Because it rains a lot. With so much rain, the plants stay very green. The earth stays very wet. Rainforests cover only 6 percent of the Earth. But they are home to 66 percent of all the different kinds of plants and animals on Earth! Today, rainforests are threatened by such things as acid rain from factory smoke emissions around the world and from farm expansion. Farmers living near rainforests cut down many trees each year to clear the land for farming. I wish I could see a rainforest. Do you?

Directions: Answer these questions about rainforests.

1. What do the plants and trees in a rainforest look like?

   _____

2. What is the soil like in a rainforest?

   _____

3. How much of the Earth is covered by rainforests?

   _____

4. What percentage of the Earth's plants and animals live there?

   _____

Comprehension: The Sloth

The sloth spends most of its life in the trees of the rainforest. The three-toed sloth, for example, is usually hanging around, using its claws to keep it there. Because it is in the trees so much, it has trouble moving on the ground. Certainly it could be caught easily by other animals of the rainforest if it was being chased. The sloth is a very slow-moving animal. Do you have any idea what the sloth eats? The sloth eats mostly leaves it finds in the treetops.

Have you ever seen a three- or two-toed sloth? If you see one in a zoo, you don't have to get close enough to count the toes. You can tell these two "cousins" apart in a different way—the three-toed sloth has some green mixed in with its fur because of the algae it gets from the trees.

Directions: Answer these questions about the sloth.

1. How does the three-toed sloth hang around the rainforest?

   a. by its tail, like a monkey

   b. by its claws, or toes

2. The main diet of the sloth is _____.

3. Why does the sloth have trouble moving around on the ground?

   _____

   _____

Comprehension: The Jaguar

The jaguar weighs between 100 and 250 pounds. It can be as long as 6 feet! This is not your ordinary house cat!

One strange feature of the jaguar is its living arrangements. The jaguar has its own territory. No other jaguar lives in its "home range." It would be very unusual for one jaguar to meet another in the rainforest. One way they mark their territory is by scratching trees.

Have you ever seen your pet cat hide in the grass and carefully and quietly sneak up on an unsuspecting grasshopper or mouse? Like its gentler, smaller "cousin," the jaguar stalks its prey in the high grass. It likes to eat small animals, such as rodents, but can attack and kill larger animals such as tapirs, deer and cattle. It is good at catching fish as well.

Directions: Answer these questions about the jaguar.

1. The jaguar lives:

    a. in large groups

    b. alone

    c. under water

2. This large cat marks its territory by:

    a. black marker

    b. roaring

    c. scratching trees

3. What does the jaguar eat?

    _____

4. How much does it weigh?

    _____

Making Inferences: State Bird — Arizona

Have you ever traveled through Arizona or other southwestern states of the United States? One type of plant you may have seen is the cactus. This plant and other desert thickets are homes to the cactus wren, the state bird of Arizona. It is interesting how this bird (which is the size of a robin) can roost on this prickly plant and keep from getting stuck on the sharp spines. The cactus wren builds its nest on top of these thorny desert plants.

The cactus wren's "song" is not a beautiful, musical sound. Instead, it is compared to the grating sound of machinery. You can also identify the bird by its coloring. It has white spots on its outer tail feathers and white eyebrows. The crown (head) of the cactus wren is a rusty color.

Directions: Answer these questions about the cactus wren.

1. In what part of the United States would you find the cactus wren?

   _____

2. What does **prickly** mean?

   a. soft   b. green   c. having sharp points

3. Do you think you would like to hear the "song" of the cactus wren? Why or why not?

   _____

   _____

   _____

Comprehension: State Bird — Maine

The chickadee may visit your bird feeder on a regular basis if you live in Maine. This bird seems to have a feeding schedule so it doesn't miss a meal! The chickadee can be tamed to eat right out of your hand. If this bird sees some insect eggs on a tree limb, it even will hang upside down to get at this treat.

The chickadee lives in forests and open woodlands throughout most of the year, but when winter comes, it moves into areas populated by people. It is colored gray with a black cap and white on its underside and cheeks.

The chickadee lives in the northern half of the United States and in southern and western Canada. The western part of Alaska is also home to this curious and tame little bird.

Directions: Answer these questions about the chickadee.

1. What does **curious** mean?

   a. underside   c. tame

   b. questioning   d. schedule

2. What does the chickadee do when winter comes?

   _____

   _____

3. One of the chickadee's favorite treats is _____.

4. Where does the chickadee live?

   _____

   _____

   _____

Main Idea: Hawks

Hawks are birds of prey. They "prey upon" birds and animals. This means they kill other animals and eat them. The hawk has long pointed wings. It uses them to soar through the air as it looks for prey. It looks at the ground while it soars.

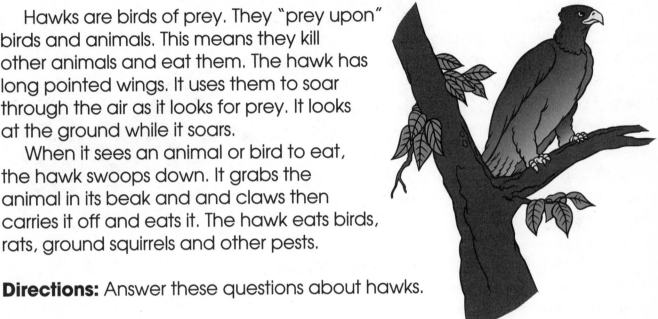

When it sees an animal or bird to eat, the hawk swoops down. It grabs the animal in its beak and and claws then carries it off and eats it. The hawk eats birds, rats, ground squirrels and other pests.

Directions: Answer these questions about hawks.

1. Circle the main idea:

   Hawks are mean because they swoop down from the sky and eat animals and birds.

   Hawks are helpful because they eat sick birds, rats, ground squirrels and other pests.

2. What kind of wings does a hawk have?

   _____

3. How does the hawk pick up its prey?

   _____

4. What does "prey upon" mean?

   _____

Name _____

Comprehension: Pet Crickets

Did you know that some people keep crickets as pets? These people always keep two crickets together. That way, the crickets do not get lonely!

Crickets are kept in a flowerpot filled with dirt. The dirt helps the crickets feel at home. They are used to being outside. Over the flowerpot is a covering that lets air inside. It also keeps the crickets in! Some people use a small net; others use cheesecloth. They make sure there is room under the covering for crickets to hop!

Pet crickets like to eat bread and lettuce. They also like raw hamburger meat. Would you like to have a pet cricket?

Directions: Answer these questions about pet crickets.

1. Where do pet crickets live?

   _____

2. Why should you put dirt in with the crickets?

   _____

3. What is placed over the flowerpot?

   _____

4. Write three things pet crickets like to eat. 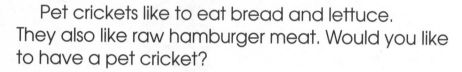 _____

   _____

   _____

Comprehension: Our Solar System

There are nine planets in our solar system. All of them circle the Sun. The planet closest to the Sun is named Mercury. The Romans said Mercury was the messenger of the gods. The second planet from the Sun is named Venus. Venus shines the brightest. Venus was the Roman goddess of beauty. Earth is the third planet from the Sun. It is about the same size as Venus. After Earth is Mars, which is named after the Roman god of war. The other five planets are Jupiter, Saturn, Uranus, Neptune and Pluto. They, too, are named after Roman gods.

Directions: Answer these questions about our solar system.

1. How many planets are in our solar system?

   _____

2. What do the planets circle?

   _____

3. What are the planets named after?

   _____

4. Which planet is closest to the Sun?

   _____

5. Which planet is about the same size as Earth?

   _____

6. Which planet comes after Earth in the solar system?

   _____

Comprehension: Moon

Our moon is not the only moon in the solar system. Some other planets have moons also. Saturn has 10 moons! Our moon is Earth's closest neighbor in the solar system. Sometimes our moon is 225,727 miles away. Other times, it is 252,002 miles away. Why? Because the Moon revolves around Earth. It does not go around Earth in a perfect circle. So, sometimes its path takes it further away from our planet.

When our astronauts visited the Moon, they found dusty plains, high mountains and huge craters. There is no air or water on the Moon. That is why life cannot exist there. The astronauts had to wear space suits to protect their skin from the bright Sun. They had to take their own air to breathe. They had to take their own food and water. The Moon was an interesting place to visit. Would you want to live there?

Directions: Answer these questions about the Moon.

1. Circle the main idea:

   The Moon travels around Earth, and the astronauts visited the Moon.

   Astronauts found that the Moon—Earth's closest neighbor—has no air or water and cannot support life.

2. Write three things our astronauts found on the Moon.

   1) _____ 2) _____ 3) _____

3. Make a list of what to take on a trip to the Moon.

   _____

   _____

Comprehension: Your Heart

Make your hand into a fist. Now look at it. That is about the size of your heart! Your heart is a strong pump. It works all the time. Right now it is beating about 90 times a minute. When you run, it beats about 150 times a minute.

Inside, your heart has four spaces. The two spaces on the top are called atria. This is where blood is pumped into the heart. The two spaces on the bottom are called ventricles. This is where blood is pumped out of the heart. The blood is pumped to every part of your body. How? Open and close your fist. See how it tightens and loosens? The heart muscle tightens and loosens, too. This is how it pumps blood.

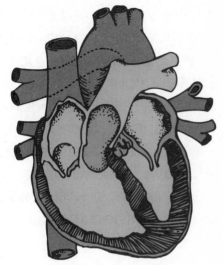

Directions: Answer these questions about your heart.

1. How often does your heart work?

   _____

2. How fast does it beat when you are sitting?

   _____

3. How fast does it beat when you are running?

   _____

4. How many spaces are inside your heart?_____

5. What are the heart's upper spaces called? What are the lower spaces called?

   _____   _____

Name _____

Making Inferences: Your Bones

Are you scared of skeletons? You shouldn't be. There is a skeleton inside of you! The skeleton is made up of all the bones in your body. These 206 bones give you your shape. They also protect your heart and everything else inside. Your bones come in many sizes. Some are short. Some are long. Some are rounded. Some are very tiny. The outside of your bones looks solid. Inside, they are filled with a soft material called marrow. This is what keeps your bones alive. Red blood cells and most white blood cells are made here. These cells help feed the body and fight disease.

Directions: Answer these questions about your bones.

1. Do you think your leg bone is short, long or rounded?

   _____

2. Do you think the bones in your head are short, long or rounded?

   _____

3. What is the size of the bones in your fingers?

   _____

4. What is the "something soft" inside your bones?

   _____

5. How many bones are in your skeleton?

   _____

Comprehension: Beavers

The beaver is not only a great lumberjack, it can also swim quite well. Its special fur helps to keep it warm; its hind legs work like fins; its tail is used as a rudder to steer it through the water. The beaver can hold its breath under water for 15 minutes, and its special eyelids are transparent, so they work like goggles!

Even though the beaver is a very good swimmer and can stay under water for a long time, it does not live under water. When the beaver builds a dam it also builds a lodge. A lodge is a dome-shaped structure above water level in which the beaver lives. The beaver enters its lodge through underwater tunnels. The lodge provides a place for the beaver to rest, eat and raise young.

Directions: Answer these questions about the beaver.

1. What is the main idea of the first paragraph?

   _____

   _____

2. Which word in the first paragraph means "able to see through"?

   _____

3. How long can the beaver hold its breath under water?

   _____

4. How does a beaver enter his lodge?

   _____

Name _____

Making Inferences: Sheep

Sheep like to stay close together. They do not run off. They move together in a flock. They live on sheep ranches. Some sheep grow 20 pounds of fleece each year. After it is cut off, the fleece is called wool. Cutting off the wool is called "shearing." It does not hurt the sheep to be sheared. The wool is very warm and is used to make clothing.

Female sheep are called "ewes" (yous). Some types of ewes have only one baby each year. The baby is called a "lamb." Other types of ewes have two or three lambs each year.

Directions: Answer these questions about sheep.

1. Why is sheep's behavior helpful to sheep ranchers?

   _____

2. If you were a sheep farmer, would you rather own the kind of sheep that has one baby each year, or one that has two or three?

   _____

   Why?

   _____

3. When it is still on the sheep, what is wool called?

   _____

4. What is a group of sheep called?

   _____

Name _____

Comprehension: Rhinos

Rhinos are the second largest land animal. Only elephants are bigger.

Most people think rhinos are ugly. Their full name is "rhinoceros" (rhy-nos-ur-us). There are five kinds of rhinos—the square-lipped rhino, black rhino, great Indian rhino, Sumatran (sue-ma-trahn) rhino and Javan rhino.

Rhinos have a great sense of smell, which helps protect them. They can smell other animals far away. They don't eat them, though. Rhinos do not eat meat. They are vegetarians.

Directions: Answer these questions about rhinos.

1. What is the largest land animal?

_____

2. What are the five kinds of rhinos?

1) _____

2) _____

3) _____

4) _____

5) _____

3. What is a "vegetarian"?

_____

_____

Comprehension: Rodents

You are surrounded by rodents (row-dents)! There are 1,500 different kinds of rodents. One of the most common rodents is the mouse. Rats, gophers (go-furs) and beavers are also rodents. So are squirrels and porcupines (pork-you-pines).

All rodents have long, sharp teeth. These sharp teeth are called "incisors" (in-size-ors). Rodents use these teeth to eat their food. They eat mostly seeds and vegetables. There is one type of rodent some children have as a pet. No, it is not a rat! It is the guinea (ginney) pig.

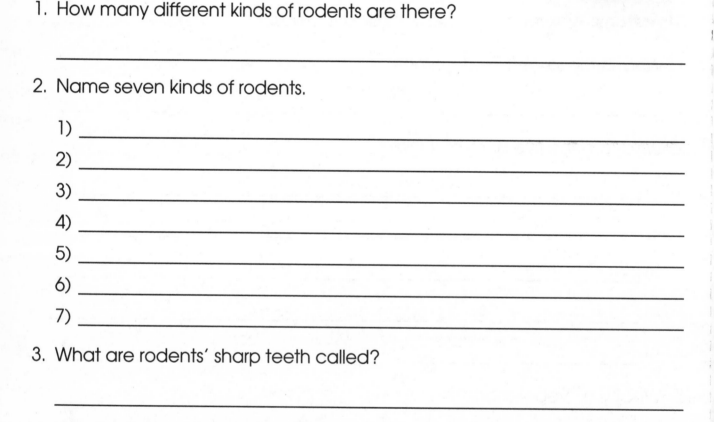

Directions: Answer these questions about rodents.

1. How many different kinds of rodents are there?

_____

2. Name seven kinds of rodents.

   1) _____

   2) _____

   3) _____

   4) _____

   5) _____

   6) _____

   7) _____

3. What are rodents' sharp teeth called?

_____

4. What rodent is sometimes a pet?

_____

Drawing Conclusions

Drawing a conclusion means to use clues to make a final decision about something. To draw a conclusion, you must read carefully.

Directions: Read each story carefully. Use the clues given to draw a conclusion about the story.

The boy and girl took turns pushing the shopping cart. They went up and down the aisles. Each time they stopped the cart, they would look at things on the shelf and decide what they needed. Jody asked her older brother, "Will I need a box of 48 crayons in Mrs. Charles' class?"

"Yes, I think so," he answered. Then he turned to their mother and said, "I need some new notebooks. Can I get some?"

1. Where are they? _____

2. What are they doing there? _____

3. How do you know? Write at least two clue words that helped you.

_____

Eric and Randy held on tight. They looked around them and saw that they were not the only ones holding on. The car moved slowly upward. As they turned and looked over the side, they noticed that the people far below them seemed to be getting smaller and smaller. "Hey, Eric, did I tell you this is my first time on one of these?" asked Randy. As they started down the hill at a frightening speed, Randy screamed, "And it may be my last!"

1. Where are they? _____

2. How do you know? Write at least two clue words that helped you.

_____

Name _____

Drawing Conclusions: A Colorful Yard

Directions: Read the story, then answer the questions.

Mrs. Posy plants roses everywhere. She plants yellow roses near her front porch. She plants red roses near the back door. There are also pink roses and white roses in her yard. Every time the postal carrier comes to her house, he sneezes. "You should not plant so many flowers," he tells Mrs. Posy. Mrs. Posy just smiles.

1. What are Mrs. Posy's favorite flowers? _____

2. Why do you think the postal carrier tells Mrs. Posy, "You should not plant so

   many flowers"? _____

   _____

3. Why does Mrs. Posy smile? _____

   _____

ENGLISH

Name _____

Alphabetical Order

Alphabetical order (or ABC order) is the order of letters in the alphabet. When putting words in alphabetical order, use the first letter of each word.

Directions: Number the words in each list from 1 to 5 in alphabetical order.

___ happy   ___ zebra   ___ banana

___ scared   ___ gorilla   ___ kiwi

___ worried   ___ monkey   ___ apple

___ amused   ___ hyena   ___ peach

___ excited   ___ kangaroo   ___ lemon

Name _____

Alphabetical Order

Directions: Alphabetical order is putting words in the order in which they appear in the alphabet. Put the eggs in alphabetical order. The first and last words are done for you.

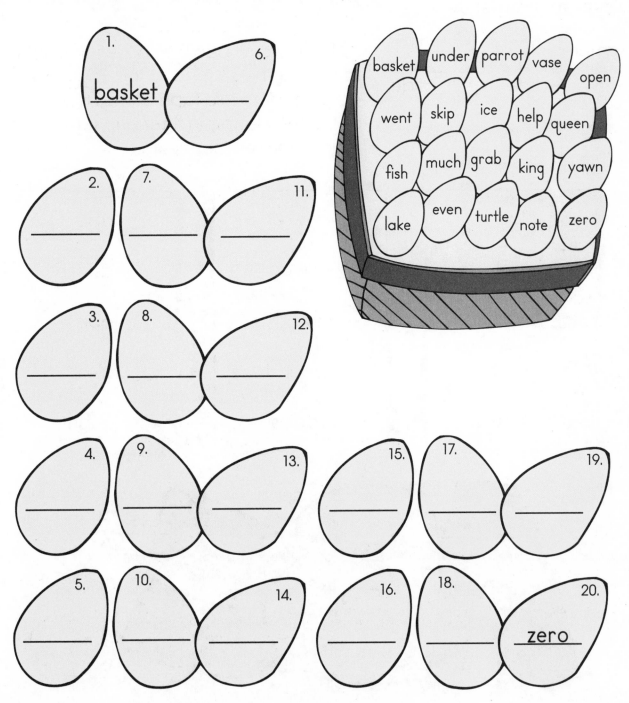

1. basket
6. _____

2. _____
7. _____
11. _____

3. _____
8. _____
12. _____

4. _____
9. _____
13. _____
15. _____
17. _____
19. _____

5. _____
10. _____
14. _____
16. _____
18. _____
20. zero

basket under parrot vase open
went skip ice help queen
fish much grab king yawn
lake even turtle note zero

Alphabetical Order

The words in these lists begin with the same letter.

Directions: Use the second or third letters of each word to put the lists in alphabetical order.

Example:

tiger	_3_	tiger
tape	_1_	tape
tide	_2_	tide

All three words begin with the same letter (**t**), so look at the second letters. The letter **a** comes before **i**, so **tape** comes first. Then look at the third letters in **tiger** and **tide** to see which word comes next.

___ glad

___ goat

___ gasoline

___ gentle

___ grumble

___ answer

___ about

___ ask

___ around

___ against

___ tape

___ taste

___ table

___ talent

___ taught

Alphabetical Order

Alphabetical order is the order in which letters come in the alphabet.

Directions: Write the words in alphabetical order. If the first letter is the same, use the second letter of each word to decide which word comes first. If the second letter is also the same, look at the third letter of each word to decide.

Example: wsh wsp wn't

1. w**a**sp
2. w**i**sh
3. w**o**n't

bench   flag   bowl

1. _____

2. _____

3. _____

egg   nod   neat

1. _____

2. _____

3. _____

dog   dart   drag

1. _____

2. _____

3. _____

skipped   stairs   stones

1. _____

2. _____

3. _____

Antonyms

An **antonym** is a word that means the opposite of another word.

Examples:

child  adult    hot    cold

Directions: Match the words that have opposite meanings. Draw a line between each pair of antonyms.

thaw	same
huge	sad
crying	friend
happy	open
enemy	freeze
asleep	thin
closed	hide
fat	tiny
seek	awake
different	laughing

Name _____

Antonyms

Directions: Complete each sentence with an antonym pair from page 196. Some pairs will not be used.

Example: Usually we wear <u>different</u> clothes, but today we are dressed the <u>same</u>.

1. A _____ is allowed in the museum if he/she is with

   an _____.

2. Mom was _____ it rained since her garden was very dry, but

   I was _____ because I had to stay inside.

3. The _____ crowd of people tried to fit into the

   _____ room.

4. The _____ baby was soon _____ and playing
   in the crib.

5. We'll _____ the meat for now, and Dad will _____
   it when we need it.

6. The windows were wide _____, but the door

   was _____.

Now, write your own sentence using one of the antonym pairs.

_____

_____

_____

Name _____

Antonyms

Antonyms are words that are opposites.

Example:  **hairy**   **bald**

Directions: Choose a word from the box to complete each sentence below.

open	right	light	full	late	below
hard	clean	slow	quiet	old	nice

Example:

My car was **dirty**, but now it's **clean**.

1. Sometimes my cat is naughty, and sometimes she's _____.

2. The sign said, "Closed," but the door was _____.

3. Is the glass half empty or half _____?

4. I bought new shoes, but I like my _____ ones better.

5. Skating is easy for me, but _____ for my brother.

6. The sky is dark at night and _____ during the day.

7. I like a noisy house, but my mother likes a _____ one.

8. My friend says I'm wrong, but I say I'm _____.

9. Jason is a fast runner, but Adam is a _____ runner.

10. We were supposed to be early, but we were _____.

Antonyms

Directions: Write the antonym pairs from each sentence in the boxes.

Example: Many things are bought and sold at the market.

bought	sold

1. I thought I lost my dog, but someone found him.

2. The teacher will ask questions for the students to answer.

3. Airplanes arrive and depart from the airport.

4. The water in the pool was cold compared to the warm water in the whirlpool.

5. The tortoise was slow, but the hare was fast.

Synonyms

Synonyms are words with nearly the same meaning.

Directions: Draw a line to match each word on the left with its synonym on the right.

infant	hello
forest	coat
bucket	grin
hi	baby
bunny	woods
cheerful	fall
jacket	repair
alike	small
smile	same
autumn	hop
little	skinny
thin	top
jump	rabbit
shirt	pail
fix	happy

Synonyms

Directions: Read each sentence. Choose a word from the box that has the same meaning as the bold word. Write the synonym on the line next to the sentence. The first one has been done for you.

skinniest	biggest	jacket	little	quickly	woods	joyful
grin	alike	trip	rabbit	fix	autumn	infant

1. The deer ran through the **forest**. _____woods_____

2. White mice are very **small** pets. _____

3. Goldfish move **fast** in the water. _____

4. The twins look exactly the **same**. _____

5. Trees lose their leaves in the **fall**. _____

6. The blue whale is the **largest** animal on Earth. _____

7. We will go to the ocean on our next **vacation**. _____

8. The **bunny** hopped through the tall grass. _____

9. The **baby** was crying because it was hungry. _____

10. Put on your **coat** before you go outside. _____

11. Does that clown have a big **smile** on his face? _____

12. That is the **thinnest** man I have ever seen. _____

13. I will **repair** my bicycle as soon as I get home. _____

14. The children made **happy** sounds when they won. _____

Synonyms

Directions: Match the pairs of synonyms.

delight •   • discover
speak •   • tidy
lovely •   • start
find •   • talk
nearly •   • beautiful
neat •   • almost
big •   • joy
sad •   • unhappy
begin •   • large

Directions: Read each sentence. Write the synonym pairs from each sentence in the boxes.

1. That unusual clock is a rare antique.

2. I am glad you are so happy!

3. Becky felt unhappy when she heard the sad news.

Homophones

Homophones are words that sound the same but are spelled differently and have different meanings.

Example:

sew   sow   so

Directions: Read the sentences and write the correct word in the blanks.

Example:

blue   blew   She has **blue** eyes.

The wind **blew** the barn down.

eye   I   He hurt his left _____ playing ball.

_____ like to learn new things.

see   sea   Can you _____ the winning runner from here?

He goes diving for pearls under the _____ .

eight   ate   The baby _____ the banana.

Jane was _____ years old last year.

one   won   Jill _____ first prize at the science fair.

I am the only _____ in my family with red hair.

be   bee   Jenny cried when a _____ stung her.

I have to _____ in bed every night at eight o'clock.

two   to   too   My father likes _____ play tennis.

I like to play, _____ .

It takes at least _____ people to play.

Name _____

Homophones

Directions: Circle the correct word to complete each sentence. Then write the word on the line.

1. I am going to _____ a letter to my grandmother.
   right, write

2. Draw a circle around the _____ answer.
   right, write

3. Wait an _____ before going swimming.
   our, hour

4. This is _____ house.
   our, hour

5. He got a _____ from his garden.
   beat, beet

6. Our football team _____ that team.
   beat, beet

7. Go to the store and _____ a loaf of bread.
   by, buy

8. We will drive _____ your house.
   by, buy

9. It will be trouble if the dog _____ the cat.
   seas, sees

10. They sailed the seven _____ .
    seas, sees

11. We have _____ cars in the garage.
    to, too, two

12. I am going _____ the zoo today.
    to, too, two

13. My little brother is going, _____ .
    to, too, two

Name _____

Homophones

Homophones are words that sound the same but have different spellings and meanings.

Directions: Complete each sentence using a word from the box.

blew	night	blue	knight	hour	in	ant	inn
our	aunt	meet	too	two	to	meat

1. A red _____ crawled up the wall.

2. It will be one _____ before we can go back home.

3. Will you _____ us later?

4. We plan to stay at an _____ during our trip.

5. The king had a _____ who fought bravely.

6. The wind _____ so hard that I almost lost my hat.

7. His jacket was _____.

8. My_____ plans to visit us this week.

9. I will come _____ when it gets too cold outside.

10. It was late at _____ when we finally got there.

11. _____ of us will go with you.

12. I will mail a note _____ someone at the bank.

13. Do you eat red _____?

14. We would like to join you, _____.

15. Come over to see _____ new cat.

Name _____

Homophones

Directions: Circle the words that are not used correctly. Write the correct word above the circled word. Use the words in the box to help you. The first one has been done for you.

road	see	one	be	so	I	brakes	piece	there
wait	not	some	hour	would	no	deer	you	heard

Jake and his family were getting close to Grandpa's. It had taken them

nearly an ~~our~~ *(hour)* to get their, but Jake knew it was worth it. In his mind, he could

already sea the pond and could almost feel the cool water. It had been sew

hot this summer in the apartment.

"Wood ewe like a peace of my apple, Jake?" asked his big sister Clare.

"Eye can't eat any more."

"Know, thank you," Jake replied. "I still have sum of my fruit left."

Suddenly, Dad slammed on the breaks. "Did you see that dear on the rode?

I always herd that if you see won, there might bee more."

"Good thinking, Dad. I'm glad you are a safe

driver. We're knot very far from

Grandpa's now. I can't weight!"

Nouns

Nouns are words that tell the names of people, places or things.

Directions: Read the words below. Then write them in the correct column.

goat	Mrs. Jackson	girl
beach	tree	song
mouth	park	Jean Rivers
finger	flower	New York
Kevin Jones	Elm City	Frank Gates
Main Street	theater	skates
River Park	father	boy

Person   **Place**   **Thing**

_____ _____ _____

_____ _____ _____

_____ _____ _____

_____ _____ _____

_____ _____ _____

_____ _____ _____

Common Nouns

Common nouns are nouns that name any member of a group of people, places or things, rather than specific people, places or things.

Directions: Read the sentences below and write the common noun found in each sentence.

Example: ___socks___ My socks do not match.

1. _____ The bird could not fly.

2. _____ Ben likes to eat jelly beans.

3. _____ I am going to meet my mother.

4. _____ We will go swimming in the lake tomorrow.

5. _____ I hope the flowers will grow quickly.

6. _____ We colored eggs together.

7. _____ It is easy to ride a bicycle.

8. _____ My cousin is very tall.

9. _____ Ted and Jane went fishing in their boat.

10. _____ They won a prize yesterday.

11. _____ She fell down and twisted her ankle.

12. _____ My brother was born today.

13. _____ She went down the slide.

14. _____ Ray went to the doctor today.

Proper Nouns

Proper nouns are names of specific people, places or things. Proper nouns begin with a capital letter.

Directions: Read the sentences below and circle the proper nouns found in each sentence.

Example: (Aunt Frances) gave me a puppy for my birthday.

1. We lived on Jackson Street before we moved to our new house.

2. Angela's birthday party is tomorrow night.

3. We drove through Cheyenne, Wyoming on our way home.

4. Dr. Charles always gives me a treat for not crying.

5. George Washington was our first president.

6. Our class took a field trip to the Johnson Flower Farm.

7. Uncle Jack lives in New York City.

8. Amy and Elizabeth are best friends.

9. We buy doughnuts at the Grayson Bakery.

10. My favorite movie is *E.T.*

11. We flew to Miami, Florida in a plane.

12. We go to Riverfront Stadium to watch the baseball games.

13. Mr. Fields is a wonderful music teacher.

14. My best friend is Tom Dunlap.

Name _____

Proper Nouns

Directions: Rewrite each sentence, capitalizing the proper nouns.

1. mike's birthday is in september.

_____

2. aunt katie lives in detroit, michigan.

_____

3. In july, we went to canada.

_____

4. kathy jones moved to utah in january.

_____

5. My favorite holiday is valentine's day in february.

_____

6. On friday, mr. polzin gave the smith family a tour.

_____

7. saturday, uncle cliff and I will go to the mall of america in minnesota.

_____

_____

Name _____

Plural Nouns

Directions: Write the plural of each noun to complete the sentences below. Remember to change the **y** to **ie** before you add **s**!

1. I am going to two birthday _____ this week.
   (party)

2. Sandy picked some _____ for Mom's pie.
   (cherry)

3. At the store, we saw lots of _____.
   (bunny)

4. My change at the candy store was three _____.
   (penny)

5. All the _____ baked cookies for the bake sale.
   (lady)

6. Thanksgiving is a special time for _____ to gather together.
   (family)

7. Boston and New York are very large _____.
   (city)

Name _____

Plural Nouns

Directions: The **singular form** of a word shows one person, place or thing. Write the singular form of each noun on the lines below.

cherries _____

lunches _____

countries _____

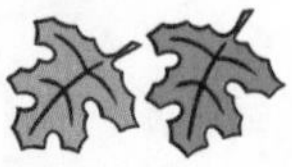

leaves _____

churches _____

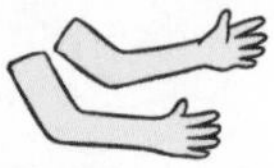

arms _____

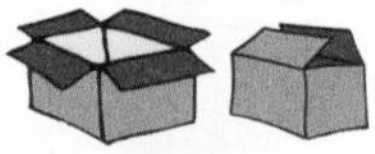

boxes _____

men _____

wheels _____

pictures _____

cities _____

places _____

ostriches _____

glasses _____

Name _____

Possessive Nouns

Possessive nouns tell who or what is the owner of something. With singular nouns, we use an apostrophe **before** the **s**. With plural nouns, we use an apostrophe **after** the **s**.

Example:

singular: one elephant

The **elephant's** dance was wonderful.

plural: more than one elephant

The **elephants'** dance was wonderful.

Directions: Put the apostrophe in the correct place in each bold word. Then write the word in the blank.

1. The **lions** cage was big. _____

2. The **bears** costumes were purple. _____

3. One **boys** laughter was very loud. _____

4. The **trainers** dogs were dancing about. _____

5. The **mans** popcorn was tasty and good. _____

6. **Marks** cotton candy was delicious. _____

7. A little **girls** balloon burst in the air. _____

8. The big **clowns** tricks were very funny. _____

9. **Lauras** sister clapped for the clowns. _____

10. The **womans** money was lost in the crowd. _____

11. **Kellys** mother picked her up early. _____

Name _____

Possessive Nouns

Directions: Circle the correct possessive noun in each sentence and write it in the blank.

Example: One ___girl's___ mother is a teacher.

(girl's)   girls'

1. The _____ tail is long.

    cat's   cats'

2. One _____ baseball bat is aluminum.

    boy's   boys'

3. The_____ aprons are white.

    waitresses'   waitress's

4. My _____ apple pie is the best!

    grandmother's   grandmothers'

5. My five _____ uniforms are dirty.

    brother's   brothers'

6. The _____ doll is pretty.

    child's   childs'

7. These_____ collars are different colors.

    dog's   dogs'

8. The _____ tail is short.

    cow's   cows'

Pronouns

Pronouns are words that are used in place of nouns.
Examples: he, she, it, they, him, them, her, him

Directions: Read each sentence. Write the
pronoun that takes the place of each noun.

Example:
 The **monkey** dropped the banana. __It__

1. **Dad** washed the car last night. _____

2. **Mary and David** took a walk in the park. _____

3. **Peggy** spent the night at her grandmother's house. _____

4. The baseball **players** lost their game. _____

5. **Mike Van Meter** is a great soccer player. _____

6. The **parrot** can say five different words. _____

7. **Megan** wrote a story in class today. _____

8. They gave a party for **Teresa**. _____

9. Everyone in the class was happy for **Ted**. _____

10. The children petted the **giraffe**. _____

11. Linda put the **kittens** near the warm stove. _____

12. **Gina** made a chocolate cake for my birthday. _____

13. **Pete and Matt** played baseball on the same team. _____

14. Give the books to **Herbie**. _____

Name _____

Pronouns

Singular Pronouns

I me my mine

you your yours

he she it her

hers his its him

Plural Pronouns

we us our ours

you your yours

they them their theirs

Directions: Underline the pronouns in each sentence.

1. Mom told us to wash our hands.

2. Did you go to the store?

3. We should buy him a present.

4. I called you about their party.

5. Our house had damage on its roof.

6. They want to give you a prize at our party.

7. My cat ate her sandwich.

8. Your coat looks like his coat.

Name _____

Possessive Pronouns

Possessive pronouns show ownership.

Example: his hat, **her** shoes, **our** dog

We can use these pronouns before a noun:
my, our, you, his, her, its, their

Example: That is **my** bike.

We can use these pronouns on their own:
mine, yours, ours, his, hers, theirs, its

Example: That is **mine**.

Directions: Write each sentence again, using a pronoun instead of the words in bold letters. Be sure to use capitals and periods.

Example:

My **dog's** bowl is brown.   **Its** bowl is brown.

1. That is **Lisa's** book. _____

2. This is **my pencil**.   _____

3. This hat is **your hat**. _____

4. Fifi is **Kevin's** cat.   _____

5. That beautiful house is **our home**.

_____

6. **The gerbil's** cage is too small.

_____

Abbreviations

An **abbreviation** is the shortened form of a word. Most abbreviations begin with a capital letter and end with a period.

Mr.	Mister	St.	Street
Mrs.	Missus	Ave.	Avenue
Dr.	Doctor	Blvd.	Boulevard
A.M.	before noon	Rd.	Road
P.M.	after noon		

Days of the week: Sun. Mon. Tues. Wed. Thurs. Fri. Sat.
Months of the year: Jan. Feb. Mar. Apr. Aug. Sept. Oct. Nov. Dec.

Directions: Write the abbreviations for each word.

street	_____	doctor	_____	Tuesday	_____
road	_____	mister	_____	avenue	_____
missus	_____	October	_____	Friday	_____
before noon	_____	March	_____	August	_____

Directions: Write each sentence using abbreviations.

1. On Monday at 9:00 before noon Mister Jones had a meeting.

_____

2. In December Doctor Carlson saw Missus Zuckerman.

_____

3. One Tuesday in August Mister Wood went to the park.

_____

Name _____

Adjectives

Adjectives are words that tell more about nouns, such as a **happy** child, a **cold** day or a **hard** problem. Adjectives can tell how many (**one** airplane) or which one (**those** shoes).

Directions: The nouns are in bold letters. Circle the adjectives that describe the nouns.

Example: Some people have (unusual) **pets**.

1. Some people keep wild **animals**, like lions and bears.

2. These **pets** need special care.

3. These **animals** want to be free when they get older.

4. Even small **animals** can be difficult if they are wild.

5. Raccoons and squirrels are not tame **pets**.

6. Never touch a wild **animal** that may be sick.

Complete the story below by writing in your own adjectives. Use your imagination.

My Cat

My cat is a very_____ animal. She has _____

and _____ fur. Her favorite toy is a _____ ball.

She has _____ claws. She has a _____ tail.

She has a _____ face and _____ whiskers.

I think she is the _____ cat in the world!

Adjectives and Nouns

Directions: Underline the nouns in each sentence below. Then draw an arrow from each adjective to the noun it describes.

Example:

A <u>platypus</u> is a furry <u>animal</u> that lives in <u>Australia</u>.

1. This animal likes to swim.

2. The nose looks like a duck's bill.

3. It has a broad tail like a beaver.

4. Platypuses are great swimmers.

5. They have webbed feet which help them swim.

6. Their flat tails also help them move through the water.

7. The platypus is an unusual mammal because it lays eggs.

8. The eggs look like reptile eggs.

9. Platypuses can lay three eggs at a time.

10. These babies do not leave their mothers for one year.

11. This animal spends most of its time hunting near streams.

Name _____

Adjectives

A chart of adjectives can also be used to help describe nouns.

Directions: Look at the pictures. Complete each chart.

Example:

Noun	What Color?	What Size?	What Number?
flower	red	small	two

Noun	What Color?	What Size?	What Number?

Noun	What Color?	What Size?	What Number?

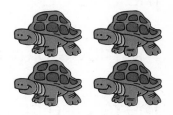

Noun	What Color?	What Size?	What Number?

Prefixes

Prefixes are special word parts added to the beginnings of words. Prefixes change the meaning of words.

Prefix	Meaning	Example
un	not	**un**happy
re	again	**re**do
pre	before	**pre**view
mis	wrong	**mis**understanding
dis	opposite	**dis**obey

Directions: Circle the word that begins with a prefix. Then write the prefix and the root word.

1. The dog was unfriendly.   _____ + _____

2. The movie preview was interesting.   _____ + _____

3. The referee called an unfair penalty.   _____ + _____

4. Please do not misbehave.   _____ + _____

5. My parents disapprove of that show.   _____ + _____

6. I had to redo the assignment.   _____ + _____

Name _____

Suffixes

Suffixes are word parts added to the ends of words. Suffixes change the meaning of words.

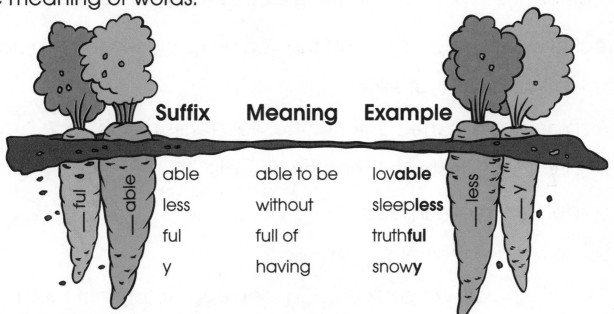

Suffix	Meaning	Example
able	able to be	lov**able**
less	without	sleep**less**
ful	full of	truth**ful**
y	having	snow**y**

Directions: Circle the suffix in each word below.

Example: fluff(y)

rainy	thoughtful	likeable
blameless	enjoyable	helpful
peaceful	careless	silky

Directions: Write a word for each meaning.

full of hope _____   having rain _____

without hope _____   able to break _____

without power _____   full of cheer _____

Verbs

A **verb** is the action word in a sentence, the word that tells what something does or that something exists. **Examples: run, jump, skip.**

Directions: Draw a box around the verb in each sentence below.

1. Spiders spin webs of silk.

2. A spider waits in the center of the web for its meals.

3. A spider sinks its sharp fangs into insects.

4. Spiders eat many insects.

5. Spiders make their nests with silk.

6. Female spiders wrap silk around their eggs to protect them.

Directions: Choose the correct verb from the box and write it in the sentences below.

| hides | swims | eats | grabs | hurt |

1. A crab spider _____ deep inside a flower where it cannot be seen.

2. The crab spider _____ insects when they land on the flower.

3. The wolf spider is good because it _____ wasps.

4. The water spider _____ under water.

5. Most spiders will not _____ people.

Name _____

Verbs

When a verb tells what one person or thing is doing now, it usually ends in **s. Example:** She **sings**.

When a verb is used with **you**, **I** or **we**, we do not add an **s**.

Example: I **sing**.

Directions: Write the correct verb in each sentence.

Example:

I ____write____ a newspaper about our street.   **writes, write**

1. My sister _____ me sometimes.   **helps, help**

2. She _____ the pictures.   **draw, draws**

3. We _____ them together.   **delivers, deliver**

4. I _____ the news about all the people.   **tell, tells**

5. Mr. Macon _____ the most beautiful flowers.   **grow, grows**

6. Mrs. Jones _____ to her plants.   **talks, talk**

7. Kevin Turner_____ his dog loose everyday.   **lets, let**

8. Little Mikey Smith _____ lost once a week.   **get, gets**

9. You may _____ I live on an interesting street.   **thinks, think**

10. We _____ it's the best street in town.   **say, says**

Helping Verbs

A **helping verb** is a word used with an action verb.

Examples: may, **shall**, and **are**

Directions: Write a helping verb from the box with each action verb.

can	could	must	will
may	would	should	do
shall	did	does	am
had	have	has	
are	were	is	
be	being	been	

Example:

Tomorrow, I ___**may**___ play soccer.

1. Mom _____ buy my new soccer shoes tonight.

2. Yesterday, my old soccer shoes _____ ripped by the cat.

3. I _____ going to ask my brother to go to the game.

4. He usually _____ not like soccer.

5. But, he _____ go with me because I am his sister.

6. He _____ promised to watch the entire soccer game.

7. He has _____ helping me with my homework.

8. I _____ spell a lot better because of his help.

9. Maybe I _____ finish the semester at the top of my class.

Name _____

Past-Tense Verbs

The **past tense** of a verb tells about something that has already happened. We add a **d** or an **ed** to most verbs to show that something has already happened.

Directions: Use the verb from the first sentence to complete the second sentence.

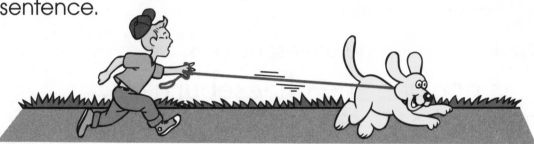

Example:

Please **walk** the dog. I already __walked__ her.

1. The flowers look good. They_____ better yesterday.

2. Please accept my gift. I _____ it for my sister.

3. I wonder who will win. I _____ about it all night.

4. He will saw the wood. He _____ some last week.

5. Fold the paper neatly. She _____ her paper.

6. Let's cook outside tonight. We _____ outside last night.

7. Do not block the way. They _____ the entire street.

8. Form the clay this way. He _____ it into a ball.

9. Follow my car. We _____ them down the street.

10. Glue the pages like this. She _____ the flowers on.

Present-Tense Verbs

The **present tense** of a verb tells about something that is happening now, happens often or is about to happen. These verbs can be written two ways: The bird sing**s**. The bird is sing**ing**.

Directions: Write each sentence again, using the verb **is** and writing the **ing** form of the verb.

Example: He cooks the cheeseburgers.

He is cooking the cheeseburgers.

1. Sharon dances to that song.

_____

2. Frank washed the car.

_____

3. Mr. Benson smiles at me.

_____

Write a verb for the sentences below that tells something that is happening now. Be sure to use the verb **is** and the **ing** form of the verb.

Example: The big, brown dog _is barking_____.

1. The little baby _____.

2. Most nine-year-olds _____.

3. The monster on television _____.

Future-Tense Verbs

The **future tense** of a verb tells about something that has not happened yet but will happen in the future. **Will** or **shall** are usually used with future tense.

Directions: Change the verb tense in each sentence to future tense.

Example: She cooks dinner.

_____ She will cook dinner. _____

1. He plays baseball.

   _____

2. She walks to school.

   _____

3. Bobby talks to the teacher.

   _____

4. I remember to vote.

   _____

5. Jack mows the lawn every week.

   _____

6. We go on vacation soon.

   _____

Name _____

Irregular Verbs

Irregular verbs are verbs that do not change from the present tense to the past tense in the regular way with **d** or **ed**.

Example: sing, **sang**

Directions: Read the sentence and underline the verbs. Choose the past-tense form from the box and write it next to the sentence.

blow — blew	fly — flew
come — came	give — gave
take — took	wear — wore
make — made	sing — sang
grow — grew	

Example:

Dad will <u>make</u> a cake tonight.   _____made_____

1. I will probably grow another inch this year.   _____

2. I will blow out the candles.   _____

3. Everyone will give me presents.   _____

4. I will wear my favorite red shirt.   _____

5. My cousins will come from out of town.   _____

6. It will take them four hours.   _____

7. My Aunt Betty will fly in from Cleveland.   _____

8. She will sing me a song when she gets here.   _____

Irregular Verbs

Directions: Circle the verb that completes each sentence.

1. Scientists will try to (find, found) the cure.

2. Eric (brings, brought) his lunch to school yesterday.

3. Everyday, Betsy (sings, sang) all the way home.

4. Jason (breaks, broke) the vase last night.

5. The ice had (freezes, frozen) in the tray.

6. Mitzi has (swims, swum) in that pool before.

7. Now I (choose, chose) to exercise daily.

8. The teacher has (rings, rung) the bell.

9. The boss (speaks, spoke) to us yesterday.

10. She (says, said) it twice already.

Name _____

Irregular Verbs

The verb **be** is different from all other verbs. The present-tense forms of **be** are **am**, **is** and **are**. The past-tense forms of **be** are **was** and **were**. The verb **to be** is written in the following ways:

singular: I am, you are, he is, she is, it is
plural: we are, you are, they are

Directions: Choose the correct form of **be** from the words in the box and write it in each sentence.

| are | am | is | was | were |

Example:

I _____ am _____ feeling good at this moment.

1. My sister _____ a good singer.

2. You _____ going to the store with me.

3. Sandy _____ at the movies last week.

4. Rick and Tom _____ best friends.

5. He _____ happy about the surprise.

6. The cat _____ hungry.

7. I _____ going to the ball game.

8. They _____ silly.

9. I _____ glad to help my mother.

Name _____

Linking Verbs

Linking verbs connect the noun to a descriptive word. Linking verbs are often forms of the verb **be**.

Directions: The linking verb is underlined in each sentence. Circle the two words that are being connected.

Example: The (cat) is (fat.)

1. My favorite food <u>is</u> pizza.

2. The car <u>was</u> red.

3. I <u>am</u> tired.

4. Books <u>are</u> fun!

5. The garden <u>is</u> beautiful.

6. Pears <u>taste</u> juicy.

7. The airplane <u>looks</u> large.

8. Rabbits <u>are</u> furry.

Adverbs

Adverbs are words that describe verbs. They tell where, how or when.

Directions: Circle the adverb in each of the following sentences.

Example: The doctor worked (carefully).

1. The skater moved gracefully across the ice.

2. Their call was returned quickly.

3. We easily learned the new words.

4. He did the work perfectly.

5. She lost her purse somewhere.

Directions: Complete the sentences below by writing your own adverbs in the blanks.

Example: The bees worked _____busily_____ .

1. The dog barked _____ .

2. The baby smiled _____ .

3. She wrote her name _____ .

4. The horse ran _____ .

Name _____

Adverbs

Directions: Read each sentence. Then answer the questions on the lines below.

Example: Charles ate hungrily.

who? _____Charles_____

what? _____ate_____

how? _____hungrily_____

1. She dances slowly.

who? _____

what? _____

how? _____

2. The girl spoke carefully.

who? _____

what? _____

how? _____

3. My brother ran quickly.

who? _____

what? _____

how? _____

4. Jean walks home often.

who? _____

what? _____

when? _____

5. The children played there.

who? _____

what? _____

where? _____

Name _____

Prepositions

Prepositions show relationships between the noun or pronoun and another noun in the sentence. The preposition comes before that noun.

Example: The <u>book</u> is on the table.

Common Prepositions

above	behind	by	near	over
across	below	in	off	through
around	beside	inside	on	under

Directions: Circle the prepositions in each sentence.

1. The dog ran fast around the house.

2. The plates in the cupboard were clean.

3. Put the card inside the envelope.

4. The towel on the sink was wet.

5. I planted flowers in my garden.

6. My kite flew high above the trees.

7. The chair near the counter was sticky.

8. Under the ground, worms lived in their homes.

9. I put the bow around the box.

10. Beside the pond, there was a playground.

Name _____

Articles

Articles are words used before nouns. **A**, **an** and **the** are articles. We use **a** before words that begin with a consonant. We use **an** before words that begin with a vowel.

Example: **a peach**    **an apple**

Directions: Write **a** or **an** in the sentences below.

Example: My bike had _____**a**_____ flat tire.

1. They brought _____ goat to the farm.

2. My mom wears _____ old pair of shoes to mow the lawn.

3. We had _____ party for my grandfather.

4. Everybody had _____ ice-cream cone after the game.

5. We bought _____ picnic table for our backyard.

6. We saw _____ lion sleeping in the shade.

7. It was _____ evening to be remembered.

8. He brought _____ blanket to the game.

9. _____ exit sign was above the door.

10. They went to _____ orchard to pick apples.

11. He ate _____ orange for lunch.

Name _____

Commas

Commas are used to separate words in a series of three or more.

Example: My favorite fruits are apples, bananas and oranges.

Directions: Put commas where they are needed in each sentence.

1. Please buy milk eggs bread and cheese.

2. I need a folder paper and pencils for school.

3. Some good pets are cats dogs gerbils fish and rabbits.

4. Aaron Mike and Matt went to the baseball game.

5. Major forms of transportation are planes trains and automobiles.

Name _____

Commas

We use commas to separate the day from the year.
Example: May 13, 1950

Directions: Write the dates in the blanks. Put the
commas in and capitalize the name of each month.

Example:

Jack and Dave were born on february 22 1982.

_____February 22, 1982_____

1. My father's birthday is may 19 1948.

_____

2. My sister was fourteen on december 13 1994.

_____

3. Lauren's seventh birthday was on november 30 1998.

_____

4. october 13 1996 was the last day I saw my lost cat.

_____

5. On april 17 1997, we saw the Grand Canyon.

_____

6. Our vacation lasted from april 2 1998 to april 26 1998.

_____   _____

7. Molly's baby sister was born on august 14 1991.

_____

8. My mother was born on june 22 1959.

_____

Capitalization

The names of **people**, **places** and **pets**, the **days of the week**, the **months of the year** and **holidays** begin with a capital letter.

Directions: Read the words in the box. Write the words in the correct column with capital letters at the beginning of each word.

ron polsky	tuesday	march	april
presidents' day	saturday	woofy	october
blackie	portland, oregon	corning, new york	molly yoder
valentine's day	fluffy	harold edwards	arbor day
bozeman, montana	sunday		

People

_____

_____

_____

Places

_____

_____

_____

Pets

_____

_____

_____

Days

_____

_____

_____

Months

_____

_____

_____

Holidays

_____

_____

_____

Name _____

Parts of Speech

Nouns, pronouns, verbs, adjectives, adverbs and prepositions are all **parts of speech**.

Directions: Label the words in each sentence with the correct part of speech.

Example: The   cat   is   fat.
article   noun   verb   adjective

1. My   cow   walks   in   the   barn.

2. Red   flowers   grow   in   the   garden.

3. The   large   dog   was   excited.

Name _____

Parts of Speech

Directions: Ask someone to give you nouns, verbs, adjectives and pronouns where shown. Write them in the blanks. Read the story to your friend when you finish.

The _____ **Adventure**
(adjective)

I went for a _____ . I found a really big _____ .
(noun)   (noun)

It was so _____ that I _____ all the
(adjective)   (verb)

way home. I put it in my _____ . To my amazement, it
(noun)

began to _____ . I _____ . I took it to my
(verb)   (past-tense verb)

_____ . I showed it to all my _____ .
(place)   (plural noun)

I decided to _____ it in a box and wrap it up with
(verb)

_____ paper. I gave it to _____ for a
(adjective)   (person)

present. When_____ opened it,_____
(pronoun)   (pronoun)

_____ . _____ shouted, "Thank you!
(past-tense verb)   (pronoun)

This is the best _____ I've ever had!"
(noun)

Name _____

Parts of Speech

Directions: Write the part of speech of each underlined word.

NOUN   PRONOUN   VERB   ADJECTIVE   ADVERB   PREPOSITION

①　　②
There are many different kinds of animals. Some animals live in the

③
wild. Some animals live in the zoo. And still others live in homes. The animals

④
that live in homes are called pets.

There are many types of pets. Some pets without fur are fish, turtles,

⑤　　⑥
snakes and hermit crabs. Trained birds can fly around your house. Some

⑦
furry animals are cats, dogs, rabbits, ferrets, gerbils or hamsters. Some animals

⑧　　　　　⑨
can successfully learn tricks that you teach them. Whatever your favorite

⑩
animal is, animals can be special friends!

1. _____   4. _____

2. _____   5. _____   7. _____   9. _____

3. _____   6. _____   8. _____   10. _____

And and But

We can use **and** or **but** to make one longer sentence from two short ones.

Directions: Use **and** or **but** to make two short sentences into a longer, more interesting one. Write the new sentence on the line below the two short sentences.

Example:

The skunk has black fur. The skunk has a white stripe.

The skunk has black fur and a white stripe.

1. The skunk has a small head. The skunk has small ears.

_____

2. The skunk has short legs. Skunks can move quickly.

_____

3. Skunks sleep in hollow trees. Skunks sleep underground.

_____

4. Skunks are chased by animals. Skunks do not run away.

_____

5. Skunks sleep during the day. Skunks hunt at night.

_____

Subjects

A **subject** tells who or what the sentence is about.

Directions: Underline the subject in the following sentences.

Example:

The zebra is a large animal.

1. Zebras live in Africa.

2. Zebras are related to horses.

3. Horses have longer hair than zebras.

4. Zebras are good runners.

5. Their feet are protected by their hooves.

6. Some animals live in groups.

7. These groups are called herds.

8. Zebras live in herds with other grazing animals.

9. Grazing animals eat mostly grass.

10. They usually eat three times a day.

11. They often travel to water holes.

Name _____

Simple Subjects

A **simple subject** is the main noun or pronoun in the complete subject.

Directions: Draw a line between the subject and the predicate. Circle the simple subject.

Example: The black (bear) | lives in the zoo.

1. Penguins look like they wear tuxedos.

2. The seal enjoys raw fish.

3. The monkeys like to swing on bars.

4. The beautiful peacock has colorful feathers.

5. Bats like dark places.

6. Some snakes eat small rodents.

7. The orange and brown giraffes have long necks.

8. The baby zebra is close to his mother.

Compound Subjects

Compound subjects are two or more nouns that have the same predicate.

Directions: Combine the subjects to create one sentence with a compound subject.

Example: Jill can swing.
Whitney can swing.
Luke can swing.

Jill, Whitney and Luke can swing.

1. Roses grow in the garden. Tulips grow in the garden.

_____

2. Apples are fruit. Oranges are fruit. Bananas are fruit.

_____

3. Bears live in the zoo. Monkeys live in the zoo.

_____

4. Jackets keep us warm. Sweaters keep us warm.

_____

Compound Subjects

Directions: Underline the simple subjects in each compound subject.

Example: <u>Dogs</u> and <u>cats</u> are good pets.

1. Blueberries and strawberries are fruit.

2. Jesse, Jake and Hannah like school.

3. Cows, pigs and sheep live on a farm.

4. Boys and girls ride the bus.

5. My family and I took a trip to Duluth.

6. Fruits and vegetables are good for you.

7. Katarina, Lexi and Mandi like to go swimming.

8. Petunias, impatiens, snapdragons and geraniums are all flowers.

9. Coffee, tea and milk are beverages.

10. Dave, Karla and Tami worked on the project together.

Name _____

Predicates

A **predicate** tells what the subject is doing, has done or will do.

Directions: Underline the predicate in the following sentences.

Example: Woodpeckers <u>live in trees.</u>

1. They hunt for insects in the trees.

2. Woodpeckers have strong beaks.

3. They can peck through the bark.

4. The pecking sound can be heard from far away.

Directions: Circle the groups of words that can be predicates.

have long tongues   pick up insects

hole in bark   sticky substance

help it to climb trees   tree bark

Now, choose the correct predicates from above to finish these sentences.

1. Woodpeckers _____ .

2. They use their tongues to _____ .

3. Its strong feet _____ .

Simple Predicates

A **simple predicate** is the main verb or verbs in the complete predicate.

Directions: Draw a line between the complete subject and the complete predicate. Circle the simple predicate.

Example: The ripe apples (fell) to the ground.

1. The farmer scattered feed for the chickens.

2. The horses galloped wildly around the corral.

3. The baby chicks were staying warm by the light.

4. The tractor was baling hay.

5. The silo was full of grain.

6. The cows were being milked.

7. The milk truck drove up to the barn.

8. The rooster woke everyone up.

Compound Predicates

Compound predicates have two or more verbs that have the same subject.

Directions: Combine the predicates to create one sentence with a compound predicate.

Example: We went to the zoo.
We watched the monkeys.
We went to the zoo and watched the monkeys.

1. Students read their books. Students do their work.

_____

2. Dogs can bark loudly. Dogs can do tricks.

_____

3. The football player caught the ball. The football player ran.

_____

4. My dad sawed wood. My dad stacked wood.

_____

5. My teddy bear is soft. My teddy bear likes to be hugged.

_____

Compound Predicates

Directions: Underline the simple predicates (verbs) in each predicate.

Example: The fans <u>clapped</u> and <u>cheered</u> at the game.

1. The coach talks and encourages the team.

2. The cheerleaders jump and yell.

3. The basketball players dribble and shoot the ball.

4. The basketball bounces and hits the backboard.

5. The ball rolls around the rim and goes into the basket.

6. Everyone leaps up and cheers.

7. The team scores and wins!

Subjects and Predicates

Directions: Write the words for the subject to answer the **who** or **what** questions. Write the words for the predicate to answer the **does**, **did**, **is** or **has** questions.

Example:

My friend has two pairs of sunglasses.   **who?** _My friend_

has? _has two pairs of sunglasses._

1. John's dog went to school with him.   **what?** _____

   did? _____

2. The Eskimo traveled by dog sled.   **who?** _____

   did? _____

3. Alex slept in his treehouse last night.   **who?** _____

   did? _____

4. Cherry pie is my favorite kind of pie.   **what?** _____

   is? _____

5. The mail carrier brings the mail to the door.   **who?** _____

   does? _____

6. We have more than enough bricks to build the wall.   **who?** _____

   has? _____

7. The bird has a worm in its beak.   **what?** _____

   has? _____

Subjects and Predicates

Directions: Draw one line under the subjects and two lines under the predicates in the sentences below.

1. My mom likes to plant flowers.

2. Our neighbors walk their dog.

3. Our car needs gas.

4. The children play house.

5. Movies and popcorn go well together.

6. Peanut butter and jelly is my favorite kind of sandwich.

7. Bill, Sue and Nancy ride to the park.

8. We use pencils, markers and pens to write on paper.

9. Trees and shrubs need special care.

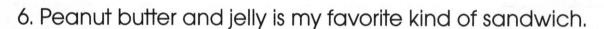

Sentences and Non-Sentences

A **sentence** tells a complete idea.

Directions: Circle the groups of words that tell a complete idea.

1. Sharks are fierce hunters.

2. Afraid of sharks.

3. The great white shark will attack people.

4. Other kinds will not.

5. Sharks have an outer row of teeth for grabbing food.

6. When the outer teeth fall out, another row of teeth moves up.

7. Keep the ocean clean by eating dead animals.

8. Not a single bone in its body.

9. Cartilage.

10. Made of the same material as the tip of your nose.

11. Unlike other fish, sharks cannot float.

12. In motion constantly.

13. Even while sleeping.

Name _____

Statements and Questions

Statements are sentences that tell about something. Statements begin with a capital letter and end with a period. **Questions** are sentences that ask about something. Questions begin with a capital letter and end with a question mark.

Directions: Rewrite the sentences using capital letters and either a period or a question mark.

Example: walruses live in the Arctic

Walruses live in the Arctic.

1. are walruses large sea mammals or fish

_____

2. they spend most of their time in the water and on ice

_____

3. are floating sheets of ice called ice floes

_____

4. are walruses related to seals

_____

5. their skin is thick, wrinkled and almost hairless

_____

Statements and Questions

Directions: Change the statements into questions and the questions into statements.

Example: Jane is happy.   Is Jane happy?
Were you late?   You were late.

1. The rainbow was brightly colored.

_____

2. Was the sun coming out?

_____

3. The dog is doing tricks.

_____

4. Have you washed the dishes today?

_____

5. Kurt was the circus ringmaster.

_____

6. Were you planning on going to the library?

_____

Exclamations

Exclamation points are used for sentences that express strong feelings. These sentences can have one or two words or be very long.

Example: Wait! or **Don't forget to call!**

Directions: Add an exclamation point at the end of sentences that express strong feelings. Add a period at the end of the statements.

1. My parents and I were watching television

2. The snow began falling around noon

3. Wow

4. The snow was really coming down

5. We turned the television off and looked out the window

6. The snow looked like a white blanket

7. How beautiful

8. We decided to put on our coats and go outside

9. Hurry

10. Get your sled

11. All the people on the street came out to see the snow

12. How wonderful

13. The children began making a snowman

14. What a great day

Name _____

Contractions

Contractions are shortened forms of two words. We use apostrophes to show where letters are missing.

Example: It is = it's

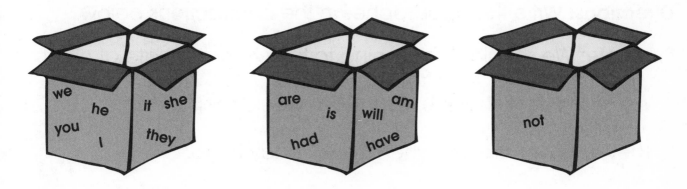

Directions: Write the words that are used in each contraction.

we're _____+_____   they'll _____+_____

you'll _____+_____   aren't _____+_____

I'm _____+_____   isn't _____+_____

Directions: Write the contraction for the two words shown.

you have _____   have not _____

had not _____   we will _____

they are _____   he is _____

she had _____   it will _____

I am _____   is not _____

Apostrophes

Apostrophes are used to show ownership by placing an **s** at the end of a single person, place or thing.

Example: Mary**'s** cat

Directions: Write the apostrophes in the contractions below.

Example: We shouldn**'**t be going to their house so late at night.

1. We didn t think that the ice cream would melt so fast.

2. They re never around when we re ready to go.

3. Didn t you need to make a phone call?

4. Who s going to help you paint the bicycle red?

Directions: Add an apostrophe and an **s** to the words to show ownership of a person, place or thing.

Example: Jill**'s** bike is broken.

1. That is Holly   flower garden.

2. Mark   new skates are black and green.

3. Mom threw away Dad   old shoes.

4. Buster   food dish was lost in the snowstorm.

Quotation Marks

Quotation marks are punctuation marks that tell what is said by a person. Quotation marks go before the first word and after the punctuation of a direct quote. The first word of a direct quote begins with a capital letter.

Example: Katie said, "Never go in the water without a friend."

Directions: Put quotation marks around the correct words in the sentences below.

Example: "Wait for me, please," said Laura.

1. John, would you like to visit a jungle? asked his uncle.

2. The police officer said, Don't worry, we'll help you.

3. James shouted, Hit a home run!

4. My friend Carol said, I really don't like cheeseburgers.

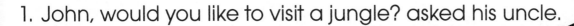

Directions: Write your own quotations by answering the questions below. Be sure to put quotation marks around your words.

1. What would you say if you saw a dinosaur?

   _____

   _____

2. What would your best friend say if your hair turned purple?

   _____

   _____

Quotation Marks

Directions: Put quotation marks around the correct words in the sentences below.

1. Can we go for a bike ride? asked Katrina.

_____

2. Yes, said Mom.

_____

3. Let's go to the park, said Mike.

_____

4. Great idea! said Mom.

_____

5. How long until we get there? asked Katrina.

_____

6. Soon, said Mike.

_____

7. Here we are! exclaimed Mom.

_____

Parts of a Paragraph

A **paragraph** is a group of sentences that all tell about the same thing. Most paragraphs have three parts: a **beginning**, a **middle** and an **end**.

Directions: Write **beginning, middle** or **end** next to each sentence in the scrambled paragraphs below. There can be more than one middle sentence.

Example:

_____middle_____ We took the tire off the car.

___beginning___ On the way to Aunt Louise's, we had a flat tire.

_____middle_____ We patched the hole in the tire.

_____end_____ We put the tire on and started driving again.

_____ I took all the ingredients out of the cupboard.

_____ One morning, I decided to bake a pumpkin pie.

_____ I forgot to add the pumpkin!

_____ I mixed the ingredients together, but something was missing.

_____ The sun was very hot and our throats were dry.

_____ We finally decided to turn back.

_____ We started our hike very early in the morning.

_____ It kept getting hotter as we walked.

Name _____

Topic Sentences

A **topic sentence** is usually the first sentence in a paragraph. It tells what the story will be about.

Directions: Read the following sentences. Circle the topic sentence that should go first in the paragraph that follows.

Rainbows have seven colors.

There's a pot of gold.

I like rainbows.

The colors are red, orange, yellow, green, blue, indigo and violet. Red forms the outer edge, with violet on the inside of the rainbow.

He cut down a cherry tree.

His wife was named Martha.

George Washington was a good president.

He helped our country get started. He chose intelligent leaders to help him run the country.

Mark Twain was a great author.

Mark Twain was unhappy sometimes.

Mark Twain was born in Missouri.

One of his most famous books is *Huckleberry Finn*. He wrote many other great books.

Name _____

Middle Sentences

Middle sentences support the topic sentence. They tell more about it.

Directions: Underline the middle sentences that support each topic sentence below.

Topic Sentence:

Penguins are birds that cannot fly.

Pelicans can spear fish with their sharp bills.

Many penguins waddle or hop about on land.

Even though they cannot fly, they are excellent swimmers.

Pelicans keep their food in a pouch.

Topic Sentence:

Volleyball is a team sport in which the players hit the ball over the net.

There are two teams with six players on each team.

My friend John would rather play tennis with Lisa.

Players can use their heads or their hands.

I broke my hand once playing handball.

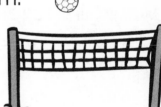

Topic Sentence:

Pikes Peak is the most famous of all the Rocky Mountains.

Some mountains have more trees than other mountains.

Many people like to climb to the top.

Many people like to ski and camp there, too.

The weather is colder at the top of most mountains.

Name _____

Ending Sentences

Ending sentences are sentences that tie the story together.

Directions: Choose the correct ending sentence for each story from the sentences below. Write it at the end of the paragraph.

A new pair of shoes!
All the corn on the cob I could eat!
A new eraser!

Corn on the Cob

   Corn on the cob used to be my favorite food. That is, until I lost my four front teeth. For one whole year, I had to sit and watch everyone else eat my favorite food without me. Mom gave me creamed corn, but it just wasn't the same. When my teeth finally came in, Dad said he had a surprise for me. I thought I was going to get a bike or a new C.D. player or something. I was just as happy to get what I did.

_____

I would like to take a train ride every year.
Trains move faster than I thought they would.
She had brought her new gerbil along for the ride.

A Train Ride

   When our family took its first train ride, my sister brought along a big box. She would not tell anyone what she had in it. In the middle of the trip, we heard a sound coming from the box. "Okay, Jan, now you have to open the box," said Mom. When she opened the box we were surprised.

_____

SPELLING

Name _____

Vocabulary: Beginning and Ending Sounds

Directions: Use the words in the box to answer the questions below.

ax	mix
beach	church
class	kiss
brush	crash

Which word:

begins with the same sound as **breakfast** and ends with the same sound as **fish**? _____

begins with the same sound as **children** and ends with the same sound as **catch**? _____

begins and ends with the same sound as **cuts**? _____

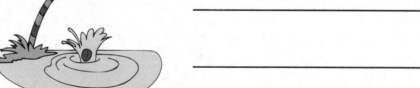

sounds like **acts**? _____

begins with the same sound as **coconut** and ends with the same sound as **splash**? _____

rhymes with **tricks**? _____

has **each** in it? _____

Name _____

Vocabulary: Sentences

Directions: Use a word from the box to complete each sentence. Use each word only once.

ax	mix	beach	church	class	kiss	brush	crash

1. Those two cars are going to _____ .

2. He chopped the wood with an _____ .

3. Grandma gave me a _____ on my cheek.

4. Before you go, _____ your hair.

5. How many students are in your _____ at school?

6. The waves bring sand to the _____ .

7. To make orange, you _____ yellow and red.

8. On Sunday, we always go to _____ .

Vocabulary: Plurals

A word that names one thing is **singular**, like **house**. A word that names more than one thing is **plural**, like **houses**.

To make a word plural, we usually add **s**.

Examples: one book — two book**s**   one tree — four tree**s**

To make plural words that end in **s**, **ss**, **x**, **sh** and **ch**, we add **es**.

Examples: one fox — two fox**es**   one bush — three bush**es**

Directions: Write the word that is missing from each pair below. Add **s** or **es** to make the plural words. The first one is done for you.

	Singular	Plural
	table	_tables_
	beach	_____
	class	_____
	_____	axes
	brush	_____
	_____	crashes

Name _____

Vocabulary: Spelling

Directions: Circle the word in each sentence which is not spelled correctly. Then write the word correctly.

1. How many clases are in your school? _____

2. Our town has six chirches. _____

3. Have you been to Maryland's beechs? _____

4. Water mixs with dirt to make mud. _____

5. We need two axs for this tree. _____

6. That car has been in three crashs. _____

7. She gave the baby lots of kises. _____

8. I lost both of my brushs at school. _____

Vocabulary: Nouns and Verbs

A **noun** names a person, place or thing. A **verb** tells what something does or what something is. Some words can be a noun one time and a verb another time.

Directions: Complete each pair of sentences with a word from the box. The word will be a noun in the first sentence and a verb in the second sentence.

mix	kiss	brush	crash

1. Did your dog ever give you a _____?
   (noun)

   I have a cold, so I can't _____ you today.
   (verb)

2. I brought my comb and my _____.
   (noun)

   I will _____ the leaves off your coat.
   (verb)

3. Was anyone hurt in the _____?
   (noun)

   If you aren't careful, you will _____ into me.
   (verb)

4. We bought a cake _____ at the store.
   (noun)

   I will _____ the eggs together.
   (verb)

Vocabulary: Nouns and Verbs

Directions: Write the correct word in each sentence. Use each word once. Write **N** above the words that are used as nouns (people, places and things). Write **V** above the words that are used as verbs (what something does or what something is).

Example:

I need a ___<u>drink</u>___ . I will ___<u>drink</u>___ milk.
        N   **V**

mix	beach	church	class	kiss	brush	crash

1. It's hot today, so let's go to the _____ .

2. The _____ was crowded.

3. I can't find my paint _____ .

4. Will you _____ my finger and make it stop hurting?

5. I will _____ the red and yellow paint to get orange.

6. The teacher asked our _____ to get in line.

7. If you move that bottom can, the rest will

_____ to the floor.

Name _____

Vocabulary: Sentences

Every sentence must have two things: a **noun** that tells who or what is doing something and a **verb** that tells what the noun is doing.

Directions: Add a **noun** or a **verb** to complete each sentence. Be sure to begin your sentences with capital letters and end them with periods.

Example: reads after school (needs a noun)

Brandy reads after school. _____

1. brushes her dog every day

_____

2. at the beach, we

_____

3. kisses me too much

_____

4. in the morning, our class

_____

5. stopped with a crash

_____

Vocabulary

Directions: Find the picture that matches each sentence below. Then complete each sentence with the word under the picture.

list

spill

search

pound

toast

load

1. I will _____ until I find it.

2. Be careful you don't _____ the paint.

3. Is that _____ too heavy for you?

4. They made _____ for breakfast.

5. Please go to the store and buy a _____ of butter.

6. Is my name on the _____?

Vocabulary

Directions: Find the picture that matches each sentence below. Then complete the sentence with the word under the picture.

hug   plan   clap

stir   drag   grab

1. She will _____ where to go on her trip.

2. _____ that big box over here, please.

3. My little brother always tries to _____ my toys.

4. May I help you _____ the soup?

5. I like to _____ my dog because he is so soft.

6. After she played, everyone started to _____.

Name _____

Vocabulary: Beginning and Ending Sounds

Directions: Write the words from the box that begin or end with the same sound as the pictures.

stir	clap	drag	hug	plan	grab

1. Which word begins with the same sound as each picture?

2. Which word (or words) ends with the same sound as each picture?

 _____   _____

 _____   _____

 _____   _____

 _____    _____

 _____

 _____   _____

Vocabulary: Explaining Sentences

Directions: Complete each sentence, explaining why each event might have happened.

She hugged me because _____

_____ .

He didn't want to play with us because _____

_____ .

We planned to go to the zoo because _____

_____ .

I grabbed it away from him because _____

_____ .

We clapped loudly because _____

_____ .

Vocabulary: Verbs

Directions: Write the verb that answers each question. Write a sentence using that verb.

stir	clap	drag	hug	plan	grab

Which verb means to put your arms around someone?

_____

_____

Which verb means to mix something with a spoon?

_____

_____

Which verb means to pull something along the ground?

_____

_____

Which verb means to take something suddenly?

_____

_____

Vocabulary: Past-Tense Verbs

The past tense of a verb tells that something already happened. To tell about something that already happened, add **ed** to most verbs. If the verb already ends in **e**, just add **d**.

Examples:

We enter**ed** the contest last week.
I fold**ed** the paper wrong.
He add**ed** two boxes to the pile.

We taste**d** the cupcakes.
They decide**d** quickly.
She share**d** her cupcake.

Directions: Use the verb from the first sentence to complete the second sentence. Add **d** or **ed** to show that something already happened.

Example:

My mom looks fine today. Yesterday, she ___looked___ tired.

1. You enter through the middle door.

   We _____ that way last week.

2. Please add this for me. I already _____ it twice.

3. Will you share your cookie with me?

   I _____ my apple with you yesterday.

4. It's your turn to fold the clothes. I _____ them yesterday.

5. May I taste another one? I already _____ one.

6. You need to decide. We _____ this morning.

Vocabulary: Past-Tense Verbs

When you write about something that already happened, you add **ed** to most verbs. For some verbs that have a short vowel and end in one consonant, you double the consonant before adding **ed**.

Examples:

He hug**ged** his pillow. The dog grab**bed** the stick.
She stir**red** the carrots. We plan**ned** to go tomorrow.
They clap**ped** for me. They drag**ged** their bags on the ground.

Directions: Use the verb from the first sentence to complete the second sentence. Change the verb in the second part to the past tense. Double the consonant and add **ed**.

Example:

We skip to school. Yesterday, we ___skipped___ the whole way.

1. It's not nice to grab things.

   When you _____ my cookie, I felt angry.

2. Did anyone hug you today? Dad _____ me this morning.

3. We plan our vacations every year. Last year, we _____ to go to the beach.

4. Is it my turn to stir the pot? You _____ it last time.

5. Let's clap for Andy, just like we _____ for Amy.

6. My sister used to drag her blanket everywhere.

   Once, she _____ it to the store.

Vocabulary: Past-Tense Verbs

When you write about something that already happened, you add **ed** to most verbs. Here is another way to write about something in the past tense.

Examples: The dog walked.   The dog was walking.
             The cats played.   The cats were playing.

Directions: Write each sentence again, writing the verb a different way.

Example: The baby pounded the pans.

The baby was pounding the pans.

1. Gary loaded the car by himself.

_____

2. They searched for a long time.

_____

3. The water spilled over the edge.

_____

4. Dad toasted the rolls.

_____

Name _____

Vocabulary: Past-Tense Verbs

Directions: Write sentences that tell about each picture using the words **is, are, was** and **were**. Use words from the box as either nouns or verbs.

| pound | spill | toast | list | load | search |

_____

_____

_____

_____

_____

_____

_____

_____

_____

_____

Name _____

Vocabulary: Present-Tense Verbs

When something is happening right now, it is in the **present tense**. There are two ways to write verbs in the present tense:

Examples: The dog **walks**.   The cats **play**.
                     The dog **is walking**.   The cats **are playing**.

Directions: Write each sentence again, writing the verb a different way.

Example:

He lists the numbers.

He is listing the numbers.

1. She is pounding the nail.

_____

2. My brother toasts the bread.

_____

3. They search for the robber.

_____

4. The teacher lists the pages.

_____

5. They are spilling the water.

_____

6. Ken and Amy load the packages.

_____

Vocabulary: Sentences

Directions: Write a word from the box to complete each sentence. Use each word only once.

glue	enter	share	add	decide	fold

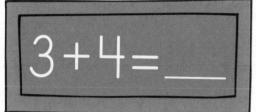

1. I know how to _____ 3 and 4.

2. Which book did you _____ to read?

3. Go in the door that says " _____ ."

4. I will _____ a yellow circle for the sun onto my picture.

5. I help _____ the clothes after they are washed.

6. She will _____ her banana with me.

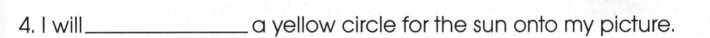

Vocabulary

Directions: Follow the directions below.

glue	enter	share	add	decide	fold

1. Add letters to these words to make words from the box.

   old _____   are _____

2. Write the two words from the box that begin with vowels.

   _____   _____

3. Change one letter of each word to make a word from the box.

   food _____   clue _____

4. Change two letters of this word to make a word from the box.

   beside _____

Vocabulary: Statements

A **statement** is a sentence that tells something.

Directions: Use the words in the box to complete the statements below. Write the words on the lines.

glue	decide	add
share	enter	fold

1. It took ten minutes for Kayla to _____ the numbers.

2. Ben wants to _____ his cookies with me.

3. "I can't _____ which color to choose," said Rocky.

4. _____ can be used to make things stick together.

5. "This is how you _____ your paper in half," said Mrs. Green.

6. The opposite of **leave** is _____ .

Write your own statement on the line.

Vocabulary: Questions

Questions are asking sentences. They begin with a capital letter and end with a question mark. Many questions begin with the words **who, what, why, when, where** and **how**. Write six questions using the question words below. Make sure to end each question with a question mark.

1. Who _____

2. What _____

3. Why _____

4. When _____

5. Where _____

6. How _____

Vocabulary: Commands

A **command** is a sentence that tells someone to do something.

Directions: Use the words in the box to complete the commands below. Write the words on the lines.

glue	decide	add	share	enter	fold

1. _____ a cup of flour to the cake batter.

2. _____ how much paper you will need to write your story.

3. Please _____ the picture of the apple onto the paper.

4. _____ through this door and leave through

   the other door.

5. Please _____ the letter and put it into an envelope.

6. _____ your toys with your sister.

Write your own command on the lines.

_____

_____

Vocabulary: Directions

A **direction** is a sentence written as a command.

Directions: Write the missing directions for these pictures. Begin each direction with one of the verbs below.

glue	enter	share	add	decide	fold

How To Make a Peanut Butter and Jelly Sandwich:

1. Spread peanut butter on bread.

2. _____

3. Cut the sandwich in half.

4. _____

How To Make a Valentine:

1. _____

2. Draw half a heart.

3. Cut along the line you drew.

4. _____

Kinds of Sentences

A **statement** is a sentence that tells something.
A **question** is a sentence that asks something.
A **command** is a sentence that tells someone to do something.

Commands begin with a verb or **please.** They usually end with a period. The noun is **you** but does not need to be part of the sentence.

Example: "Come here, please." means "**You** come here, please."

Examples of commands: Stand next to me.
Please give me some paper.

Directions: Write **S** in front of the statements, **Q** in front of the questions and **C** in front of the commands. End each sentence with a period or a question mark.

Example:

_____C_____ Stop and look before you cross the street.

_____ 1. Did you do your math homework

_____ 2. I think I lost my math book

_____ 3. Will you help me find it

_____ 4. I looked everywhere

_____ 5. Please open your math books to page three

_____ 6. Did you look under your desk

_____ 7. I looked, but it's not there

_____ 8. Who can add seven and four

_____ 9. Come up and write the answer on the board

_____ 10. Chris, where is your math book

_____ 11. I don't know for sure

_____ 12. Please share a book with a friend

Name _____

Kinds of Sentences

Remember: a **statement** tells something, a **question** asks something and a **command** tells someone to do something.

Directions: On each line, write a statement, question or command. Use a word from the box in each sentence.

glue	share	decide
enter	add	fold

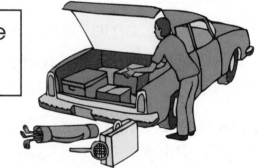

Example:

Question:

Can he add anything else?

1. Statement:

_____

2. Question:

_____

3. Command:

_____

4. Statement:

_____

5. Question:

_____

Kinds of Sentences

Directions: Use the group of words below to write three sentences: a **statement**, a **question** and a **command**.

| add | can | these | he | quickly | numbers |

Example:

Statement:

He can add these numbers quickly.

Question:

Can he can add these numbers quickly?

Command:

Add these numbers quickly.

| fold | here | should | we | it |

1. Statement:

_____

2. Question:

_____

3. Command:

_____

Name _____

Vocabulary: Completing a Story

Directions: Use verbs to complete the story below. The verbs that tell about things that happened in the past will end in **ed**.

Last week, Amy and I _____ a contest. We were supposed to make a card to give to a child in a hospital. First, we _____ a big sheet of white paper in half to make the card. Then we _____ to draw a rainbow on the front. Amy started coloring the rainbow all by herself. "Wait!" I said. "We both _____ the contest. Let me help!" "Okay," Amy said. "Let's _____ . You _____ a color, and then I'll _____ a color." It was more fun when we _____ . When we finished making the rainbow, we _____ to _____ a sun to the picture. I cut one out of yellow paper. Then Amy _____ it just above the rainbow. Well, our card didn't win the contest, but it did make a little boy with a broken leg smile. Amy and I felt so happy! We _____ to go right home and make some more cards!

Name _____

Homophones

Homophones are words that sound the same but are spelled differently and have different meanings.

Directions: Use the homophones in the box to answer the riddles below.

main	meat	peace	dear	to
mane	meet	piece	deer	too

1. Which word has the word **pie** in it? _____

2. Which word rhymes with **ear** and is an animal? _____

3. Which word rhymes with **shoe** and means **also**? _____

4. Which word has the word **eat** in it and is something you might eat? _____

5. Which word has the same letters as the word **read** but in a different order? _____

6. Which word rhymes with **train** and is something on a pony? _____

7. Which word, if it began with a capital letter, might be the name of an important street? _____

8. Which word sounds like a number but has only two letters? _____

9. Which word rhymes with and is a synonym for **greet**? _____

10. Which word rhymes with the last syllable in **police** and can mean quiet? _____

Name _____

Homophones: Sentences

Directions: Write a word from the box to complete each sentence.

main	meat	peace	dear	two
mane	meet	piece	deer	too

1. The horse had a long, beautiful _____ .

   The _____ idea of the paragraph was boats.

2. Let's _____ at my house to do our homework.

   The lion was fed _____ at mealtime.

3. We had _____ kittens.

   Mike has a red bike. Tom does, _____ .

4. The _____ ran in front of the car.

   I begin my letters with " _____ Mom."

Homophones: Spelling

Directions: Circle the word in each sentence which is not spelled correctly. Then write the word correctly.

1. Please meat me at the park.   _____

2. I would like a peace of pie.   _____

3. There were too cookies left.   _____

4. The horse's main needed to be brushed. _____

5. We saw a dear in the forest.   _____

Name _____

Homophones: Rhymes

Directions: Use homophones to create two-lined rhymes.

Example: I found it a **pain**

To comb the horse's **mane**!

1. _____

_____

2. _____

_____

3. _____

_____

Name _____

Short Vowels

Short vowel patterns usually have a single vowel followed by a consonant sound.

Short a is the sound you hear in the word **can**.

Short e is the sound you hear in the word **men**.

Short i is the sound you hear in the word **pig**.

Short o is the sound you hear in the word **pot**.

Short u is the sound you hear in the word **truck**.

fast	stop
spin	track
wish	lunch
bread	block

Directions: Use the words in the box to answer the questions below.

Which word:

begins with the same sound as **blast** and ends with the same sound as **look**? _____

rhymes with **stack**? _____

begins with the same sound as **phone** and ends with the same sound as **lost**? _____

has the same vowel sound as **hen**? _____

rhymes with **crunch**? _____

begins with the same sound as **spot** and ends with the same sound as **can**? _____

begins with the same sound as **win** and ends with the same sound as **crush**? _____

has the word **top** in it? _____

Name _____

Short Vowels: Sentences

Directions: Use the words in the box to complete each sentence.

fast	wish	truck	bread	sun
best	stop	track	lunch	block

Race cars can go very _____ .

Carol packs a _____ for Ted before school.

Throw a penny in the well and make a _____ .

The _____ had a flat tire.

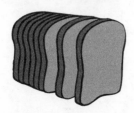

My favorite kind of _____ is whole wheat.

Name _____

Short Vowels: Spelling

Directions: Circle the word in each sentence which is not spelled correctly. Then write the word correctly.

1. Be sure to stopp at the red light. _____

2. The train goes down the trak. _____

3. Please put the bred in the toaster. _____

4. I need another blok to finish. _____

5. The beasst player won a trophy. _____

6. Blow out the candles and make a wiish. _____

7. The truk blew its horn. _____

Name _____

Long Vowels

Long vowels are the letters **a, e, i, o** and **u** which say the letter name sound.

Long a is the sound you hear in **cane**.

Long e is the sound you hear in **green**.

Long i is the sound you hear in **pie**.

Long o is the sound you hear in **bowl**.

Long u is the sound you hear in **cube**.

lame	goal
pain	few
street	fright
nose	gray
bike	fuse

Directions: Use the words in the box to answer the questions below.

1. Add one letter to each of these words to make words from the box.

   ray _____ use _____ right _____

2. Change one letter from each word to make a word from the box.

   pail _____ goat _____

   late _____ bite _____

3. Write the word from the box that . . .

   has the long **e** sound. _____

   rhymes with **you**. _____

   is a homophone for **knows**. _____

   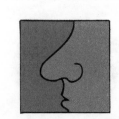

Name _____

Long Vowels: Sentences

Directions: Use the words in the box to complete each sentence.

lame	goal	pain	few	bike
street	fright	nose	gray	fuse

1. Look both ways before crossing the _____ .

2. My _____ had a flat tire.

3. Our walk through the haunted house

   gave us such a _____ .

4. I kicked the soccer ball and scored a _____ .

5. The _____ clouds mean rain is coming.

6. Cover your _____ when you sneeze.

7. We blew a _____ at my house last night.

Name _____

Long Vowels

Directions: Use long vowel words from the box to answer the clues below. Write the letters of the words on the lines.

| few bike dime goal fuse lame street nose fright pain |

1. ___ ___ ___ ___ ___ ☐ (rhymes with **night**)

2. ___ ☐ ___ ___ ___ (could be Main or Maple)

3. ___ ☐ ___ (synonym for **a couple**)

4. ___ ___ ☐ ___ (rhymes with **tame**)

5. ___ ___ ___ ☐ (can be ridden on a trail)

6. ___ ___ ___ ☐ (homophone for **pane**)

7. ☐ ___ ___ ___ (ten of these make a dollar)

8. ___ ☐ ___ ___ (changing one letter of this word makes **goat**)

9. ___ ☐ ___ ___ (has the word **use** in it)

10. ___ ___ ☐ ___ (homophone for **knows**)

Now, read the letters in the boxes from top to bottom to find out what kind of a job you did!

202

Name _____

Adjectives

Directions: Use the words in the box to answer the questions below. Use each word only once.

| polite | careless | neat | shy | selfish | thoughtful |

1. Someone who is quiet and needs some time to make new friends is _____.

2. A person who says "please" and "thank you" is _____.

3. Someone who always puts all the toys away is _____.

4. A person who won't share with others is being _____.

5. A person who leaves a bike out all night is being _____.

6. Someone who thinks of others is _____.

Name _____

Adjectives

Directions: Use the adjectives in the box to answer the questions below.

polite	careless	neat	shy	selfish	thoughtful

1. Change a letter in each word to make an adjective.

near   _____

why   _____

2. Write the word that rhymes with each of these.

fell dish   _____

not full   _____

hair mess   _____

3. Find these words in the adjectives. Write the adjective.

at   _____

are   _____

it   _____

Name _____

Adjectives: Spelling

Directions: Circle the word in each sentence which is not spelled correctly. Then write the word correctly.

1. John isn't shelfish at all. _____

2. He sharred his lunch with me today. _____

3. I was careles and forgot to bring mine. _____

4. My father says if I planed better,
   that wouldn't happen all the time. _____

5. John is kind of quiet, and I used
   to think he was shie. _____

6. Now, I know he is really thotful. _____

7. He's also very polyte and always
   asks before he borrows anything. _____

8. He would never just reach over
   and grabb something he wanted. _____

9. I'm glad John desided to be my friend. _____

Adjectives: Explaining Sentences

Directions: Use a word from the box to tell about a person in each picture below. Then write a sentence that explains why you chose that word.

| polite neat careless shy selfish thoughtful |

The word I picked: _____

I think so because . . .

_____

The word I picked: _____

I think so because . . .

_____

The word I picked: _____

I think so because . . .

_____

Adjectives

Directions: Look at each picture. Then add adjectives to the sentences. Use colors, numbers, words from the box and any other words you need to describe each picture.

Example:

polite	neat	careless
shy	selfish	thoughtful

The boy shared his pencil.

The polite boy shared his red pencil.

The girl dropped her coat.

_____

The boy played with cars.

_____

The boy put books away.

_____

Name _____

C, K, CK Words: Spelling

Directions: Write the words from the box that answer the questions.

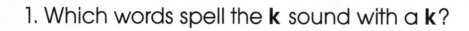

| crowd | keeper | cost | pack | kangaroo | thick |

1. Which words spell the **k** sound with a **k**?

_____

2. Which words spell the **k** sound with a **c**?

_____

3. Which words spell the **k** sound with **ck**?

_____

4. Circle the letters that spell **k** in these words:

cook   black   cool   kite

cake   pocket   poke

5. Which words from the box rhyme with each of these?

tossed _____   deeper _____

proud _____   all in blue _____

C, K, CK Words: Sentences

The **k** sound can be spelled with a **c**, **k** or **ck** after a short vowel sound.

Directions: Use the words from the box to complete the sentences. Use each word only once.

crowd	keeper
cost	pack
kangaroo	thick

1. On sunny days, there is always a _____ of people at the zoo.

2. It doesn't _____ much to get into the zoo.

3. We always get hungry, so we _____ a picnic lunch.

4. We like to watch the _____ .

5. Its _____ tail helps it jump and walk.

6. The _____ always makes sure the cages are clean.

C, K, CK Words: **Sentences**

Remember: every sentence must have a noun that tells who or what is doing something and a verb that tells what the noun is doing.

Directions: Parts of each sentence below are missing. Rewrite each sentence, adding a noun or a verb, periods and capital letters.

Example:

read a book every day (needs a noun)

Leon reads a book every day.

1. packed a lunch

_____

2. the crowd at the beach

_____

3. cost too much

_____

4. kangaroos and their babies

_____

5. was too thick to chew

_____

MATH

Name _____

Addition

Directions: Add.
Example:

Add the ones.

```
  26
+21
───
   7
```

Add the tens.

```
  26
+21
───
  47
```

```
  18        24        38        49        52
+11       +35       +21       +50       +33
```

```
  75        83        67        44        28
+12       +16       +32       +25       +41
```

68 + 20 = ____   54 + 25 = ____   71 + 17 = ____

The Lions scored 42 points. The Clippers scored 21 points.
How many points were scored in all? _____

Name _____

Subtraction

Subtraction means "taking away" or subtracting one number from another to find the difference. For example, 10 - 3 = 7.

Directions: Subtract.

Example:

Subtract the ones.
```
  39
 -24
   5
```

Subtract the tens.
```
  39
 -24
 | 5
```

```
  48        95        87        55
 -35       -22       -16       -43
```

```
  37        69        44        99
 -14       -57       -23       -78
```

66 - 44 = ____   57 - 33 = ____

The yellow car traveled 87 miles per hour. The orange car traveled 66 miles per hour. How much faster was the yellow car traveling?

_____

Place Value

The place value of a digit, or numeral, is shown by where it is in the number. For example, in the number 1,234, 1 has the place value of thousands, 2 is hundreds, 3 is tens and 4 is ones.

Hundred Thousands	Ten Thousands	Thousands	Hundreds	Tens	Ones
9	4	3	8	5	2

9 4 3 , 8 5 2

Directions: Match the numbers in Column A with the words in Column B.

A	B
62,453	two hundred thousand
7,641	three thousand
486,113	four hundred thousand
11,277	eight hundreds
813,463	seven tens
594,483	five ones
254,089	six hundreds
79,841	nine ten thousands
27,115	five tens

Name _____

Addition: Regrouping

Addition means "putting together" or adding two or more numbers to find the sum. For example, 3 + 5 = 8. To regroup is to use ten ones to form one ten, ten tens to form one 100 and so on.

Directions: Add using regrouping.

Example:

Add the ones.	Add the tens with regrouping.
88 +21 9	88 +21 109

37 +72	56 +67	51 +88	37 +55	70 +68

93 +54	47 +82	81 +77	23 +92	36 +71

92 + 13 = ____   73 + 83 = ____   54 + 61 = ____

The Blues scored 63 points. The Reds scored 44 points.
How many points were scored in all?

_____

Subtraction: Regrouping

Subtraction means "taking away" or subtracting one number from another to find the difference. For example, 10 - 3 = 7. To regroup is to use one ten to form ten ones, one 100 to form ten tens and so on.

Directions: Study the example. Subtract using regrouping.

Example:

$$
\begin{array}{rcl}
32 &=& 2 \text{ tens} + 12 \text{ ones} \\
-13 &=& 1 \text{ ten} + 3 \text{ ones} \\
\hline
19 &=& 1 \text{ ten} + 9 \text{ ones}
\end{array}
$$

$$
\begin{array}{cccc}
33 & 86 & 92 & 71 \\
-28 & -59 & -37 & -48 \\
\end{array}
$$

$$
\begin{array}{cccc}
63 & 45 & 31 & 55 \\
-47 & -18 & -22 & -39 \\
\end{array}
$$

82 - 69 = _____   73 - 36 = _____

The Yankees won 85 games.
The Cubs won 69 games.
How many more games
did the Yankees win? _____

Name _____

Addition and Subtraction: Regrouping

Addition means "putting together" or adding two or more numbers to find the sum. Subtraction means "taking away" or subtracting one number from another to find the difference. To regroup is to use one ten to form ten ones, one 100 to form ten tens and so on.

Directions: Add or subtract. Regroup when needed.

92 -47	58 +26	63 +18	77 -38
27 -17	31 +42	56 -29	67 +33
72 +19	87 -58	93 -89	54 +27

The soccer team scored 83 goals this year. The soccer team scored 68 goals last year. How many goals did they score in all? _____

How many more goals did they score this year than last year? _____

Name _____

Addition: Regrouping

Directions: Study the example. Add using regrouping.

Examples:

Add the ones. Regroup.	Add the tens. Regroup.	Add the hundreds.

```
  1                        1    11                 1
156        6           5      156              156
+267      +7          +6     +267             +267
  3       13          12      23               423
```

```
 29        81         52        49
 46        78         67        37        162
+12       +33        +23       +19       +349
```

```
273       655        783       385        428
+198      +297       +148      +169       +122
```

Sally went bowling. She had scores of 115, 129 and 103. What was her total score for three games? _____

Name _____

Addition: Regrouping

Directions: Add using regrouping. Then use the code to discover the name of a United States president.

$$\begin{array}{r} 348 \\ +752 \\ \hline 1,100 \end{array} \qquad \begin{array}{r} 642 \\ +277 \\ \hline \end{array} \qquad \begin{array}{r} 386 \\ +787 \\ \hline \end{array} \qquad \begin{array}{r} 184 \\ +875 \\ \hline \end{array} \qquad \begin{array}{r} 578 \\ +874 \\ \hline \end{array}$$

$$\begin{array}{r} 653 \\ +768 \\ \hline \end{array} \qquad \begin{array}{r} 653 \\ +359 \\ \hline \end{array} \qquad \begin{array}{r} 946 \\ +239 \\ \hline \end{array} \qquad \begin{array}{r} 393 \\ +257 \\ \hline \end{array} \qquad \begin{array}{r} 199 \\ +843 \\ \hline \end{array}$$

$$\begin{array}{r} 721 \\ +679 \\ \hline \end{array}$$

___ . ___ ___ ___ ___ ___ ___ ___ ___ ___

1012	1173	1059	1421	919	650	1452	1042	1100	1400	1185
N	A	S	I	W	T	H	O	G	N	G

Addition: Regrouping

Directions: Study the example. Add using regrouping.

Example:

Steps:

5,356
+3,976
9,332

1. Add the ones.
2. Regroup the tens. Add the tens.
3. Regroup the hundreds. Add the hundreds.
4. Add the thousands.

```
  6,849        1,846        9,221
+ 3,276      + 8,384      + 6,769
```

```
  2,758        5,299        7,932
+ 3,663      + 8,764      + 6,879
```

A plane flew 1,838 miles on the first day. It flew 2,347 miles on the second day. How many miles did it fly in all?

_____

Name _____

Addition: Mental Math

Directions: Try to do these addition problems in your head without using paper and pencil.

7	6	8	10	2	6
+4	+3	+1	+ 2	+9	+6

10	40	80	60	50	100
+20	+20	+100	+30	+70	+ 40

350	300	400	450	680	900
+150	+500	+800	+ 10	+100	+ 70

	4,000	300	8,000		7,000
1,000	400	200	500	9,800	300
+ 200	+ 30	+ 80	+ 60	+ 150	+ 30

Name _____

Subtraction: Regrouping

Directions: Regrouping for subtraction is the opposite of regrouping for addition. Study the example. Subtract using regrouping. Then use the code to color the flowers.

Example:

647
-453
194

Steps:
1. Subtract ones.
2. Subtract tens. Five tens cannot be subtracted from 4 tens.
3. Regroup tens by regrouping 6 hundreds (5 hundreds + 10 tens).
4. Add the 10 tens to the four tens.
5. Subtract 5 tens from 14 tens.
6. Subtract the hundreds.

If the answer has:
1 one, color it red;
8 ones, color it pink;
5 ones, color it yellow.

222

Math

Subtraction: Regrouping

Directions: Study the example. Follow the steps. Subtract using regrouping.

Example:

```
 634
-455
 179
```

Steps:
1. Subtract ones. You cannot subtract five ones from 4 ones.
2. Regroup ones by regrouping 3 tens to 2 tens + 10 ones.
3. Subtract 5 ones from 14 ones.
4. Regroup tens by regrouping hundreds (5 hundreds + 10 tens).
5. Subtract 5 tens from 12 tens.
6. Subtract hundreds.

635 -169	553 -174	832 -563	944 -578
423 -268	941 -872	733 -498	266 -197
387 -198	594 -385	960 -759	887 -598

Sue goes to school 185 days a year. Yoko goes to school 313 days a year. How many more days of school does Yoko attend each year?

_____

Name _____

Subtraction: Regrouping

Directions: Study the example. Follow the steps. Subtract using regrouping. If you have to regroup to subtract ones and there are no tens, you must regroup twice.

Example:

$$\begin{array}{r} 300 \\ -182 \\ \hline 118 \end{array}$$

Steps:
1. Subtract ones. You cannot subtract 2 ones from 0 ones.
2. Regroup. No tens. Regroup hundreds (2 hundreds + 10 tens).
3. Regroup tens (9 tens + 10 ones).
4. Subtract 2 ones from ten ones.
5. Subtract 8 tens from 9 tens.
6. Subtract 1 hundred from 2 hundreds.

602	306	600	807	703
-423	-128	-263	-499	-328

800	206	400	508	909
-557	-137	-224	-379	-769

207	604	308	700	900
-138	-397	-199	-531	-278

Name _____

Subtraction: Regrouping

Directions: Subtract. Regroup when necessary. The first one is done for you.

```
  7,354        4,214        8,437        6,837
 -5,295       -3,185       -5,338       -4,318
  2,059
```

```
  5,735        1,036        6,735        3,841
 -3,826       -  947       -6,646       -1,953
```

Columbus discovered America in 1492. The pilgrims landed in America in 1620. How many years difference was there between these two events?

_____

Name _____

Subtraction: Mental Math

Directions: Try to do these subtraction problems in your head without using paper and pencil.

9 − 3	12 − 6	7 − 6	5 −1	15 − 5	2 −0

40 −20	90 − 80	100 − 50	20 −20	60 −10	70 − 40

450 −250	500 − 300	250 − 20	690 −100	320 − 20	900 − 600

1,000 − 400	8,000 − 500	7,000 − 900	4,000 −2,000	9,500 − 4,000	5,000 −2,000

Review

Directions: Add or subtract using regrouping.

28	82	33	67
56	49	75	94
+93	+51	+128	+248

683	756	818	956
-495	+139	-387	+267

1,588	4,675	8,732	2,938
- 989	-2,976	-5,664	+3,459

To drive from New York City to Los Angeles is 2,832 miles. To drive from New York City to Miami is 1,327 miles. How much farther is it to drive from New York City to Los Angeles than from New York City to Miami? _____

Name _____

Rounding: The Nearest Ten

If the ones number is 5 or greater, "round up" to the nearest 10. If the ones number is 4 or less, the tens number stays the same and the ones number becomes a zero.

Examples: 15 round <u>up</u> to 20   23 round <u>down</u> to 20   47 round <u>up</u> to 50

7	____	58	____
12	____	81	____
33	____	94	____
27	____	44	____
73	____	88	____
25	____	66	____
39	____	70	____

Name _____

Rounding: The Nearest Hundred

If the tens number is 5 or greater, "round up" to the nearest hundred. If the tens number is 4 or less, the hundreds number remains the same.

REMEMBER... Look at the number directly to the right of the place you are rounding to.

Example:

230 round down to 200

470 round up to 500

150 round up to 200

732 round down to 700

456 ____

120 ____

340 ____

923 ____

867 ____

550 ____

686 ____

231 ____

770 ____

492 ____

Name _____

Front-End Estimation

Front-end estimation is useful when you don't need to know the exact amount, but a close answer will do.

When we use front-end estimation, we use only the first number, and then add the numbers together to get the estimate.

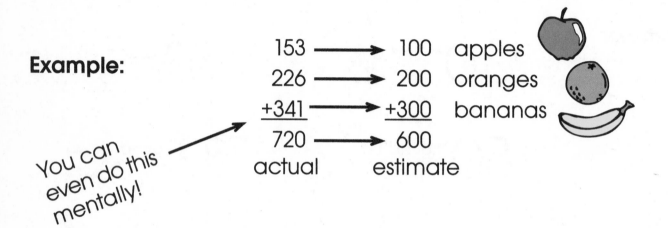

Example:

153 ⟶ 100 apples
226 ⟶ 200 oranges
+341 ⟶ +300 bananas
720 ⟶ 600
actual   estimate

You can even do this mentally!

Directions: Estimate the sum of these numbers.

456 ⟶
121 ⟶
+438 ⟶   + _____

910 ⟶
280 ⟶
+320 ⟶   + _____

686 ⟶
307 ⟶
+711 ⟶   + _____

Name _____

Multiplication

Multiplication is a short way to find the sum of adding the same number a certain amount of times. For example, we write 7 x 4 = 28 instead of 7 + 7 + 7 + 7 = 28.

Directions: Study the example. Multiply.

Example:

There are two groups of seashells.
There are 3 seashells in each group.   2 x 3 = 6
How many seashells are there in all?

4 + 4 = _____

2 x 4 = _____

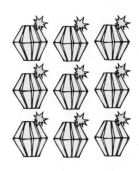

3 + 3 + 3 = _____

3 x 3 = _____

2 x3	3 x5	4 x3	6 x2	7 x3
5 x2	6 x3	4 x2	7 x2	8 x3
5 x5	9 x4	8 x5	6 x6	9 x3

Multiplication

Directions: Multiply.

3 x5	4 x6	3 x8

5 x5	4 x8	5 x4

6 x7	3 x9	2 x8	7 x6	9 x4

6 x8	5 x6	7 x7	5 x3	8 x9

A riverboat makes 3 trips a day every day.
How many trips does it make in a week?

_____

Multiplication

Factors are the numbers multiplied together in a multiplication problem. The answer is called the product. If you change the order of the factors, the product stays the same.

Example:

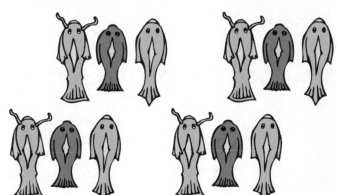

There are 4 groups of fish.
There are 3 fish in each group.
How many fish are there in all?

$$4 \times 3 = 12$$
factor x factor = product

Directions: Draw 3 groups of 4 fish.

$$3 \times 4 = 12$$

Compare your drawing and answer with the example. What did you notice?

Directions: Fill in the missing numbers. Multiply.

5 x 4 = _____   3 x 6 = _____   4 x 2 = _____

4 x 5 = _____   6 x 3 = _____   2 x 4 = _____

3	7	2	9	8	4
x7	x3	x9	x2	x4	x8

5	2	6	3	5	6
x2	x5	x3	x6	x6	x5

Multiplication: Zero and One

Any number multiplied by zero equals zero. One multiplied by any number equals that number. Study the example. Multiply.

Example:

How many full sails are there in all?

2 boats x **1** sail on each boat = **2** sails

How many full sails are there now?

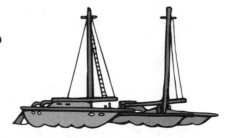

2 boats x **0** sails = **0** sails

Directions: Multiply.

1	2	3	4	0	7
x5	x1	x0	x1	x6	x0

9	8	3	4	7	6
x1	x0	x1	x0	x1	x1

Name _____

Multiplication

Directions: Time yourself as you multiply. How quickly can you complete this page?

3 x2	8 x7	1 x0	1 x6	3 x4	0 x4
4 x1	4 x4	2 x5	9 x3	9 x9	5 x3
0 x8	2 x6	9 x6	8 x5	7 x3	4 x2
3 x5	2 x0	4 x6	1 x3	0 x0	3 x3

Name _____

Multiplication Table

Directions: Complete the multiplication table. Use it to practice your multiplication facts.

X	0	1	2	3	4	5	6	7	8	9	10
0	0										
1		1									
2			4								
3				9							
4					16						
5						25					
6							36				
7								49			
8									64		
9										81	
10											100

Name _____

Division

Division is a way to find out how many times one number is contained in another number. For example, $28 \div 4 = 7$ means that there are seven groups of four in 28.

Directions: Study the example. Divide.

Example:

There are 6 oars.
Each canoe needs 2 oars.
How many canoes can be used?

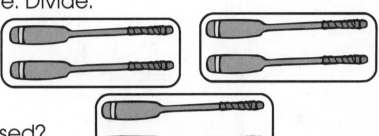

Circle groups of 2.
There are 3 groups of 2.

$$\underset{\text{oars}}{6} \div \underset{\substack{\text{number} \\ \text{of oars} \\ \text{needed} \\ \text{per canoe}}}{2} = \underset{\text{canoes}}{3}$$

$9 \div 3 =$ _____ $8 \div 2 =$ _____ $16 \div 4 =$ _____

$15 \div 5 =$ _____ $18 \div 2 =$ _____ $20 \div 4 =$ _____

$21 \div 7 =$ _____ $24 \div 6 =$ _____ $12 \div 2 =$ _____

Name _____

Division

Directions: Divide. Draw a line from the boat to the sail with the correct answer.

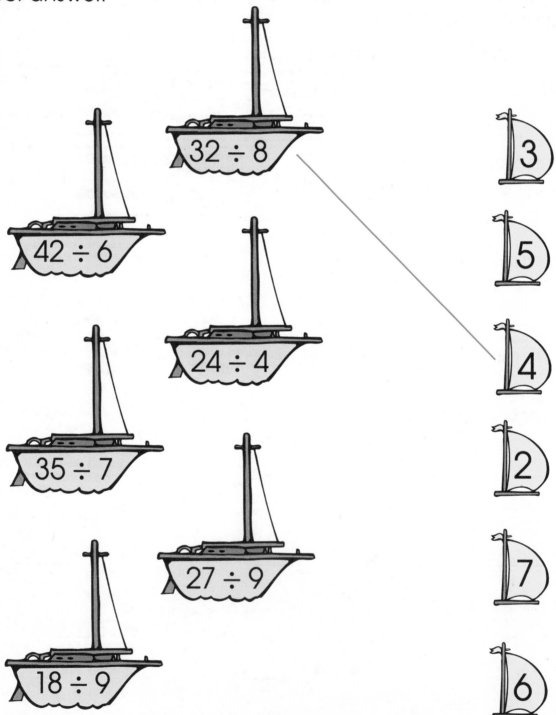

Order of Operations

When you solve a problem that involves more than one operation, this is the order to follow:

( ) Parentheses first
x Multiplication
÷ Division
+ Addition
− Subtraction

Example: 2 + (3 x 5) - 2 = 15
2 + 15 - 2 = 15
17 - 2 = 15

Directions: Solve the problems using the correct order of operations.

(5 - 3) + 4 x 7 = ____   1 + 2 x 3 + 4 = ____

6 x 3 - 1 = ____   (8 ÷ 2) x 4 = ____

9 ÷ 3 x 3 + 0 = ____   5 - 2 x 1 + 2 = ____

Order of Operations

Directions: Use +, –, x and ÷ to complete the problems so the number sentence is true.

Example: 4 __+__ 2 __–__ 1 = 5

(8 _____ 2) _____ 4 = 8

(1 _____ 2) _____ 3 = 1

9 _____ 3 _____ 9 = 3

(7 _____ 5) _____ 1 = 2

8 _____ 5 _____ 4 = 10

5 _____ 4 _____ 1 = 1

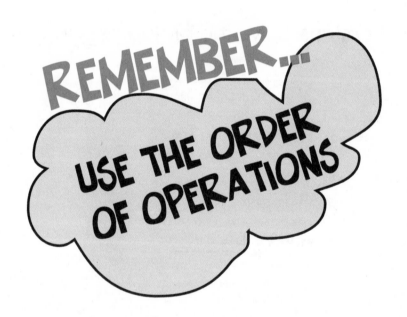

REMEMBER... USE THE ORDER OF OPERATIONS

Name _____

Review

Directions: Multiply or divide. Fill in the blanks with the missing numbers or x or ÷ signs. The first one is done for you.

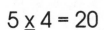

5 x 4 = 20

6 x 8 = ____

7 x ____ = 14

3 _ 6 = 18

7 x 2 = ____

____ x 3 = 24

6 _ 2 = 3

24 ÷ 6 = ____

6 x 5 = ____

25 _ 5 = 5

49 ÷ 7 = ____

8 x ____ = 32

3 _ 8 = 24

18 ÷ 3 = ____

9 x 5 = ____

12 _ 3 = 4

9 x 8 = ____

6 x ____ = 36

Name _____

Division

Division is a way to find out how many times one number is contained in another number. The ÷ sign means "divided by." Another way to divide is to use ⌐ . The dividend is the larger number that is divided by the smaller number, or divisor. The answer of a division problem is called the quotient.

Directions: Study the example. Divide.

Example:

$$20 \div 4 = 5$$

dividend   divisor   quotient

quotient

$$4\overline{)20}$$

divisor dividend

$35 \div 7 =$ _____ $7\overline{)35}$ $42 \div 6 =$ _____ $6\overline{)42}$

$2\overline{)12}$ $3\overline{)18}$ $4\overline{)36}$ $5\overline{)50}$

$6\overline{)24}$ $7\overline{)21}$ $8\overline{)32}$ $9\overline{)27}$

$36 \div 6 =$ _____ $28 \div 4 =$ _____ $15 \div 5 =$ _____ $12 \div 2 =$ _____

A tree farm has 36 trees. There are 4 rows of trees. How many trees are there in each row? _____

Name _____

Division: Zero and One

Directions: Study the rules of division and the examples. Divide, then write the number of the rule you used to solve each problem.

Examples:

Rule 1: $1\overline{)5}$ = 5   Any number divided by 1 is that number.

Rule 2: $5\overline{)5}$ = 1   Any number except 0 divided by itself is 1.

Rule 3: $7\overline{)0}$ = 0   Zero divided by any number is zero.

Rule 4: $0\overline{)7}$ You cannot divide by zero.

$1\overline{)6}$ Rule ____ $4 \div 1 =$ ____   Rule ____

$7\overline{)7}$ Rule ____   **ZERO** $9 \div 9 =$ ____   Rule ____

$9\overline{)0}$ Rule ____   **ONE** $7 \div 1 =$ ____   Rule ____

$1\overline{)4}$ Rule ____ $6 \div 0 =$ ____   Rule ____

Name _____

Division: Remainders

Division is a way to find out how many times one number is contained in another number. For example, 28 ÷ 4 = 7 means that there are seven groups of four in 28. The dividend is the larger number that is divided by the smaller number, or divisor. The quotient is the answer in a division problem. The remainder is the amount left over. The remainder is always less than the divisor.

Directions: Study the example. Find each quotient and remainder.

Example:

There are 11 dog biscuits.
Put them in groups of 3.
There are 2 left over.

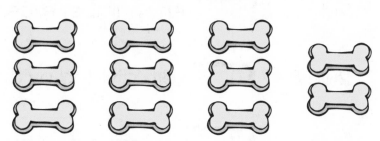

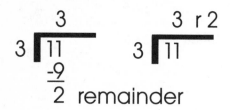

Remember: The remainder must be less than the **divisor**!

$$3\overline{)13}\qquad 4\overline{)17}\qquad 6\overline{)32}\qquad 5\overline{)26}$$

9 ÷ 4 = _____   12 ÷ 5 = _____   26 ÷ 4 = _____   49 ÷ 9 = _____

The pet store has 7 cats.
Two cats go in each
cage. How many cats
are left over?

_____

Divisibility Rules

A number is divisible... by 2 if the last digit is 0 or even (2, 4, 6, 8).
by 3 if the sum of all digits is divisible by 3.
by 4 if the last two digits are divisible by 4.
by 5 if the last digit is a 0 or 5.
by 10 if the last digit is 0.

Example: 250 is divisible by   <u>2, 5, 10</u>

Directions: Tell what numbers each of these numbers is divisible by.

3,732 _____   439 _____

50 _____   444 _____

7,960 _____   8,212 _____

104,924 _____   2,345 _____

Factor Trees

Factors are the smaller numbers multiplied together to make a larger number. Factor trees are one way to find all the factors of a number.

Example:

Name _____

Percentages

A percentage is the amount of a number out of 100. This is the percent sign: %

Directions: Fill in the blanks.

Example: $70\% = \dfrac{70}{100}$ $\underline{40}\% = \dfrac{40}{100}$

$30\% = \dfrac{}{100}$ $10\% = \dfrac{}{100}$

$90\% = \dfrac{}{100}$ $40\% = \dfrac{}{100}$

$70\% = \dfrac{}{100}$ $80\% = \dfrac{}{100}$

$\underline{}\% = \dfrac{20}{100}$ $\underline{}\% = \dfrac{60}{100}$

$\underline{}\% = \dfrac{30}{100}$ $\underline{}\% = \dfrac{10}{100}$

$\underline{}\% = \dfrac{50}{100}$ $\underline{}\% = \dfrac{90}{100}$

Name _____

Fractions

A fraction is a number that names part of a whole, such as $\frac{1}{2}$ or $\frac{1}{3}$.

Directions: Write the fraction that tells what part of each figure is colored. The first one is done for you.

Example:

2 parts shaded
5 parts in the whole figure

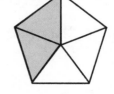

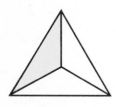

$\frac{1}{3}$
_____

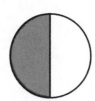

_____

_____

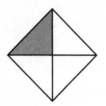

_____

_____

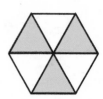

_____

_____

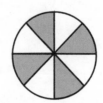

_____

_____

Name _____

Fractions: Equivalent

Fractions that name the same part of a whole are equivalent fractions.

Example:

$$\frac{1}{2} = \frac{2}{4}$$

Directions: Fill in the numbers to complete the equivalent fractions.

$$\frac{1}{4} = \frac{\boxed{}}{8}$$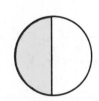

$$\frac{2}{3} = \frac{\boxed{}}{6}$$

$$\frac{1}{6} = \frac{\boxed{}}{12}$$

$$\frac{2}{3} = \frac{\boxed{}}{6}$$

$$\frac{1}{3} = \frac{\boxed{}}{12}$$

$$\frac{1}{5} = \frac{\boxed{}}{15}$$

$$\frac{1}{4} = \frac{\boxed{}}{8}$$

$$\frac{1}{2} = \frac{\boxed{}}{6}$$

$$\frac{2}{3} = \frac{\boxed{}}{9}$$

$$\frac{2}{6} = \frac{\boxed{}}{18}$$

Name _____

Fractions: Division

A fraction is a number that names part of an object. It can also name part of a group.

Directions: Study the example. Divide by the bottom number of the fraction to find the answers.

Example:
There are 6 cheerleaders.
$\frac{1}{2}$ of the cheerleaders are boys.
How many cheerleaders are boys?

6 cheerleaders ÷ 2 groups = 3 boys

$\frac{1}{2}$ of 6 = 3 $\frac{1}{2}$ of 8 = __4__

$\frac{1}{2}$ of 10 = ____ $\frac{1}{3}$ of 9 = ____ $\frac{1}{5}$ of 10 = ____

$\frac{1}{4}$ of 12 = ____ $\frac{1}{8}$ of 32 = ____ $\frac{1}{3}$ of 27 = ____

$\frac{1}{5}$ of 30 = ____ $\frac{1}{2}$ of 14 = ____ $\frac{1}{9}$ of 18 = ____

$\frac{1}{6}$ of 24 = ____ $\frac{1}{3}$ of 18 = ____ $\frac{1}{10}$ of 50 = ____

Name _____

Fractions: Comparing

Directions: Circle the fraction in each pair that is larger.

Example:

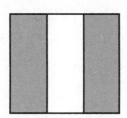

$\left(\dfrac{2}{3}\right)$

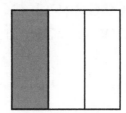

$\dfrac{1}{3}$

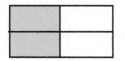

$\dfrac{2}{4}$

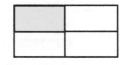

$\dfrac{1}{4}$

$\dfrac{1}{8}$

$\dfrac{2}{8}$

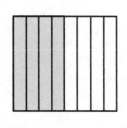

$\dfrac{1}{2}$

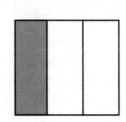

$\dfrac{1}{3}$

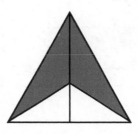

$\dfrac{2}{3}$

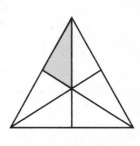

$\dfrac{1}{6}$

$\dfrac{1}{4}$ or $\dfrac{1}{6}$

$\dfrac{1}{5}$ or $\dfrac{1}{7}$

$\dfrac{1}{8}$ or $\dfrac{1}{4}$

Name _____

Decimals

A decimal is a number with one or more numbers to the right of a decimal point. A decimal point is a dot placed between the ones place and the tens place of a number, such as 2.5.

Example:

$\frac{3}{10}$ can be written as .3   They are both read as three-tenths.

Directions: Write the answer as a decimal for the shaded parts.

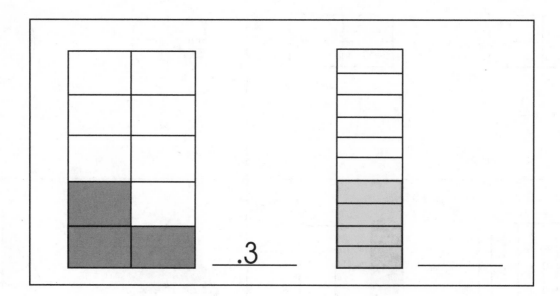

____.3____   _____

Directions: Color parts of each object to match the decimals given.

.7   .6   .5

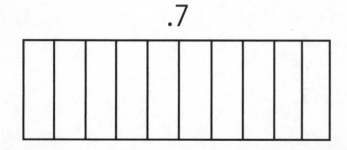   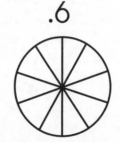   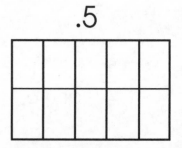

Name _____

Decimals

A decimal is a number with one or more numbers to the right of a decimal point, such as 6.5 or 2.25. Equivalent means numbers that are equal.

Directions: Draw a line between the equivalent numbers.

.8	$\frac{5}{10}$
five-tenths	$\frac{8}{10}$
.7	$\frac{6}{10}$
.4	.3
six-tenths	$\frac{2}{10}$
three-tenths	$\frac{7}{10}$
.2	$\frac{9}{10}$
nine-tenths	$\frac{4}{10}$

Math   253   Total Basic Skills Grade 3

Name _____

Decimals Greater Than 1

Directions: Write the decimal for the part that is shaded.

Example: $2\frac{4}{10}$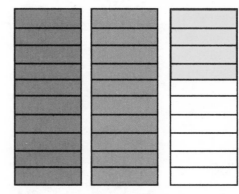

Write: 2.4   Read: two and four-tenths

$1\frac{2}{10}$ = ____

$3\frac{6}{10}$ = ____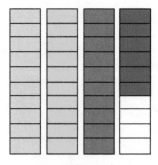

$2\frac{3}{10}$ = ____

$2\frac{7}{10}$ = ____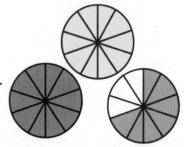

Directions: Write each number as a decimal.

four and two-tenths = ____   seven and one-tenth = ____

$3\frac{4}{10}$ = ____ $6\frac{9}{10}$ = ____ $8\frac{3}{10}$ = ____ $7\frac{5}{10}$ = ____

Decimals: Addition and Subtraction

Decimals are added and subtracted in the same way as other numbers. Simply carry down the decimal point to your answer.

Directions: Add or subtract.

Examples:

$$\begin{array}{r} 1.3 \\ +2.8 \\ \hline 4.1 \end{array}$$

$$\begin{array}{r} 4.5 \\ -2.2 \\ \hline 2.3 \end{array}$$

$$\begin{array}{r} 1.3 \\ +2.2 \\ \hline \end{array}$$
$$\begin{array}{r} 4.6 \\ -3.4 \\ \hline \end{array}$$
$$\begin{array}{r} 5.1 \\ +8.8 \\ \hline \end{array}$$
$$\begin{array}{r} 6.7 \\ -4.3 \\ \hline \end{array}$$

$$\begin{array}{r} 7.9 \\ -3.7 \\ \hline \end{array}$$
$$\begin{array}{r} 6.4 \\ +8.7 \\ \hline \end{array}$$
$$\begin{array}{r} 11.4 \\ -\ 9.5 \\ \hline \end{array}$$
$$\begin{array}{r} 0.5 \\ +3.6 \\ \hline \end{array}$$

9.3 + 1.2 = _____   2.5 - 0.7 = _____   1.2 + 5.0 = _____

Bob jogs around the school every day. The distance for one time around is .7 of a mile. If he jogs around the school two times, how many miles does he jog each day? _____

Patterns

Directions: Write the one that would come next in each pattern.

0 2 0 4 0 6 _____

1 3 5 7 9 11 _____

5 10 20 40 80 _____

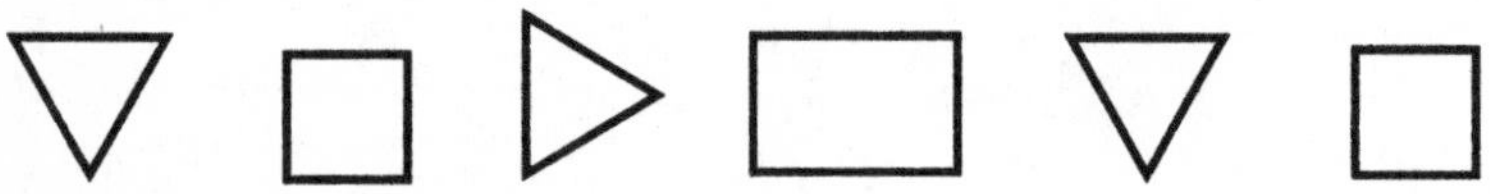

▽ □ ▷ ▭ ▽ □ _____

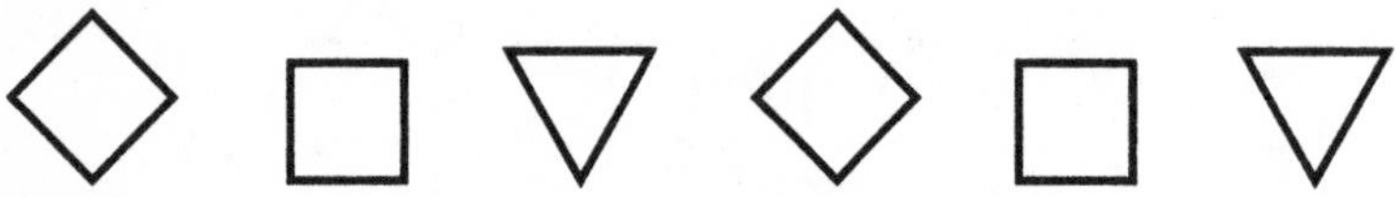

◇ □ ▽ ◇ □ ▽ _____

○ ◯ ● ⬤ ○ ◯ _____

1 A 2 B 3 C _____

A B C 1 2 3 _____

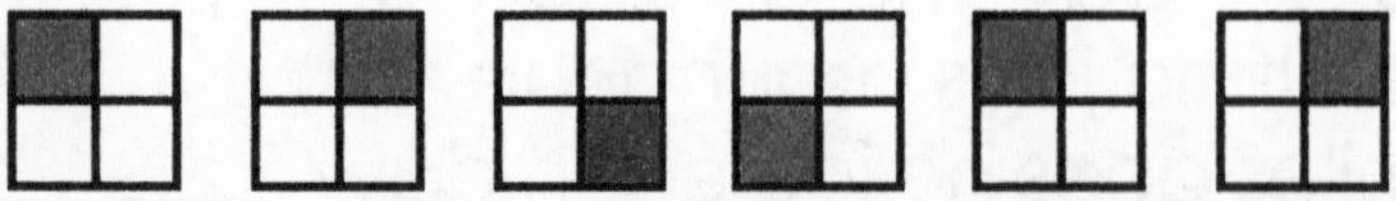

▦ ▦ ▦ ▦ ▦ ▦ _____

Pattern Maze

Directions: Follow the pattern: ⬤ ◼ ▲ ☆ to get through the maze.

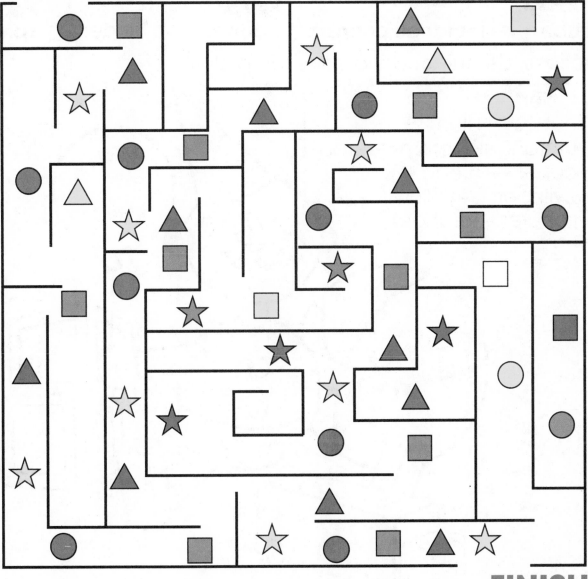

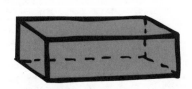 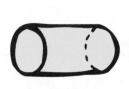 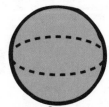

Name _____

Geometry

Geometry is the branch of mathematics that has to do with points, lines and shapes.

cube   rectangular prism   cone   cylinder   sphere

Directions: Use the code to color the picture.

Color:
cubes — blue
rectangular prisms — red
cones — green
cylinders — yellow
spheres —orange

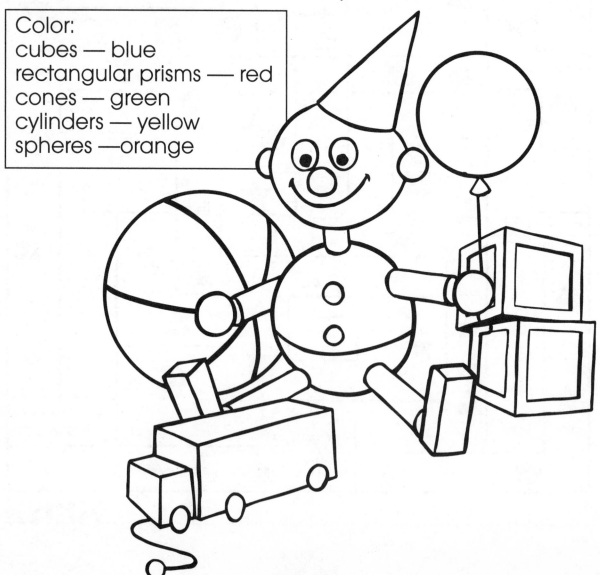

Tangram

Directions: Cut out the tangram below. Use the shapes to make a cat, a chicken, a boat and a large triangle.

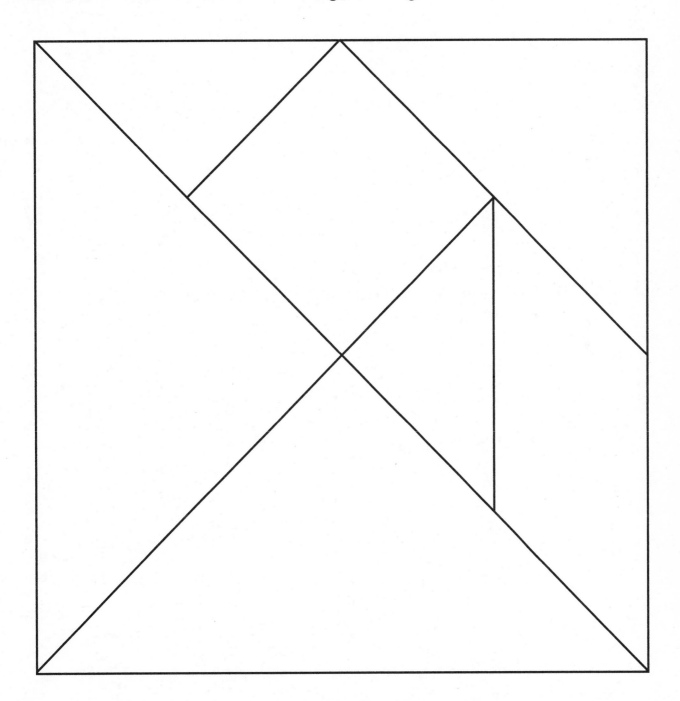

Page is blank for cutting exercise on previous page.

Name _____

Geometric Coloring

Directions: Color the geometric shapes in the box below.

Name _____

Geometry: Lines Segments, Rays, Angles

Geometry is the branch of mathematics that has to do with points, lines and shapes.

A **line** goes on and on in both directions. It has no end points.

 Line CD

A **segment** is part of a line. It has two end points.

 Segment AB

A **ray** has a line segment with only one end point. It goes on and on in the other direction.

 Ray EF

An **angle** has two rays with the same end point.

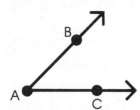 Angle BAC

Directions: Write the name for each figure.

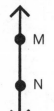

__line__

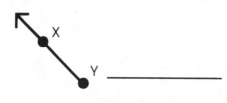 _____

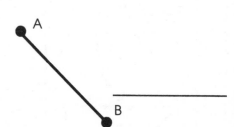 _____

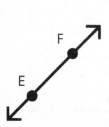 _____

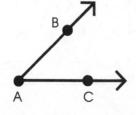 _____

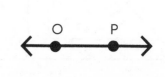 _____

Geometry Game

Directions: 1. Cut out the cards at the bottom of the page. Put them in a pile.

2. Cut out the game boards on the next page.

3. Take turns drawing cards.

4. If you have the figure that the card describes on your gameboard, cover it.

5. The first one to get three in a row, wins.

cube	point	angle	cylinder	rectangular prism
line	square	cone	circle	sphere
triangle	segment	rectangle	tangram	ray

Page is blank for cutting exercise on previous page.

Name _____

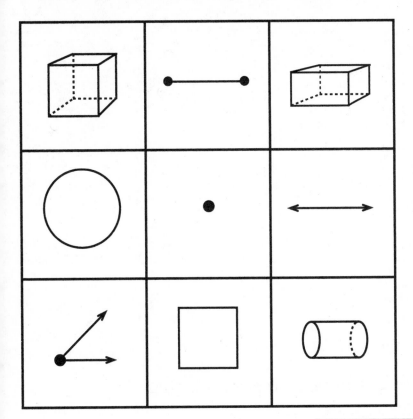

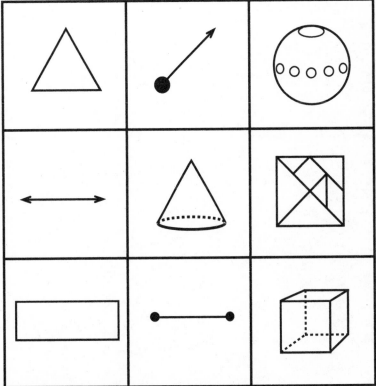

265

Page is blank for cutting exercise on previous page.

Name _____

Geometry: Perimeter

The perimeter is the distance around an object. Find the perimeter by adding the lengths of all the sides.

Directions: Find the perimeter for each object (ft. = feet).

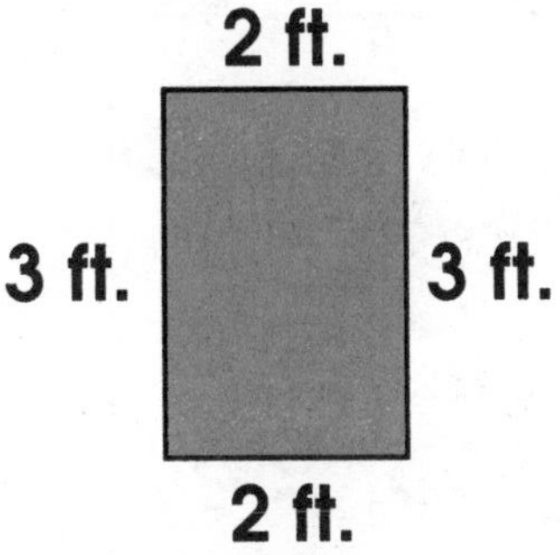

2 ft.

3 ft.   3 ft.

2 ft.

6 ft.

6 ft.   6 ft.

6 ft.   6 ft.

6 ft.

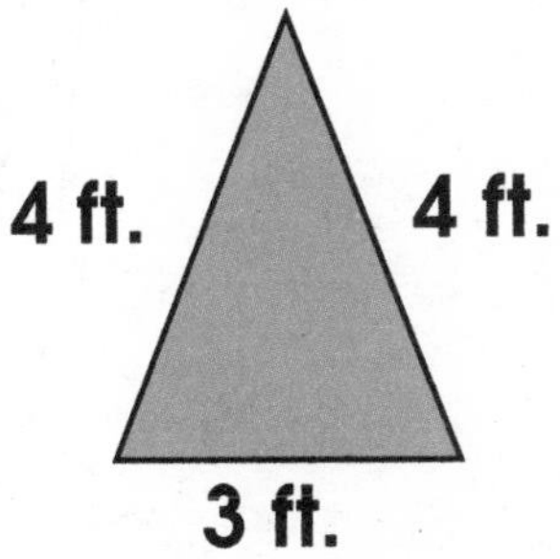

4 ft.   4 ft.

3 ft.

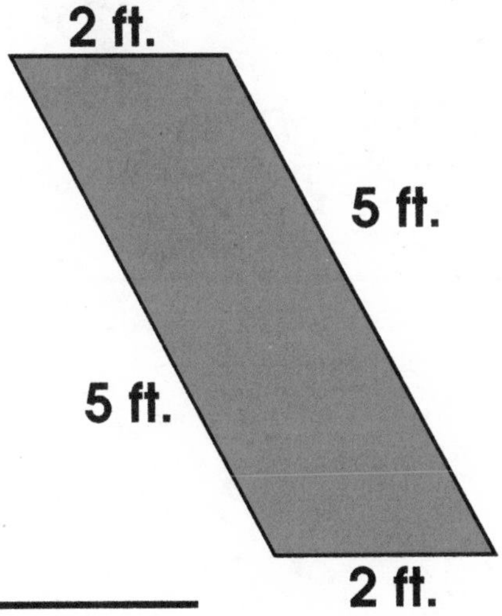

__10 ft.__

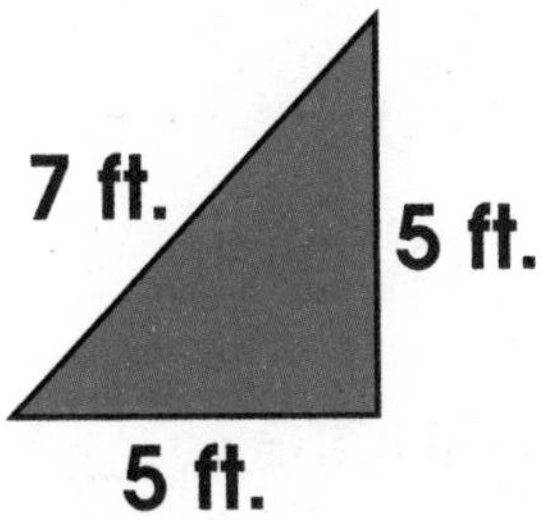

_____

_____

2 ft.

5 ft.

5 ft.

2 ft.

_____

10 ft.

3 ft.   3 ft.

10 ft.

_____

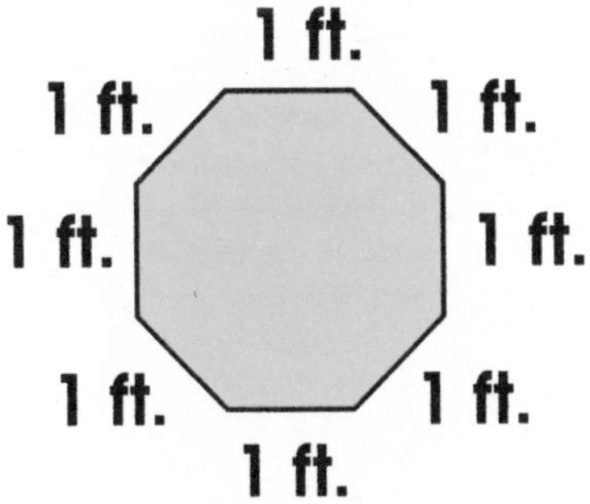

1 ft.

1 ft.   1 ft.

1 ft.   1 ft.

1 ft.   1 ft.

1 ft.

7 ft.   5 ft.

5 ft.

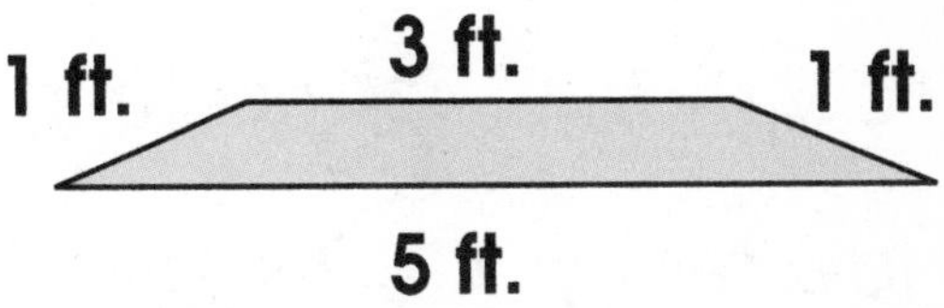

1 ft.   3 ft.   1 ft.

5 ft.

_____

_____

_____

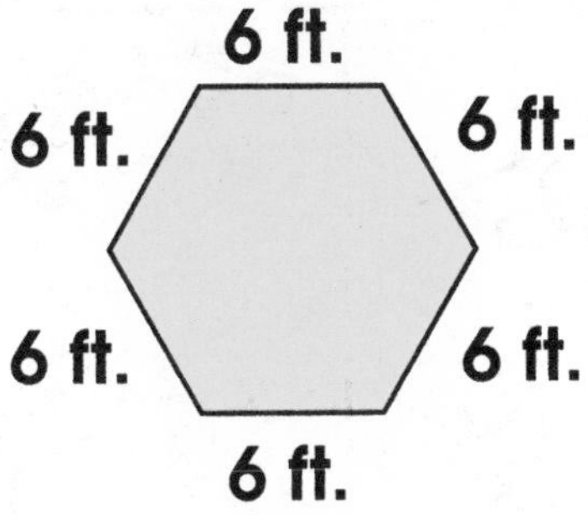

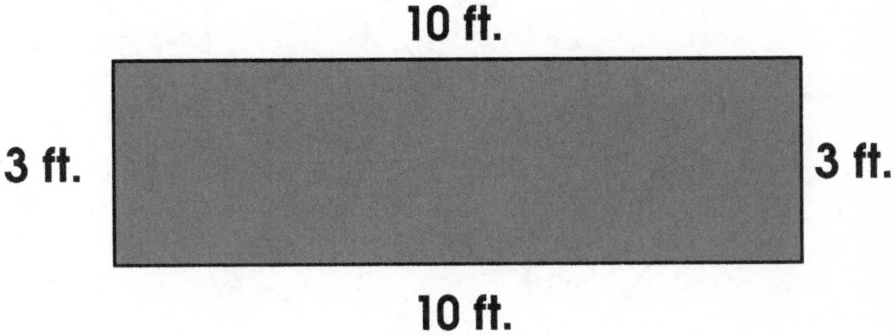

Name _____

Flower Power

Directions: Count the flowers and answer the questions.

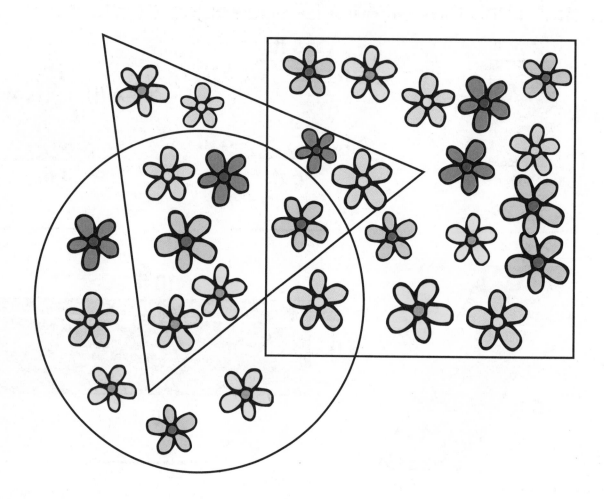

How many s are in the circle? _____

How many s are in the triangle? _____

How many s are in the square? _____

How many s in all? _____

Map Skills: Scale

A **map scale** shows how far one place is from another. This map scale shows that 1 inch on this page equals 1 mile at the real location.

Directions: Use a ruler and the map scale to find out how far it is from Ann's house to other places. Round to the nearest inch.

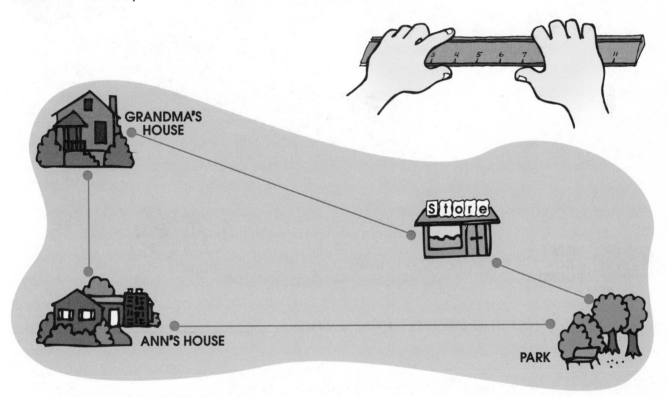

1. How far is it from Ann's house to the park? _____

2. How far is it from Ann's house to Grandma's house? _____

3. How far is it from Grandma's house to the store? _____

4. How far did Ann go when she went from her house
   to Grandma's and then to the store? _____

Name _____

Map Skills: Scale

Directions: Use a ruler and the map scale to measure the map and answer the questions. Round to the nearest inch.

Map Scale
1 inch = 10 feet

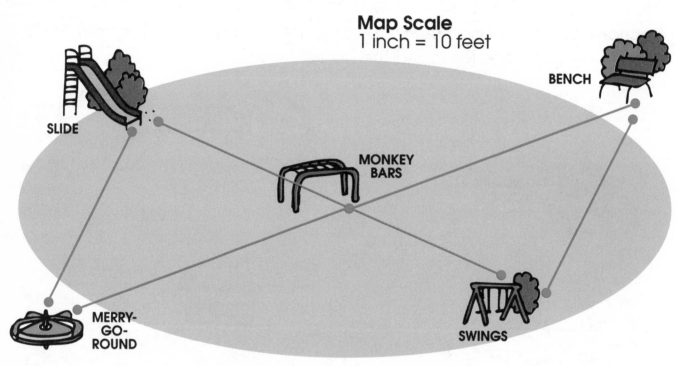

1. How far is it from the bench to the swings?_____

2. How far is it from the bench to the monkey bars?_____

3. How far is it from the monkey bars to the merry-go-round?_____

4. How far is it from the bench to the merry-go-round?_____

5. How far is it from the merry-go-round to the slide?_____

6. How far is it from the slide to the swings?_____

Graphs

A graph is a drawing that shows information about numbers.

Directions: Color the picture. Then tell how many there are of each object by completing the graph.

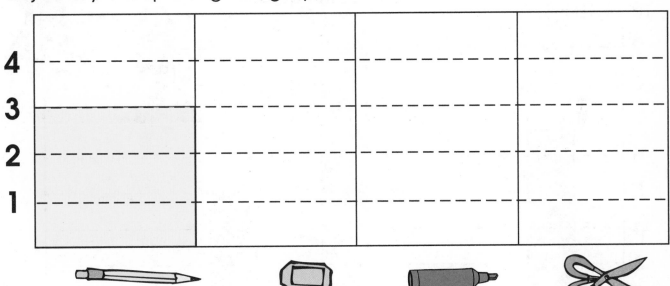

Math

271

Total Basic Skills Grade 3

Name _____

Graphs

Directions: Answer the questions about the graph.

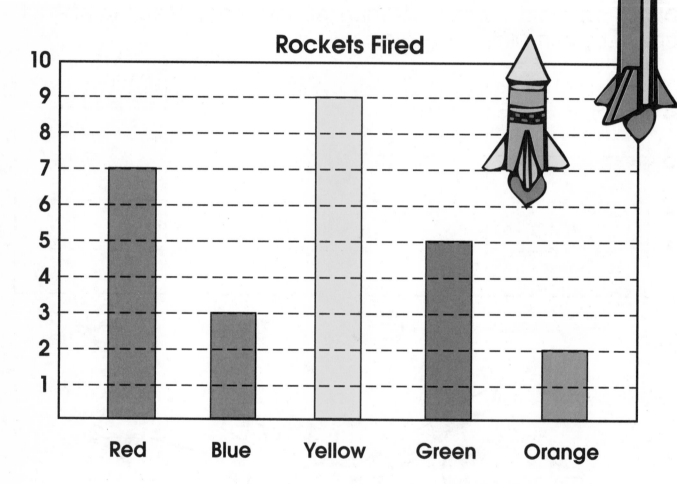

Rockets Fired

How many rockets did the Red Club fire? _____

How many rockets did the Green Club fire? _____

The Yellow Club fired 9 rockets. How many more rockets did it fire than the Blue Club? _____

How many rockets were fired in all? _____

Name _____

Measurement: Ounce and Pound

Ounces and pounds are measurements of weight in the standard measurement system. The ounce is used to measure the weight of very light objects. The pound is used to measure the weight of heavier objects. 16 ounces = 1 pound.

Example:

8 ounces   15 pounds

Directions: Decide if you would use ounces or pounds to measure the weight of each object. Circle your answer.

ounce   pound   ounce   pound

ounce   pound   ounce   pound

a chair: ounce   pound   **a table:**   ounce   pound

a shoe: ounce   pound   **a shirt:**   ounce   pound

Name _____

Measurement: Inches

An inch is a unit of length in the standard measurement system.

Directions: Use a ruler to measure each object to the nearest $\frac{1}{4}$ inch. Write **in.** to stand for inch.

Example:

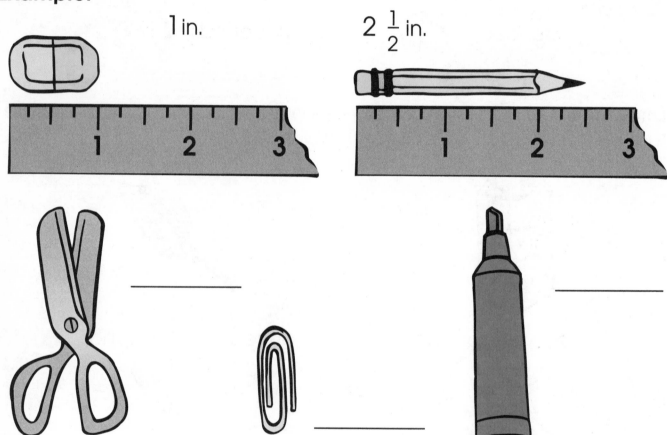

1 in.

$2\frac{1}{2}$ in.

_____

_____

_____

_____

Math

Name _____

Measurement: Centimeter

A centimeter is a unit of length in the metric system. There are 2.54 centimeters in an inch.

Directions: Use a centimeter ruler to measure each object to the nearest half of a centimeter. Write **cm** to stand for centimeter.

Example:

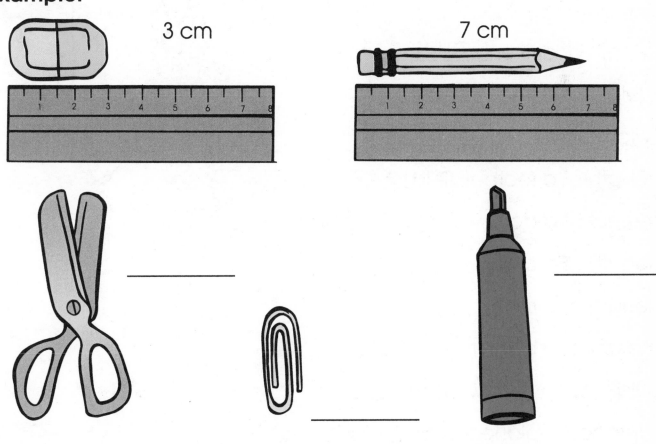

3 cm

7 cm

_____

_____

_____

_____

_____

275

Measurement: Foot, Yard, Mile

Directions: Decide whether you would use foot, yard or mile to measure each object.

1 foot = 12 inches
1 yard = 36 inches or 3 feet
1 mile = 1,760 yards

length of a river ___miles___

height of a tree _____

width of a room _____

length of a football field _____

height of a door _____

length of a dress _____

length of a race _____

height of a basketball hoop _____

width of a window _____

distance a plane travels _____

Directions: Solve the problem.

Tara races Tom in the 100-yard dash. Tara finishes 10 yards in front of Tom. How many feet did Tara finish in front of Tom?

_____

Name _____

Measurement: Meter and Kilometer

Meters and kilometers are units of length in the metric system. A meter is equal to 39.37 inches. A kilometer is equal to about $\frac{5}{8}$ of a mile.

Directions: Decide whether you would use meter or kilometer to measure each object.

1 meter = 100 centimeters
1 kilometer = 1,000 meters

length of a river ___kilometer___

height of a tree _____

width of a room _____

length of a football field _____

height of a door _____

length of a dress _____

length of a race _____

height of a basketball pole _____

width of a window _____

distance a plane travels _____

Directions: Solve the problem.

Tara races Tom in the 100-meter dash. Tara finishes 10 meters in front of Tom. How many centimeters did Tara finish in front of Tom?

_____

Name _____

Coordinates

Directions: Locate the points on the grid and color in each box.

What animal did you form?_____

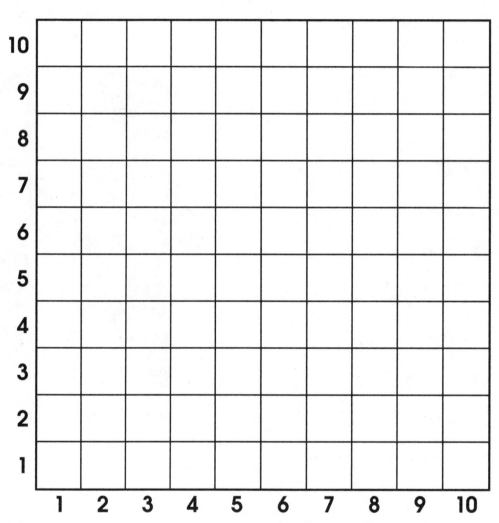

(across, up)

(4, 7)	(4, 1)	(7, 1)	(3, 5)	(2, 8)	(8, 6)	(4, 8)	(3, 7)
(5, 4)	(6, 5)	(5, 5)	(6, 6)	(7, 3)	(8, 5)	(10, 5)	(4, 3)
(7, 6)	(4, 6)	(1, 8)	(6, 4)	(7, 2)	(4, 5)	(9, 6)	(4, 9)
(3, 6)	(7, 5)	(5, 6)	(4, 2)	(4, 4)	(7, 4)	(2, 7)	(3, 8)

Math

Roman Numerals

Another way to write numbers is to use Roman numerals.

I	1	VII	7
II	2	VIII	8
III	3	IX	9
IV	4	X	10
V	5	XI	11
VI	6	XII	12

Directions: Fill in the Roman numerals on the watch.

What time is it on the watch?

_____ o'clock

Name _____

Roman Numerals

I	1	VII	7
II	2	VIII	8
III	3	IX	9
IV	4	X	10
V	5	XI	11
VI	6	XII	12

Directions: Write the number.

V _____   VII _____

X _____   IX _____

II _____   XII _____

Directions: Write the Roman numeral.

4 _____   5 _____

10 _____   8 _____

6 _____   3 _____

Name _____

Time: Hour, Half-Hour, Quarter-Hour, 5 Min. Intervals

Directions: Write the time shown on each clock.

Example:

7:15

7:00

_____

_____

_____

_____

_____

_____

_____

_____

_____

Name _____

Time: a.m. and p.m.

In telling time, the hours between 12:00 midnight and 12:00 noon are a.m. hours. The hours between 12:00 noon and 12:00 midnight are p.m. hours.

Directions: Draw a line between the times that are the same.

Example:

7:30 in the morning   7:30 a.m.
half-past seven a.m.
seven thirty in the morning

9:00 in the evening   9:00 p.m.
nine o'clock at night

six o'clock in the evening	8:00 a.m.
3:30 a.m.	six o'clock in the morning
4:15 p.m.	6:00 p.m.
eight o'clock in the morning	eleven o'clock in the evening
quarter past five in the evening	three thirty in the morning
11:00 p.m.	four fifteen in the evening
6:00 a.m.	5:15 p.m.

Name _____

Time: Minutes

A minute is a measurement of time. There are sixty seconds in a minute and sixty minutes in an hour.

Directions: Write the time shown on each clock.

Example:

Each mark is one minute.
The hand is at mark number 6.

Write: 5:06
Read: six minutes after five.

_____

_____

_____

_____

_____

_____

_____

_____

_____

_____

_____

_____

Time: Addition

Directions: Add the hours and minutes together.
(Remember, 1 hour equals 60 minutes.)

Example:

```
  2 hours 10 minutes
+ 1 hour  50 minutes
  3 hours(60 minutes)
        (1 hour)
  4 hours
```

```
  4 hours 20 minutes
+ 2 hours 10 minutes
  6 hours 30 minutes
```

```
  9 hours
+ 2 hours
```

```
  1 hour
+ 5 hours
```

```
  6 hours
+ 3 hours
```

```
  6 hours 15 minutes
+ 1 hour  15 minutes
```

```
 10 hours 30 minutes
+ 1 hour   10 minutes
```

```
  3 hours 40 minutes
+ 8 hours 20 minutes
```

```
 11 hours 15 minutes
+ 1 hour   30 minutes
```

```
  4 hours 15 minutes
+ 5 hours 45 minutes
```

```
  7 hours 10 minutes
+ 1 hour   30 minutes
```

Time: Subtraction

Directions: Subtract the hours and minutes.
(Remember, 1 hour equals 60 minutes.)
"Borrow" from the "hours" if you need to.

Example:

```
   5       70
   6 hours 10 minutes
 - 2 hours 30 minutes
   3 hours 40 minutes
```

```
  12 hours            5 hour              2 hours
 - 2 hours          - 3 hours           - 1 hour
```

```
  5 hours 30 minutes     9 hours 45 minutes     11 hours 50 minutes
 - 2 hours 15 minutes   - 3 hours 15 minutes    - 4 hours 35 minutes
```

```
  12 hours               7 hours 15 minutes     8 hours 10 minutes
 - 6 hours 30 minutes   - 5 hours 30 minutes    - 4 hours 40 minutes
```

Money: Coins and Dollars

 penny =
1¢ or $.01

 quarter =
25¢ or $.25

 nickel =
5¢ or $.05

 half-dollar =
50¢ or $.50

dollar = 100¢ or $1.00

 dime =
10¢ or $.10

Directions: Write the amount for each group of money shown. Use a dollar sign and decimal point. The first one is done for you.

 $.07

   _____

   _____

   _____

   _____

_____   _____

Money: Five-Dollar Bill and Ten-Dollar Bill

Directions: Write the amount for each group of money shown. Use a dollar sign and decimal point. The first one is done for you.

Five-dollar bill =
5 one dollar bills

Ten-dollar bill =
2 five-dollar bills or
10 one-dollar bills

$15.00

_____

_____   _____

7 one-dollar bills, 2 quarters _____

2 five-dollar bills, 3 one-dollar bills, half-dollar _____

3 ten-dollar bills, 1 five-dollar bill, 3 quarters_____

Name _____

Money: Counting Change

Directions: Subtract the money using decimals to show how much change a person would receive in each of the following.

Example:

Bill had 3 dollars.
He bought a baseball for $2.83.
How much change did he receive?

$3.00
-$2.83
$ .17

Paid 2 dollars.

_____

Paid 1 dollar.

_____

Paid 5 dollars.

_____

Paid 10 dollars.

_____

Paid 4 dollars.

_____

Paid 7 dollars.

_____

Name _____

Money: Comparing

Directions: Compare the amount of money in the left column with the price of the object in the right column. Is the amount of money in the left column enough to purchase the object in the right column? Circle yes or no.

Example:

Alice has 2 dollars. She wants to buy a box of crayons for $1.75. Does she have enough money?   (Yes) No

    Yes No

    Yes No

     Yes No

Name _____

Review

Directions: Complete each clock to show the time written below it.

7:15   3:07   6:25

Directions: Write the time using a.m. or p.m.

seven twenty-two in the evening _____

three fifteen in the morning _____

eight thirty at night _____

Directions: Write the correct amount of money.

_____   _____

   Joey paid $4.67 for a model car. He gave the clerk a five-dollar bill. How much change should he receive?

_____

Name _____

Review

Directions: Read and solve each of the problems.

The baker sets out 9 baking pans with 6 rolls on each one. How many rolls are there in all?

_____

A dozen brownies cost $1.29. James pays for a dozen brownies with a five-dollar bill. How much change does he receive?

_____

Theresa has four quarters, a nickel and three pennies. How much more money does she need to buy brownies?

_____

The baker made 24 loaves of bread. At the end of the day, he has one-fourth left. How many did he sell?

_____

Two loaves of bread weigh a pound. How many loaves are needed to make five pounds?

_____

The bakery opens at 8:30 a.m. It closes nine and a half hours later. What time does it close?

_____

Name _____

Review

Place Value

Directions: Write the number's value in each place: **678,421**.

_____ ones   _____ hundred thousands

_____ thousands   _____ hundreds

_____ tens   _____ ten thousands

Addition and Subtraction

Directions: Add or subtract. Remember to regroup, if you need to.

88	46	75	93	76
- 19	+ 39	+ 24	- 68	- 59

		84	97	
683	855	49	54	9,731
- 496	+ 138	+ 62	+ 361	- 4,664

Rounding

Directions: Round to the nearest 10, 100 or 1,000.

72 _____   49 _____   31 _____   66 _____

151 _____   296 _____   917 _____   621 _____

Name _____

Multiplication and Division

$$\begin{array}{r} 3 \\ \times 6 \\ \hline \end{array}$$
$$\begin{array}{r} 3 \\ \times 8 \\ \hline \end{array}$$
$$\begin{array}{r} 9 \\ \times 8 \\ \hline \end{array}$$
$$\begin{array}{r} 9 \\ \times 5 \\ \hline \end{array}$$
$$\begin{array}{r} 7 \\ \times 2 \\ \hline \end{array}$$

$$5\overline{)25} \qquad 2\overline{)6} \qquad 3\overline{)18} \qquad 8\overline{)24} \qquad 7\overline{)49}$$

Fractions

$\frac{1}{3}$ of 12 = _____

$\frac{1}{7}$ of 28 = _____

$\frac{1}{9}$ of 45 = _____

Directions: Color parts to match the fractions given.

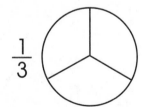

$\frac{1}{3}$

$\frac{2}{4}$

$\frac{2}{6}$

Decimals

Directions: Write the decimal for each fraction.

$\frac{4}{10}$ = _____ $3\frac{3}{10}$ = _____ $\frac{9}{10}$ = _____ $21\frac{3}{10}$ = _____

Directions: Add or Subtract.

8.2 + 1.1 = _____   3.6 - 1.8 = _____   3.9 + 2.6 = _____

Geometry

Directions: Write the name for each figure.

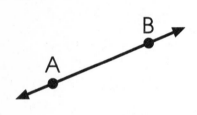  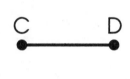 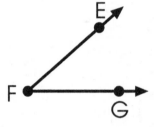

_____   _____   _____   _____

Directions: Find the perimeter of each object.

4 ft.
4 ft. [ ] 4 ft.
4 ft.

5 ft.
1 ft. [ ] 1 ft.
5 ft.

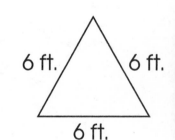
6 ft. 6 ft.
6 ft.

_____   _____   _____

Name _____

Graphing

Directions: Answer the questions.

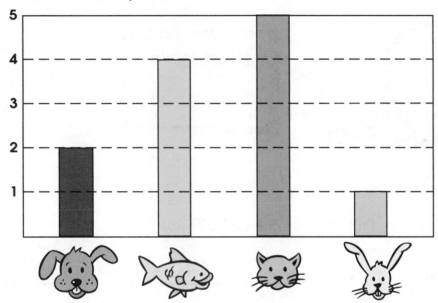

Which animal is there the most of?   _____

Which animal is there the fewest of?   _____

How many animals altogether?   _____

Measurements

Directions: Answer the questions.

What unit of measure would you use to measure...

Example: ...a cow?   _pound_

...a mouse?   _____

...length of a pencil?   _____

...length of a semi-truck?   _____

...length of a river?   _____

...width of a river?   _____

...height of a flag pole?   _____

Name _____

Time

Directions: Complete each clock to show the time written below it.

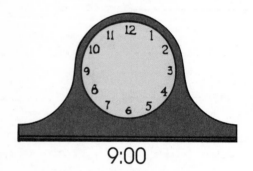

9:00

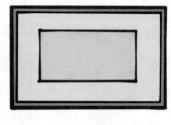

10:15

2:35

Directions: Write the time, using a.m. or p.m.

six twenty-two in the evening _____

nine forty-six in the morning _____

Directions: Add or subtract.

$$\begin{array}{r} 2 \text{ hours } 15 \text{ minutes} \\ + \ 4 \text{ hours } 30 \text{ minutes} \\ \hline \end{array}$$

$$\begin{array}{r} 1 \text{ hour } \ 30 \text{ minutes} \\ + \ 4 \text{ hours } 30 \text{ minutes} \\ \hline \end{array}$$

$$\begin{array}{r} 12 \text{ hours } 45 \text{ minutes} \\ - \ 4 \text{ hours } 30 \text{ minutes} \\ \hline \end{array}$$

$$\begin{array}{r} 8 \text{ hours } 30 \text{ minutes} \\ - \ 3 \text{ hours } 45 \text{ minutes} \\ \hline \end{array}$$

Name _____

Problem-Solving: Addition, Subtraction

Directions: Read and solve each problem. The first one is done for you.

The clown started the day with 200 balloons. He gave away 128 of them. Some broke. At the end of the day he had 18 balloons left. How many of the balloons broke?

54
_____

On Monday, there were 925 tickets sold to adults and 1,412 tickets sold to children. How many more children attended the fair than adults?

_____

At one game booth, prizes were given out for scoring 500 points in three attempts. Sally scored 178 points on her first attempt, 149 points on her second attempt and 233 points on her third attempt. Did Sally win a prize?

_____

The prize-winning steer weighed 2,348 pounds. The runner-up steer weighed 2,179 pounds. How much more did the prize steer weigh?

_____

There were 3,418 people at the fair on Tuesday, and 2,294 people on Wednesday. What was the total number of people there for the two days?

_____

Name _____

Problem-Solving: Multiplication, Division

Directions: Read and solve each problem.

Jeff and Terry are planting a garden. They plant 3 rows of green beans with 8 plants in each row. How many green bean plants are there in the garden? _____

There are 45 tomato plants in the garden. There are 5 rows of them. How many tomato plants are in each row? _____

The children have 12 plants each of lettuce, broccoli and spinach. How many plants are there in all? _____

Jeff planted 3 times as many cucumber plants as Terry. He planted 15 of them. How many did Terry plant? _____

Terry planted 12 pepper plants. He planted twice as many green pepper plants as red pepper plants. How many green pepper plants are there? _____

How many red pepper plants? _____

Name _____

Problem-Solving: Fractions, Decimals

A fraction is a number that names part of a whole, such as $\frac{1}{2}$ or $\frac{1}{3}$.

Directions: Read and solve each problem.

There are 20 large animals on the Browns' farm. Two-fifths are horses, two-fifths are cows and the rest are pigs. Are there more pigs or cows on the farm? _____

Farmer Brown had 40 eggs to sell. He sold half of them in the morning. In the afternoon, he sold half of what was left. How many eggs did Farmer Brown have at the end of the day? _____

There is a fence running around seven-tenths of the farm. How much of the farm does not have a fence around it? Write the amount as a decimal. _____

The Browns have 10 chickens. Two are roosters and the rest are hens. Write a decimal for the number that are roosters and for the number that are hens. _____ roosters _____ hens

Mrs. Brown spends three-fourths of her day working outside and the rest working inside. Does she spend more time inside or outside? _____

Name _____

Problem-Solving: Measurement

Directions: Read and solve each problem.

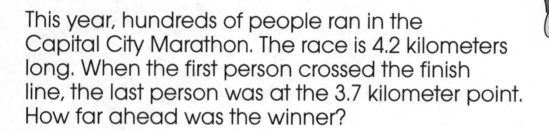

This year, hundreds of people ran in the
Capital City Marathon. The race is 4.2 kilometers
long. When the first person crossed the finish
line, the last person was at the 3.7 kilometer point.
How far ahead was the winner?

_____

Dennis crossed the finish line 10 meters ahead of Lucy.
Lucy was 5 meters ahead of Sam. How far ahead of Sam
was Dennis?

_____

Tony ran 320 yards from school to his home. Then he ran
290 yards to Jay's house. Together Tony and Jay ran 545
yards to the store. How many yards in all did Tony run?

_____

The teacher measured the heights of three children in her
class. Marsha was 51 inches tall, Jimmy was 48 inches tall
and Ted was $52\frac{1}{2}$ inches tall. How much taller is Ted than
Marsha?

_____

How much taller is he than Jimmy?

_____

Problem-Solving

Directions: Read and solve each problem.

Ralph has $8.75. He buys a teddy bear and a puzzle.
How much money does he have left?   _____

Kelly wants to buy a teddy bear and a ball. She has $7.25.
How much more money does she need?   _____

Kim paid a five-dollar bill, two one-dollar bills, two quarters,
one dime and eight pennies for a book.
How much did it cost?   _____

Michelle leaves for school at 7:45 a.m.
It takes her 20 minutes to get there.
On the clock, draw the time that she
arrives at school.

Frank takes piano lessons every
Saturday morning at 11:30.
The lesson lasts for an hour and
15 minutes. On the clock, draw
the time his piano lesson ends.
Is it a.m. or p.m.?
Circle the correct answer.

Page 6

Phonics

Some words are more difficult to read because they have one or more silent letters. Many words you already know are like this.

Examples: wrong and **night**.

Directions: Circle the silent letters in each word. The first one is done for you.

ⓦrong   ansⓦer   autumⓝ   ⓦhole
ⓚnife   ⓗour   ⓦrap   comⓑ
sigⓗ   straigⓗt   ⓚnee   ⓚnown
lamⓑ   tauⓖⓗt   sⓒent   daugⓗter
whisⓣle   ⓦrote   ⓚnew   crumⓑ

Directions: Draw a line between the rhyming words. The first one is done for you.

knew — try
sees — bowl
taut — stone
wrote — true
comb — song
straight — trees
sigh — home
known — great
wrong — caught
whole — boat

Page 7

Phonics

Sometimes letters make sounds you don't expect. Two consonants can work together to make the sound of one consonant. The **f** sound can be made by **ph**, as in the word **elephant**. The consonants **gh** are most often silent, as in the words **night** and **though**. But they also can make the **f** sound as in the word **laugh**.

Directions: Circle the letters that make the **f** sound. Write the correct word from the box to complete each sentence.

| ele**ph**ant | cou**gh** | lau**gh** | tele**ph**one | **ph**onics |
| dol**ph**ins | enou**gh** | tou**gh** | al**ph**abet | rou**gh** |

1. The **dolphins** were playing in the sea.
2. Did you have ____enough____ time to do your homework?
3. A cold can make you ____cough____ and sneeze.
4. The ____elephant____ ate peanuts with his trunk.
5. The road to my school is ____rough____ and bumpy.
6. You had a ____telephone____ call this morning.
7. The ____tough____ meat was hard to chew.
8. Studying ____phonics____ will help you read better.
9. The ____alphabet____ has 26 letters in it.
10. We began to ____laugh____ when the clowns came in.

Page 8

Phonics

There are several consonants that make the **k** sound: **c** when followed by a, o or u as in **cow** or **cup**; the letter **k** as in **milk**; the letters **ch** as in **Christmas** and **ck** as in **black**.

Directions: Read the following words. Circle the letters that make the **k** sound. The first one is done for you.

a**ch**e	s**ch**ool	mar**k**et	**c**omb
camera	de**ck**	dar**k**ness	**Ch**ristmas
ne**ck**lace	do**ct**or	stoma**ch**	**cr**a**ck**
ni**ck**el	s**k**in	thi**ck**	es**c**ape

Directions: Use your own words to finish the following sentences. Use words with the **k** sound.

1. If I had a nickel, I would ____Answers will vary.____

2. My doctor is very _____

3. We bought ripe, juicy tomatoes at the _____

4. If I had a camera now,
   I would take a picture of _____

5. When my stomach aches, _____

Page 9

Phonics

In some word "families," the vowels have a long sound when you would expect them to have a short sound. For example, the **i** has a short sound in **chill**, but a long sound in **child**. The **o** has a short sound in **cost**, but a long sound in **most**.

Directions: Read the words in the word box below. Write the words that have a long vowel sound under the word **LONG**, and the words that have a short vowel sound under the word **SHORT**. (Remember, a long vowel says its name—like **a** in **ate**.)

| old | odd | gosh | gold | sold | soft | toast | frost | lost | most |
| doll | roll | bone | done | kin | mill | mild | wild | blink | blind |

LONG

bone   sold
old   toast
roll   mild
most   wild
gold   blind

SHORT

doll   soft
odd   mill
gosh   frost
done   lost
kin   blink

Page 10

Syllables

All words can be divided into **syllables**. Syllables are word parts which have one vowel sound in each part.

Directions: Draw a line between the syllable part and write the word on the correct line below. The first one is done for you.

little   bumble|bee   pil|low
truck   daz|zle   dog
pen|cil   flag   an|gel|ic
re|joi|cing   ant   tele|phone

1 SYLLABLE	2 SYLLABLES	3 SYLLABLES
truck	little	rejoicing
flag	pencil	bumblebee
ant	dazzle	angelic
dog	pillow	telephone

Page 11

Syllables

When the letters **le** come at the end of a word, they sometimes have the sound of **ul**, as in raffle.

Directions: Draw a line to match the syllables so they make words. The first one is done for you.

can-	gle
tur	cle
pur	ple
cir	zle
spar	dle
raf	fle
ea	tle
siz	

Directions: Use the words you made to complete the sentences. One is done for you.

1. Will you buy a ticket for our school <u>raffle</u>?
2. The <u>turtle</u> pulled his head into his shell.
3. We could hear the bacon <u>sizzle</u> in the pan.
4. The baby had one <u>candle</u> on her birthday cake.
5. My favorite color is <u>purple</u>.
6. Look at that diamond <u>sparkle</u>.
7. The bald <u>eagle</u> is our national bird.
8. Draw a <u>circle</u> around the correct answer.

Page 12

Compound Words

A compound word is two small words put together to make one new word. Compound words are usually divided into syllables between the two words.

Directions: Read the words. Then divide them into syllables. The first one is done for you.

1. playground <u>play</u> <u>ground</u>
2. sailboat <u>sail</u> <u>boat</u>
3. doghouse <u>dog</u> <u>house</u>
4. dishpan <u>dish</u> <u>pan</u>
5. pigpen <u>pig</u> <u>pen</u>
6. outdoors <u>out</u> <u>doors</u>
7. beehive <u>bee</u> <u>hive</u>
8. airplane <u>air</u> <u>plane</u>
9. cardboard <u>card</u> <u>board</u>
10. nickname <u>nick</u> <u>name</u>
11. hilltop <u>hill</u> <u>top</u>
12. broomstick <u>broom</u> <u>stick</u>
13. sunburn <u>sun</u> <u>burn</u>
14. oatmeal <u>oat</u> <u>meal</u>
15. campfire <u>camp</u> <u>fire</u>
16. somewhere <u>some</u> <u>where</u>
17. starfish <u>star</u> <u>fish</u>
18. birthday <u>birth</u> <u>day</u>
19. sidewalk <u>side</u> <u>walk</u>
20. seashore <u>sea</u> <u>shore</u>

Page 13

Compound Words

Directions: Read the compound words in the word box. Then use them to answer the questions. The first one is done for you.

sailboat	blueberry	bookcase	tablecloth	beehive
dishpan	pigpen	classroom	playground	bedtime
broomstick	treetop	fireplace	newspaper	sunburn

Which compound word means . . .

 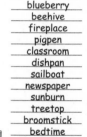

1. a case for books? <u>bookcase</u>
2. a berry that is blue? <u>blueberry</u>
3. a hive for bees? <u>beehive</u>
4. a place for fires? <u>fireplace</u>
5. a pen for pigs? <u>pigpen</u>
6. a room for a class? <u>classroom</u>
7. a pan for dishes? <u>dishpan</u>
8. a boat to sail? <u>sailboat</u>
9. a paper for news? <u>newspaper</u>
10. a burn from the sun? <u>sunburn</u>
11. the top of a tree? <u>treetop</u>
12. a stick for a broom? <u>broomstick</u>
13. the time to go to bed? <u>bedtime</u>
14. a cloth for the table? <u>tablecloth</u>
15. ground to play on? <u>playground</u>

Page 14

Transportation Vocabulary

Directions: Unscramble the words to spell the names of kinds of transportation. The first one is done for you.

behelwworar	wheel<u>b a r r o</u>w
anirt	<u>t r a i n</u>
moobattor	moto<u>r b o a</u>t
crattor	<u>t r a c t o r</u>
ceicbly	<u>b i c y c l e</u>
tocker	<u>r o c k e</u>t
etobimuloa	aut<u>o m o b i l</u>e
rilanape	<u>a i r p l a n e</u>

Directions: Use a word from above to complete each sentence.

1. My mother uses a <u>wheelbarrow</u> to move dirt to her garden.
2. The <u>rocket</u> blasted the spaceship off the launching pad.
3. We flew on an <u>airplane</u> to visit my aunt in Florida.
4. My grandfather drives a very old <u>automobile</u>.
5. We borrowed Fred's <u>motorboat</u> to go water skiing.
6. You should always look both ways when crossing a <u>train</u> track.
7. I hope I get a new <u>bicycle</u> for my birthday.

Page 15

Space Vocabulary

Directions: Unscramble each word. Use the numbers below the letters to tell you what order they belong in. Write the word by its definition.

```
i r t b o
4 2 5 3 1

u t o n c w d n o        u l e f
3 5 7 9 1 8 6 4 2        2 4 3 1

a t s r a t n o u        t e h t s u l
7 9 2 4 1 3 6 5 8        5 7 2 4 1 3 6
```

A member of the team that flies a spaceship. <u>astronaut</u>

A rocket-powered spaceship that travels between Earth and space. <u>shuttle</u>

The material, such as gas, used for power. <u>fuel</u>

The seconds just before take-off. <u>countdown</u>

The path of a spaceship as it goes around Earth. <u>orbit</u>

Page 16

Weather Vocabulary

Directions: Use the weather words in the box to complete the sentences.

sunny	temperature	foggy	puddles	rainy
windy	rainbow	cloudy	lightning	snowy

1. My friends and I love <u>snowy</u> days, because we can have snowball fights!
2. On <u>rainy</u> days, we like to stay indoors and play board games.
3. Today was hot and <u>sunny</u>, so we went to the beach.
4. We didn't see the sun at all yesterday. It was <u>cloudy</u> all day.
5. <u>Windy</u> weather is perfect for flying kites.
6. It was so <u>foggy</u>, Mom had to use the headlights in the car so we wouldn't get lost.
7. While it was still raining, the sun began to shine and created a beautiful <u>rainbow</u>.
8. We like to jump in the <u>puddles</u> after it rains.
9. <u>Lightning</u> flashed across the sky during the thunderstorm.
10. The <u>temperature</u> outside was so low, we needed to wear hats, mittens and scarves.

Page 17

Vocabulary Word Lists

Directions: Complete the vocabulary word lists. Be creative!

Answers may include:

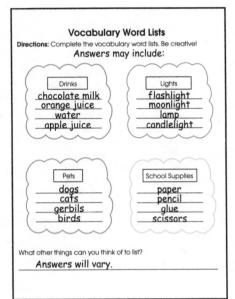

Drinks
chocolate milk
orange juice
water
apple juice

Lights
flashlight
moonlight
lamp
candlelight

Pets
dogs
cats
gerbils
birds

School Supplies
paper
pencil
glue
scissors

What other things can you think of to list?

Answers will vary.

Page 18

Sequencing

Directions: Fill in the blank spaces with what comes next in the series. The first one is done for you.

year	Wednesday	day	sixth	large
twenty	February	night	seventeen	mile
paragraph	winter	ocean		

1. Sunday, Monday, Tuesday, _____ Wednesday
2. third, fourth, fifth, _____ sixth
3. November, December, January, _____ February
4. tiny, small, medium, _____ large
5. fourteen, fifteen, sixteen, _____ seventeen
6. morning, afternoon, evening, _____ night
7. inch, foot, yard, _____ mile
8. day, week, month, _____ year
9. spring, summer, autumn, _____ winter
10. five, ten, fifteen, _____ twenty
11. letter, word, sentence, _____ paragraph
12. second, minute, hour, _____ day
13. stream, lake, river, _____ ocean

Page 19

Sequencing

When words are in a certain order, they are in sequence.

Directions: Complete each sequence using a word from the box. There are extra words in the box. The first one has been done for you.

| below | three | fifteen | December | twenty | above |
| after | go | third | hour | March | yard |

1. January, February, ___March___
2. before, during, ___after___
3. over, on, ___above___
4. come, stay, ___go___
5. second, minute, ___hour___
6. first, second, ___third___
7. five, ten, ___fifteen___
8. inch, foot, ___yard___

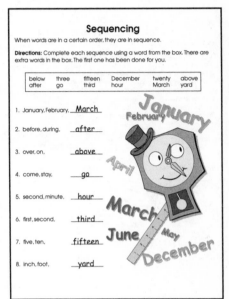

Page 20

Sequencing

Directions: Read each story. Circle the phrase that tells what happened before.

1. Beth is very happy now that she has someone to play with. She hopes that her new sister will grow up quickly!
   A few days ago . . .
   Beth was sick.
   (Beth's mother had a baby.)
   Beth got a new puppy.

2. Sara tried to mend the tear. She used a needle and thread to sew up the hole.
   While playing, Sara had . . .
   broken her bicycle.
   lost her watch.
   (Torn her shirt.)

3. The movers took John's bike off the truck and put it in the garage. Next, they moved his bed into his new bedroom.
   John's family . . .
   (bought a new house.)
   went on vacation.
   bought a new truck.

4. Katie picked out a book about dinosaurs. Jim, who likes sports, chose two books about baseball.
   Katie and Jim . . .
   (went to the library.)
   went to the playground.
   went to the grocery.

Page 21

Sequencing

Directions: Number these sentences from 1 to 5 to show the correct order of the story.

Building a Treehouse
_4_ They had a beautiful treehouse!
_2_ They got wood and nails.
_1_ Jay and Lisa planned to build a treehouse.
_5_ Now, they like to eat lunch in their treehouse.
_3_ Lisa and Jay worked in the backyard for three days building the treehouse.

A School Play
_5_ Everyone clapped when the curtain closed.
_4_ The girl who played Snow White came onto the stage.
_2_ All the other school children went to the gym to see the play.
_3_ The stage curtain opened.
_1_ The third grade was going to put on a play about Snow White.

Page 22

Following Directions

Directions: Learning to follow directions is very important. Use the map to find your way to different houses.

1. Color the start house yellow.
2. Go north 2 houses, and east two houses.
3. Go north 2 houses, and west 4 houses.
4. Color the house green.

5. Start at the yellow house.
6. Go east 1 house, and north 3 houses.
7. Go west 3 houses, and south 3 houses.
8. Color the house blue.

North
West — East
South

Page 23

Following Directions

Directions: Read each sentence and do what it says to do.

1. Count the syllables in each word. Write the number on the line by the word.
2. Draw a line between the two words in each compound word.
3. Draw a circle around each name of a month.
4. Draw a box around each food word.
5. Draw an X on each noise word.
6. Draw a line under each day of the week.
7. Write the three words from the list you did not use. Draw a picture of each of those words.

2	(April)	4	vegetable	3	table|cloth
1	ba~~ng~~	1	(June)	1	meat
2	side|walk	3	Saturday	1	cr~~as~~h
3	astronaut	1	(March)	2	ji~~ngl~~e
1	moon	2	card|board	2	rocket
2	Friday	1	meat	2	Monday

moon   astronaut   rocket

Page 24

Following Directions: A Recipe

Following directions means doing what the directions say to do. Following directions is an important skill to know. When you are trying to find a new place, build a model airplane or use a recipe, you should follow the directions given.

Directions: Read the following recipe. Then answer the questions on page 35.

Fruit Salad

1 fresh pineapple	2 oranges
1 cantaloupe	1 pear
2 bananas	1 cup seedless grapes
1 cup strawberries	lemon juice

- Cut the pineapple into chunks.
- Use a small metal scoop to make balls of the cantaloupe.
- Slice the pear, bananas and strawberries.
- Peel the oranges and divide them into sections. Cut each section into bite-sized pieces.
- Dip each piece of fruit in lemon juice, then combine them in a large bowl.
- Cover and chill.
- Pour a fruit dressing of your choice over the chilled fruit, blend well and serve cold.

Makes 4 large servings.

Page 25

Following Directions: A Recipe

Directions: Using the recipe on page 34, answer the questions below.

1. How many bananas does the recipe require? **2**

2. Does the recipe explain why you must dip the fruit in lemon juice? **no**
   Why would it be important to do this? **It keeps the fruit from turning brown quickly.**

3. Would your fruit salad be as good if you did not cut the pineapple or section the oranges? Why or why not? **No, because it would be harder to eat such big chunks of food.**

4. Which do you do first?
   (Check one.)
   ___ Pour dressing over the fruit.
   _✓_ Slice the pear.
   ___ Serve the fruit salad.

5. Which three fruits do you slice?
   pear
   bananas
   strawberries

Page 26

Main Idea

Directions: Read about spiders. Then answer the questions.

Many people think spiders are insects, but they are not. Spiders are the same size as insects, and they look like insects in some ways. But there are three ways to tell a spider from an insect. Insects have six legs, and spiders have eight legs. Insects have antennae, but spiders do not. An insect's body is divided into three parts; a spider's body is divided into only two parts.

1. The main idea of this story is:
   ~~Spiders are like insects.~~
   (Spiders are like insects in some ways, but they are not insects.)

2. What are three ways to tell a spider from an insect?
   1) **Spiders have eight legs; insects have six.**
   2) **Insects have antennae; spiders do not.**
   3) **Insects have three body parts; spiders have two.**

Circle the correct answer.

3. Spiders are the same size as insects.   (True)   False

Page 27

Main Idea

Directions: Read about the giant panda. Then answer the questions.

Giant pandas are among the world's favorite animals. They look like big, cuddly stuffed toys. There are not very many pandas left in the world. You may have to travel a long way to see one.

The only place on Earth where pandas live in the wild is in the bamboo forests of the mountains of China. It is hard to see pandas in the forest because they are very shy. They hide among the many bamboo trees. It also is hard to see pandas because there are so few of them. Scientists think there may be less than 1,000 pandas living in the mountains of China.

1. Write a sentence that tells the main idea of this story:
   There are very few pandas left in the world.

2. What are two reasons that it is hard to see pandas in the wild?
   1) **They hide among the bamboo trees.**
   2) **There are very few pandas.**

3. How many pandas are believed to be living in the mountains of China?
   fewer than 1,000

Page 28

Main Idea

Directions: Read the story. Then answer the questions.

Because bamboo is very important to pandas, they have special body features that help them eat it. The panda's front foot is like a hand. But, instead of four fingers and a thumb, the panda has five fingers and an extra-long wrist bone. With its special front foot, the panda can easily pick up the stalks of bamboo. It also can hold the bamboo more tightly than it could with a hand like ours.

Bamboo stalks are very tough. The panda uses its big heavy head, large jaws and big back teeth to chew. Pandas eat the bamboo first by peeling the outside of the stalk. They do this by moving their front feet from side to side while holding the stalk in their teeth. Then they bite off a piece of the bamboo and chew it with their strong jaws.

1. Write a sentence that tells the main idea of this story.
   Pandas have special body features to help them eat bamboo.

2. Instead of four fingers and a thumb, the panda has
   five fingers and an extra-long wrist bone.

3. Bamboo is very tender.   True   (False)

Page 29

Main Idea

The **main idea** of a paragraph is the most important point. Often, the first sentence in a paragraph tells the main idea. Most of the other sentences are details that support the main idea. One of the sentences in each paragraph below does not belong in the story.

Directions: Circle the sentence that does not support the main idea.

My family and I went to the zoo last Saturday. It was a beautiful day. The tigers napped in the sun. I guess they liked the warm sunshine as much as we did! Mom and Dad laughed at the baby monkeys. They said the monkeys reminded them of how we act. My sister said the bald eagle reminded her of Dad! I know I'll remember that trip to the zoo for a long time. (My cousin is coming to visit the weekend before school starts.)

Thanksgiving was a special holiday in our <u>classroom. Each child dressed</u> up as either a Pilgrim or a Native American. (My baby sister learned to walk last week.) We prepared food for our "feast" on the last day of school before the holiday. We all helped shake the jar full of cream to make real butter. Our teacher cooked applesauce. It smelled delicious!

Page 30

Main Idea: Inventing the Bicycle

Directions: Read about the bicycle, then answer the questions.

One of the first bicycles was made out of wood. It was created in 1790 by an inventor in France. The first bicycle had no pedals. It looked like a horse on wheels. The person who rode the bicycle had to push it with his/her legs. Pedals weren't invented until nearly 50 years later.

Bikes became quite popular in the United States during the 1890s. Streets and parks were filled with people riding them. But those bicycles were still different from the bikes we ride today. They had heavier tires, and the brakes and lights weren't very good. Bicycling is still very popular in the United States. It is a great form of exercise and a handy means of transportation.

1. Who invented the bicycle? __an inventor in France__

2. What did it look like? __no pedals, wooden, looked like a horse on wheels__

3. When did bikes become popular in the United States? __during the 1890s__

4. Where did people ride bikes? __streets and parks__

5. How is biking good for you? __good for exercise__

6. How many years have bikes been popular in the United States? __109 years__

Page 31

Main Idea: Chewing Gum

Directions: Read about chewing gum, then answer the questions.

Thomas Adams was an American inventor. In 1870, he was looking for a substitute for rubber. He was working with chicle (chick-ul), a substance that comes from a certain kind of tree in Mexico. Years ago, Mexicans chewed chicle. Thomas Adams decided to try it for himself. He liked it so much he started selling it. Twenty years later, he owned a large factory that produced chewing gum.

1. Who was the American inventor who started selling chewing gum? __Thomas Adams__

2. What was he hoping to invent? __a substitute for rubber__

3. When did he invent chewing gum? __in 1870__

4. Where does the chicle come from? __a tree in Mexico__

5. Why did Thomas Adams start selling chewing gum? __He liked it so much.__

6. How long was it until Adams owned a large factory that produced chewing gum? __20 years__

Page 32

Main Idea: The Peaceful Pueblos

Directions: Read about the Pueblo Native Americans, then answer the questions.

The Pueblo (pooh-eb-low) Native Americans live in the southwestern United States in New Mexico and Arizona. They have lived there for hundreds of years. The Pueblos have always been peaceful Native Americans. They never started wars. They only fought if attacked first.

The Pueblos love to dance. Even their dances are peaceful. They dance to ask the gods for rain or sunshine. They dance for other reasons, too. Sometimes the Pueblos wear masks when they dance.

1. The main idea is: (Circle one.)

> Pueblos are peaceful Native Americans who still live in parts of the United States.

Pueblo Native Americans never started wars.

2. Do Pueblos like to fight? __No__

3. What do the Pueblos like to do? __They love to dance.__

Page 33

Main Idea: Clay Homes

Directions: Read about adobe houses, then answer the questions.

Pueblo Native Americans live in houses made of clay. They are called adobe (ah-doe-bee) houses. Adobe is a yellow-colored clay that comes from the ground. The hot sun in New Mexico and Arizona helps dry the clay to make strong bricks. The Pueblos have used adobe to build their homes for many years.

Pueblos use adobe for other purposes, too. The women in the tribes make beautiful pottery out of adobe. While the clay is still damp, they form it into shapes. After they have made the bowls and other containers, they paint them with lovely designs.

1. What is the subject of this story? __adobe__

2. Who uses clay to make their houses? __Pueblo Native Americans__

3. How long have they been building adobe houses? __many years__

4. Why do adobe bricks need to be dried? __to make the clay bricks strong__

5. How do the Pueblos make pottery from adobe? __by forming damp clay__

Page 34

Noting Details

Directions: Read the story. Then answer the questions.

Thomas Edison was one of America's greatest inventors. An **inventor** thinks up new machines and new ways of doing things. Edison was born in Milan, Ohio in 1847. He went to school for only three months. His teacher thought he was not very smart because he asked so many questions.

Edison liked to experiment. He had many wonderful ideas. He invented the light bulb and the phonograph (record player).

Thomas Edison died in 1931, but we still use many of his inventions today.

1. What is an inventor?

__A person who thinks up new machines and new ways of doing things.__

2. Where was Thomas Edison born?

__Milan, Ohio__

3. How long did he go to school?

__three months__

4. What are two of Edison's inventions?

__the light bulb and the phonograph__

Page 35

Noting Details

Directions: Read the story. Then answer the questions.

The giant panda is much smaller than a brown bear or a polar bear. In fact, a horse weighs about four times as much as a giant panda. So why is it called "giant"? It is giant next to another kind of panda called the red panda.

The red panda also lives in China. The red panda is about the size of a fox. It has a long, fluffy, striped tail and beautiful reddish fur. It looks very much like a raccoon.

Many people think the giant pandas are bears. They look like bears. Even the word panda is Chinese for "white bear." But because of its relationship to the red panda, many scientists now believe that the panda is really more like a raccoon!

1. Why is the giant panda called "giant"?
   It is larger than the red panda.

2. Where does the red panda live?
   in China

3. How big is the red panda?
   about the size of a fox

4. What animal does the red panda look like?
   a raccoon

5. What does the word panda mean?
   "white bear"

Page 36

Inference

Inference is using logic to figure out what is not directly told.

Directions: Read the story. Then answer the questions.

In the past, thousands of people went to the National Zoo each year to see Hsing-Hsing, the panda. Sometimes, there were as many as 1,000 visitors in one hour! Like all pandas, Hsing-Hsing spent most of his time sleeping. Because pandas are so rare, most people think it is exciting to see even a sleeping panda!

1. Popular means well-liked. Do you think giant pandas are popular?
   Yes.

2. What clue do you have that pandas are popular?
   They had as many as 1,000 visitors an hour.

3. What did most visitors see Hsing-Hsing doing?
   sleeping

Page 37

Inference

Directions: Read the messages on the memo board. Then answer the questions.

1. What kind of lesson does Katie have? **dance**
2. What time is Amy's birthday party? **1:00 PM**
3. What kind of appointment does Jeff have on September 3rd? **doctor**
4. Who goes to choir practice? **mom**
5. Where is Dad's meeting? **fire station**
6. What time does Jeff go to the doctor? **4:00 PM**

Page 38

Reading for Information

Directions: Read the story. List the four steps or changes a caterpillar goes through as it becomes a butterfly. Draw the stages in the boxes at the bottom of the page.

The Life Cycle of the Butterfly

One of the most magical changes in nature is the metamorphosis of a caterpillar. There are four stages in the transformation. The first stage is the embryonic stage. This is the stage in which tiny eggs are deposited on a leaf. The second stage is the larvae stage. We usually think of caterpillars at this stage. Many people like to capture the caterpillars hoping that while they have the caterpillar, it will turn into pupa. Another name for the pupa stage is the cocoon stage. Many changes happen inside the cocoon that we cannot see. Inside the cocoon, the caterpillar is changing into an adult. The adult breaks out of the cocoon as a beautiful butterfly!

1. embryonic stage
2. larvae stage
3. pupa stage (cocoon stage)
4. butterfly stage

Life Cycle of the Butterfly

Page 39

Reading for Information

Telephone books contain information about people's addresses and phone numbers. They also list business addresses and phone numbers. The information in a telephone book is listed in alphabetical order.

Directions: Use your telephone book to find the following places in your area. Ask your mom or dad for help if you need it.

Can you find . . .

	Name	Phone number
. . . a pizza place?	Answers will vary.	
. . . a bicycle store?		
. . . a pet shop?		
. . . a toy store?		
. . . a water park?		

What other telephone numbers would you like to have?

Page 40

Analogies

Analogies compare how things are related to each other.

Directions: Complete the other analogies.

Example: Finger is to **hand** as toe is to **foot**.

1. Apple is to tree   as   flower is to **plant**

2. Tire is to car   as   wheel is to **bike**

3. Foot is to leg   as   hand is to **arm**

Page 41

Analogies

Directions: Complete each analogy using a word from the box. The first one has been done for you.

week	bottom	month	tiny	sentence	lake	out	eye

1. **Up** is to **down** as **In** is to **out**
2. **Minute** is to **hour** as **day** is to **week**
3. **Month** is to **year** as **week** is to **month**
4. **Over** is to **under** as **top** is to **bottom**
5. **Big** is to **little** as **giant** is to **tiny**
6. **Sound** is to **ear** as **sight** is to **eye**
7. **Page** is to **book** as **word** is to **sentence**
8. **Wood** is to **tree** as **water** is to **lake**

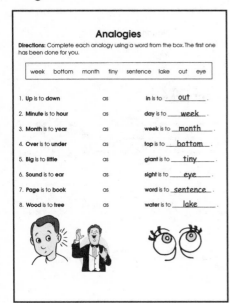

Page 42

Classifying: Seasons

Directions: Each word in the box can be grouped by seasons. Complete the pyramids for each season with a word from the box.

July 4	hot	football	bike rides
kite	froze	sled ride	swimming
snowman	bunnies	ice	jack-o-lantern
windy	baseball	leaves	Thanksgiving

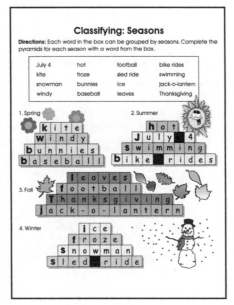

1. Spring
```
k i t e
w i n d y
b u n n i e s
b a s e b a l l
```

2. Summer
```
h o t
J u l y   4
S w i m m i n g
b i k e   r i d e s
```

3. Fall
```
l e a v e s
f o o t b a l l
T h a n k s g i v i n g
j a c k - o - l a n t e r n
```

4. Winter
```
i c e
f r o z e
s n o w m a n
S l e d   r i d e
```

Page 43

Classifying

Directions: Look at the three words in each box and add one more that is like the others. **Answers may include:**

cars	trucks	cows	pigs
airplanes	**trains**	chickens	**horses**
bread	bagels	pens	pencils
muffins	**toast**	paints	**crayons**
square	triangle	violets	tulips
rectangle	**circle**	iris	**roses**
milk	yogurt	mom	dad
cheese	**ice cream**	sister	**brother**
merry-go-round	swings	snowpants	boots
sandbox	**slide**	jacket	**hat**

Challenge: Can you list the theme of each group?

transportation	farm animals
grain products	school supplies
shapes	flowers
dairy products	family members
playground equipment	winter clothing

Page 44

Classifying

Directions: Write a word from the word box to complete each sentence. If the word you write names an article of clothing, write **1** on the line. If it names food, write **2** on the line. If it names an animal, write **3** on the line. If the word names furniture, write **4** on the line.

jacket	chair	shirt	owl	mice
bed	cheese	dress	bread	chocolate

- **1** 1. Danny tucked his **shirt** into his pants.
- **2** 2. **Chocolate** is my favorite kind of candy.
- **3** 3. The wise old **owl** sat in the tree and said, "Who-o-o."
- **4** 4. We can't sit on the **chair** because it has a broken leg.
- **1** 5. Don't forget to wear your **jacket** because it is chilly today.
- **2** 6. Will you please buy a loaf of **bread** at the store?
- **1** 7. She wore a very pretty **dress** to the dance.
- **3** 8. The cat chased the **mice** in the barn.
- **4** 9. I was so sleepy that I went to **bed** early.
- **2** 10. We put **cheese** in the mouse trap to help catch the mice.

Page 45

Classifying: Comparisons

Directions: Compare the people of Wackyville to each other. Read the sentences and answer the questions. The first one has been done for you.

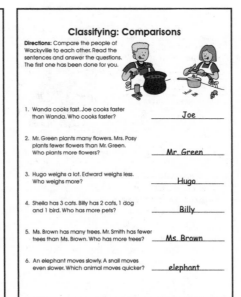

1. Wanda cooks fast. Joe cooks faster than Wanda. Who cooks faster? **Joe**

2. Mr. Green plants many flowers. Mrs. Posy plants fewer flowers than Mr. Green. Who plants more flowers? **Mr. Green**

3. Hugo weighs a lot. Edward weighs less. Who weighs more? **Hugo**

4. Sheila has 3 cats. Billy has 2 cats, 1 dog and 1 bird. Who has more pets? **Billy**

5. Ms. Brown has many trees. Mr. Smith has fewer trees than Ms. Brown. Who has more trees? **Ms. Brown**

6. An elephant moves slowly. A snail moves even slower. Which animal moves quicker? **elephant**

Page 46

Webs

Webs are another way to classify information. Look at the groups below. Add more words in each group.

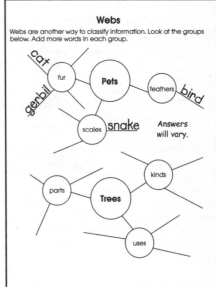

cat, gerbil, fur — Pets — feathers, bird

scales, snake

Answers will vary.

parts — Trees — kinds, uses

Page 47

Story Webs

All short stories have a plot, characters, setting and a theme.
The **plot** is what the story is about.
The **characters** are the people or animals in the story.
The **setting** is where and when the story occurs.
The **theme** is the message or idea of the story.

Directions: Use the story "Snow White" to complete this story web.

plot
The wicked stepmother tries to get rid of Snow White.

characters
Snow White, the seven dwarves, Snow White's stepmother the Prince

title of story:
"Snow White"

setting
the palace, the dwarves' cabin in the woods

theme
Good will triumph over evil.

Page 48

Fiction and Nonfiction

Fiction writing is a story that has been invented. The story might be about things that could really happen (realistic) or about things that couldn't possibly happen (fantasy). **Nonfiction** writing is based on facts. It usually gives information about people, places or things. A person can often tell while reading whether a story or book is fiction or nonfiction.

Directions: Read the paragraphs below and on page 49. Determine whether each paragraph is fiction or nonfiction. Circle the letter **F** for fiction or the letter **N** for nonfiction.

"Do not be afraid, little flowers," said the oak. "Close your yellow eyes in sleep and trust in me. You have made me glad many a time with your sweetness. Now I will take care that the winter shall do you no harm." (F) N

The whole team watched as the ball soared over the outfield fence. The game was over! It was hard to walk off the field and face parents, friends and each other. It had been a long season. Now, they would have to settle for second place. (F) N

Be careful when you remove the dish from the microwave. It will be very hot, so take care not to get burned by the dish or the hot steam. If time permits, leave the dish in the microwave for 2 or 3 minutes to avoid getting burned. It is a good idea to use a potholder, too. F (N)

Page 49

Fiction and Nonfiction

Megan and Mariah skipped out to the playground. They enjoyed playing together at recess. Today, it was Mariah's turn to choose what they would do first. To Megan's surprise, Mariah asked, "What do you want to do, Megan? I'm going to let you pick since it's your birthday!" (F) N

It is easy to tell an insect from a spider. An insect has three body parts and six legs. A spider has eight legs and no wings. Of course, if you see the creature spinning a web, you will know what it is. An insect wouldn't want to get too close to the web or it would be stuck. It might become dinner! F (N)

My name is Lee Chang, and I live in a country that you call China. My home is on the other side of the world from yours. When the sun is rising in my country, it is setting in yours. When it is day at your home, it is night at mine. F (N)

Henry washed the dog's foot in cold water from the brook. The dog lay very still, for he knew that the boy was trying to help him. (F) N

Page 50

Compare and Contrast

To **compare** means to discuss how things are similar. To contrast means to discuss how things are different.

Directions: Compare and contrast how people grow gardens. Write at least two answers for each question.

Many people in the country have large gardens. They have a lot of space, so they can plant many kinds of vegetables and flowers. Since the gardens are usually quite large, they use a wheelbarrow to carry the tools they need. Sometimes they even have to carry water or use a garden hose.

People who live in the city do not always have enough room for a garden. Many people in big cities live in apartment buildings. They can put in a window box or use part of their balcony space to grow things. Most of the time, the only garden tools they need are a hand trowel to loosen the dirt and a watering can to make sure the plant gets enough water.

1. Compare gardening in the country with gardening in the city.

Both can plant vegetables and flowers. They both have to use tools and water.

2. Contrast gardening in the country with gardening in the city.

City gardeners usually have smaller gardens and do not need as many tools as the country gardeners.

Page 51

Compare and Contrast

Directions: Look for similarities and differences in the following paragraphs. Then answer the questions.

Phong and Chris both live in the city. They live in the same apartment building and go to the same school. Phong and Chris sometimes walk to school together. If it is raining or storming, Phong's dad drives them to school on his way to work. In the summer, they spend a lot of time at the park across the street from their building.

Phong lives in Apartment 12-A with his little sister and mom and dad. He has a collection of model race cars that he put together with his dad's help. He even has a bookshelf full of books about race cars and race car drivers.

Chris has a big family. He has two older brothers and one older sister. When Chris has time to do anything he wants, he gets out his butterfly collection. He notes the place he found each specimen and the day he found it. He also likes to play with puzzles.

1. Compare Phong and Chris. List at least three similarities.

They both live in the city.
Phong and Chris spend a lot of time at the park.
They go to the same school.

2. Contrast Phong and Chris. List two differences.

Phong has a little sister; Chris has two brothers and one sister. Chris has a butterfly collection; Phong collects model race cars.

Page 52

Compare and Contrast: Venn Diagram

Directions: List the similarities and differences you find below on a chart called a **Venn diagram**. This kind of chart shows comparisons and contrasts.

Butterflies and moths belong to the same group of insects. They both have two pairs of wings. Their wings are covered with tiny scales. Both butterflies and moths undergo metamorphosis, or a change, in their lives. They begin their lives as caterpillars.

Butterflies and moths are different in some ways. Butterflies usually fly during the day, but moths generally fly at night. Most butterflies have slender, hairless bodies; most moths have plump, furry bodies. When butterflies land, they hold their wings together straight over their bodies. When moths land, they spread their wings out flat.

1. List three ways that butterflies and moths are alike.
Both have two pairs of wings.
Their wings are covered with tiny scales.
Both begin their lives as caterpillars.

2. List three ways that butterflies and moths are different.
Butterflies fly during the day; moths fly at night.
Butterflies' bodies are slender and hairless; moths'
plump and furry. Butterflies land wings up and moths
land wings spread out.

3. Combine your answers from questions 1 and 2 into a Venn diagram. Write the differences in the circle labeled for each insect. Write the similarities in the intersecting part.

Moths — Fly at night, Plump, furry body

Butterflies — Fly during the day, Slender, hairless body

Both — 2 pairs of wings, Wings have tiny scales, Have been caterpillars

Land wings spread out / Land wings straight up

Page 53

Cause and Effect

A **cause** is the reason for an event. An **effect** is what happens as a result of a cause.

Directions: Circle the cause and underline the effect in each sentence. They may be in any order. The first one has been done for you.

1. (The truck hit an icy patch) and skidded off the road.

2. (When the door slammed shut,) the baby woke up crying.

3. Our soccer game was cancelled (when it began to storm.)

4. Dad and Mom are adding a room onto the house (since our family is growing.)

5. (Our car ran out of gas on the way to town) so we had to walk.

6. (The home run in the ninth inning) helped our team win the game.

7. We had to climb the stairs (because the elevator was broken.)

8. We were late to school (because the bus had a flat tire.)

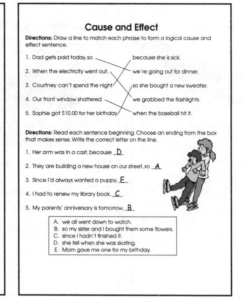

Page 54

Cause and Effect

Directions: Draw a line to match each phrase to form a logical cause and effect sentence.

1. Dad gets paid today, so — because she is sick.

2. When the electricity went out, — we're going out for dinner.

3. Courtney can't spend the night — so she bought a new sweater.

4. Our front window shattered — we grabbed the flashlights.

5. Sophie got $10.00 for her birthday, — when the baseball hit it.

Directions: Read each sentence beginning. Choose an ending from the box that makes sense. Write the correct letter on the line.

1. Her arm was in a cast, because __D__

2. They are building a new house on our street, so __A__

3. Since I'd always wanted a puppy, __E__

4. I had to renew my library book, __C__

5. My parents' anniversary is tomorrow, __B__

A. we all went down to watch.
B. so my sister and I bought them some flowers.
C. since I hadn't finished it.
D. she fell when she was skating.
E. Mom gave me one for my birthday.

Page 55

Causes

Directions: Complete each sentence by writing a possible cause.

1. I bought my best friend this book _____

2. Dad's back was really sore because _____

3. Our ~~Answers will vary.~~

4. We don't have any homework this weekend so _____

Write two sentences that show a cause-and-effect relationship.

1. _____

2. _____

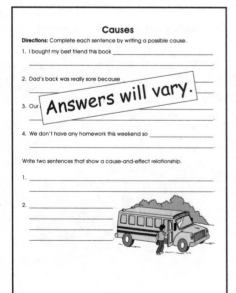

Page 56

Effects

Directions: Complete each sentence by writing a possible effect.

1. The front door was locked, so _____

2. Bec~~Answers will vary.~~

3. Since I spent all my money, _____

4. When my alarm clock did not wake me this morning, _____

Page 58

Main Idea: Iguanodon

Millions of years ago, many kinds of dinosaurs roamed the Earth. The name of one kind of dinosaur was Iguanodon (ee-gwan-eh-don). The Iguanodon looked like a giant lizard. It had tough skin. The Iguanodon's skin must have felt like leather! Iguanodons ate plants.

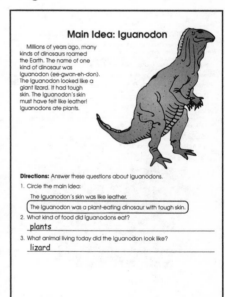

Directions: Answer these questions about Iguanodons.

1. Circle the main idea:

The Iguanodon's skin was like leather.

The Iguanodon was a plant-eating dinosaur with tough skin.

2. What kind of food did Iguanodons eat?
__plants__

3. What animal living today did the iguanodon look like?
__lizard__

Page 59

Comprehension: Tyrannosaurus Rex

One of the biggest dinosaurs was Tyrannosaurus Rex (ty-ran-oh-saur-us recks). This dinosaur walked on its two big back legs. It had two small, short front legs. From the top of its head to the tip of its tail, Tyrannosaurus Rex measured 50 feet long. Its head was 4 feet long! Are you taller than this dinosaur's head? Tyrannosaurus was a meat eater. It had many small, sharp teeth. Its favorite meal was a smaller dinosaur that had a bill like a duck. This smaller dinosaur lived near water.

Directions: Answer these questions about Tyrannosaurus Rex.

1. What is the story about?
   Tyrannosaurus Rex
2. What size was this dinosaur?
   50 feet long; its head was 4 feet long
3. When this. dinosaur was hungry, what did it eat?
   Meat. Its favorite meal was a smaller dinosaur with a bill like a duck.
4. Where did this dinosaur find its favorite meal?
   near the water
5. Why did this dinosaur need many sharp teeth?
   It was a meat eater.

Page 60

Comprehension: Cold-Blooded Animals

Like snakes, dinosaurs were cold-blooded. Cold-blooded animals cannot keep themselves warm. Because of this, dinosaurs were not very active when it was cold. In the early morning they did not move much. When the sun grew warm, the dinosaurs became active. When the sun went down in the evening, they slowed down again for the night. The sun warmed the dinosaurs and gave them the energy they needed to move about.

Directions: Answer these questions about dinosaurs.

1. Why were dinosaurs inactive when it was cold?
   They were cold-blooded and could not keep themselves warm.
2. What time of day were the dinosaurs active?
   in the afternoon
3. What times of day were the dinosaurs not active?
   early morning and evening
4. Why did dinosaurs need the sun?
   to warm them up and give them energy

Page 61

Main Idea: Dinosaur Models

Some people can build models of dinosaurs. The models are fakes, of course. But they are life-size and they look real! The people who build them must know the dinosaur inside and out. First, they build a skeleton. Then they cover it with fake "skin." Then they paint it. Some models have motors in them. The motors can make the dinosaur's head or tail move. Have you ever seen a life-size model of a dinosaur?

Directions: Answer these questions about dinosaur models.

1. Circle the main idea:
   Some models of dinosaurs have motors in them.
   ⬭Some people can build life-size models of dinosaurs that look real.⬭
2. What do the motors in model dinosaurs do?
   The motors can make the dinosaur's head or tail move.
3. What is the first step in making a model dinosaur?
   build a skeleton
4. Why do dinosaur models look real?
   They have skin and move like real dinosaurs.

Page 62

Comprehension: Kareem Abdul-Jabbar

Have you heard of a basketball star named Kareem Abdul-Jabbar? When he was born, Kareem's name was Lew Alcindor. He was named after his father. When he was in college, Kareem changed his religion from Christianity to Islam. That was when he took the Muslim name of Kareem Abdul-Jabbar.

Directions: Answer these questions about Kareem Abdul-Jabbar.

1. What was Kareem Abdul-Jabbar's name when he was born?
   Lew Alcindor
2. Who was Kareem named after?
   his father
3. When did Kareem become a Muslim?
   when he was in college
4. When did he change his name to Kareem Abdul-Jabbar?
   when he became Muslim

Page 63

Comprehension: Michael Jordan

Michael Jordan was born February 17, 1963, in Brooklyn, New York. His family moved to North Carolina when he was just a baby. As a young boy, his favorite sport was baseball, but he soon found that he could play basketball as well. At age 17, he began to show people just how talented he really was.

Throughout his basketball career, Michael Jordan has won many scoring titles. Many boys and girls look up to Michael Jordan as their hero. Did you know he had a hero, too, when he was growing up? He looked up to his older brother, Larry.

Michael Jordan, a basketball superstar, is not just a star on the basketball court. He also works hard to raise money for many children's charities. He encourages children to develop their talents by practice, practice, practice!

Directions: Answer these questions about Michael Jordan.

1. Michael says children can develop their talents by lots of __practice__.
2. Who was Michael's hero when he was growing up?
   his older brother
3. Where was Michael Jordan born?
   Brooklyn, New York
4. At first, he played __baseball__ instead of basketball.

Page 64

Recalling Details: The Home Run Race

The summer of 1998 was exciting for the sport of baseball. Even if you were not a big fan of this sport, you couldn't help but hear about two great sluggers—Mark McGwire and Sammy Sosa. By mid-summer, many baseball fans realized that several men were getting close to the home run record. The record of 61 home runs in a single season had been set by Roger Maris 37 years before!

On Tuesday, September 8, 1998, that record was broken. Mark McGwire, who plays for the St. Louis Cardinals, hit his 62nd home run in a game with the Chicago Cubs.

To make the home run race more interesting, a player for the Chicago Cubs, Sammy Sosa, was also close to breaking the 61 home run record. On Sunday, September 13, Sammy Sosa also hit his 62nd home run.

Directions: Write the letter of the correct answer in the blanks.

A. Sept. 13   B. McGwire   C. 37   D. Maris   E. Chicago Cubs

1. Had the home run record __D__
2. First to hit 62 home runs __B__
3. Sosa broke the home run record __A__
4. Years record had stood __C__
5. Sosa's team __E__

Page 65

Comprehension: Christopher Columbus

What do you know about Christopher Columbus? He was a famous sailor and explorer. Columbus was 41 years old when he sailed from southern Spain on August 3, 1492, with three ships. On them was a crew of 90 men. Thirty-three days later, he landed on Watling Island in the Bahamas. The Bahamas are islands located in the West Indies. The West Indies are a large group of islands between North America and South America.

Directions: Answer these questions about Christopher Columbus.

1. How old was Columbus when he set sail from southern Spain?

   41 years old

2. How many ships did he take?

   three ships

3. How many men were with him?

   90 men

4. How long did it take him to reach land?

   33 days

5. Where did Columbus land?

   Watling Island in the Bahamas

6. What are the West Indies?

   a large group of islands between North and South America

Page 66

Comprehension: Lewis and Clark

In 1801, President Thomas Jefferson chose an army officer named Meriwether Lewis to lead an expedition through our country's "new frontier." He knew Lewis would not be able to make the journey by himself, so he chose William Clark to travel with him. The two men had known each other in the army. They decided to be co-leaders of the expedition.

The two men and a group of about 45 others made the trip from the state of Missouri, across the Rocky Mountains all the way to the Pacific Coast. They were careful in choosing the men who would travel with them. They wanted men who were strong and knew a lot about the wilderness. It was also important that they knew some of the Native American languages.

Directions: Answer these questions about Lewis and Clark.

1. Which president wanted an expedition through the "new frontier"?

   Thomas Jefferson

2. Look at a United States map or a globe. In what direction did Lewis and Clark travel? (Circle one.)

   north   south   east   (west)

3. About how many people made up the entire expedition, including Lewis and Clark?

   47 people

Lewis and Clark Expedition
1804-1806

Page 67

Comprehension: George Washington

George Washington was the first president of the United States. He was born in Wakefield, Virginia, on February 22, 1732. His father was a wealthy Virginia planter. As he grew up, George Washington became interested in surveying and farming. When George was only 11 years old, his father died. George moved in with his older brother, Lawrence.

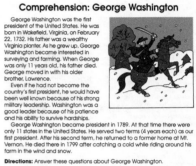

Even if he had not become the country's first president, he would have been well known because of his strong military leadership. Washington was a good leader because of his patience and his ability to survive hardships.

George Washington became president in 1789. At that time there were only 11 states in the United States. He served two terms (4 years each) as our first president. After his second term, he returned to a former home at Mt. Vernon. He died there in 1799 after catching a cold while riding around his farm in the wind and snow.

Directions: Answer these questions about George Washington.

1. In what year did George Washington become president? 1789

2. Besides being our country's first president, how else did he serve our country?

   as a strong military leader

3. Where was he born?

   Wakefield, Virginia

Page 68

Comprehension: Benjamin Franklin

Benjamin Franklin was born in Boston, Massachusetts, on January 17, 1706. Even though he only attended school to age 10, he worked hard to improve his mind and character. He taught himself several foreign languages and learned many skills that would later be a great help to him.

Ben Franklin played a very important part in our history. One of his many accomplishments was as a printer. He was a helper (apprentice) to his half-brother, James, and later moved to the city of Philadelphia where he worked in another print shop.

Another skill that he developed was writing. He wrote and published *Poor Richard's Almanac* in December 1732. Franklin was also a diplomat. He served our country in many ways, both in the United States and in Europe. As an inventor he experimented with electricity. Have you heard about the kite and key experiment? Benjamin Franklin was able to prove that lightning has an electrical discharge.

Directions: Answer these questions about Benjamin Franklin.

1. Circle the main idea:

   (Benjamin Franklin was a very important part of our history.)
   Benjamin Franklin wrote *Poor Richard's Almanac*.
   He flew a kite with a key on the string.

2. How old was Ben Franklin when he left school? 10 years old

3. Write three of Ben Franklin's accomplishments.

   1) He wrote Poor Richards Almanac.
   2) He was a diplomat.
   3) He proved lightning has an electrical discharge.

Page 69

Main Idea: Unusual Plants

Do you have a cat? Do you have catnip growing around your home? If you don't know, your cat probably does. Cats love the catnip plant and can be seen rolling around in it. Some cat toys have catnip inside them because cats love it so much.

People can enjoy catnip, too. Some people make catnip tea with the leaves of the plant. It is like the mint with which people make tea.

Another refreshing drink can be made with the berries of the sumac bush or tree. Native Americans would pick the red berries, crush them and add water to make a thirst-quenching drink. The berries were sour, but they must have believed that the cool, tart drink was refreshing. Does this remind you of lemonade?

Directions: Answer these questions about unusual plants.

1. What is the main idea of the first two paragraphs above?

   Cats and people can both enjoy catnip.

2. Write two ways cats show that they love catnip.

   1) by rolling around in it
   2) by playing with a catnip toy

3. How can people use catnip?

   They can make tea with it.

Page 70

Comprehension: Rainforests

The soil in rainforests is very dark and rich. The trees and plants that grow there are very green. People who have seen one say a rainforest is "the greenest place on Earth." Why? Because it rains a lot. With so much rain, the plants stay very green. The earth stays very wet. Rainforests cover only 6 percent of the Earth. But they are home to 66 percent of all the different kinds of plants and animals on Earth! Today, rainforests are threatened by such things as acid rain from factory smoke emissions around the world and from farm expansion. Farmers living near rainforests cut down many trees each year to clear the land for farming. I wish I could see a rainforest. Do you?

Directions: Answer these questions about rainforests.

1. What do the plants and trees in a rainforest look like?

   They are very green.

2. What is the soil like in a rainforest?

   very dark and rich

3. How much of the Earth is covered by rainforests?

   6 percent

4. What percentage of the Earth's plants and animals live there?

   66 percent

Page 71

Comprehension: The Sloth

The sloth spends most of its life in the trees of the rainforest. The three-toed sloth, for example, is usually hanging around, using its claws to keep it there. Because it is in the trees so much, it has trouble moving on the ground. Certainly it could be caught easily by other animals of the rainforest if it was being chased. The sloth is a very slow-moving animal. Do you have any idea what the sloth eats? The sloth eats mostly leaves it finds in the treetops.

Have you ever seen a three- or two-toed sloth? If you see one in a zoo, you don't have to get close enough to count the toes. You can tell these two "cousins" apart in a different way—the three-toed sloth has some green mixed in with its fur because of the algae it gets from the trees.

Directions: Answer these questions about the sloth.

1. How does the three-toed sloth hang around the rainforest?

   a. by its tail, like a monkey

   (b. by its claws, or toes)

2. The main diet of the sloth is __leaves__.

3. Why does the sloth have trouble moving around on the ground?

__because it is in the trees so much__

Page 72

Comprehension: The Jaguar

The jaguar weighs between 100 and 250 pounds. It can be as long as 6 feet! This is not your ordinary house cat!

One strange feature of the jaguar is its living arrangements. The jaguar has its own territory. No other jaguar lives in its "home range." It would be very unusual for one jaguar to meet another in the rainforest. One way they mark their territory is by scratching trees.

Have you ever seen your pet cat hide in the grass and carefully and quietly sneak up on an unsuspecting grasshopper or mouse? Like its gentler, smaller "cousin," the jaguar stalks its prey in the high grass. It likes to eat small animals, such as rodents, but can attack and kill larger animals such as tapirs, deer and cattle. It is good at catching fish as well.

Directions: Answer these questions about the jaguar.

1. The jaguar lives:

   a. in large groups

   (b. alone)

   c. under water

2. This large cat marks its territory by:

   a. a black marker

   b. roaring

   (c. scratching trees)

3. What does the jaguar eat?

__small animals, tapirs, deer and cattle__

4. How much does it weigh?

__between 100 and 250 pounds__

Page 73

Making Inferences: State Bird — Arizona

Have you ever traveled through Arizona or other southwestern states of the United States? One type of plant you may have seen is the cactus. This plant and other desert thickets are homes to the cactus wren, the state bird of Arizona. It is interesting how this bird (which is the size of a robin) can roost on this prickly plant and keep from getting stuck on the sharp spines. The cactus wren builds its nest on top of these thorny desert plants.

The cactus wren's "song" is not a beautiful, musical sound. Instead, it is compared to the grating sound of machinery. You can also identify the bird by its coloring. It has white spots on its outer tail feathers and white eyebrows. The crown (head) of the cactus wren is a rusty color.

Directions: Answer these questions about the cactus wren.

1. In what part of the United States would you find the cactus wren?

__the southwestern states__

2. What does **prickly** mean?

   a. soft   b. green   (c. having sharp points)

3. Do you think you would like to hear the "song" of the cactus wren? Why or why not?

__Answers will vary.__

Page 74

Comprehension: State Bird — Maine

The chickadee may visit your bird feeder on a regular basis if you live in Maine. This bird seems to have a feeding schedule so it doesn't miss a meal! The chickadee can be tamed to eat right out of your hand. If this bird sees some insect eggs on a tree limb, it even will hang upside down to get at this treat.

The chickadee lives in forests and open woodlands throughout most of the year, but when winter comes, it moves into areas populated by people. The chickadee lives in the northern half of the United States and in southern and western Canada. The western part of Alaska is also home to this curious and tame little bird.

Directions: Answer these questions about the chickadee.

1. What does **curious** mean?

   a. underside   c. tame

   (b. questioning)   d. schedule

2. What does the chickadee do when winter comes?

__It moves into areas populated by people.__

3. One of the chickadee's favorite treats is __insect eggs__.

4. Where does the chickadee live?

__in forests and open woodlands in the northern__
__half of the United States and in southern and__
__western Canada__

Page 75

Main Idea: Hawks

Hawks are birds of prey. They "prey upon" birds and animals. This means they kill other animals and eat them. The hawk has long pointed wings. It uses them to soar through the air as it looks for prey. It looks at the ground while it soars.

When it sees an animal or bird to eat, the hawk swoops down. It grabs the animal in its beak and and claws then carries it off and eats it. The hawk eats birds, rats, ground squirrels and other pests.

Directions: Answer these questions about hawks.

1. Circle the main idea:

   Hawks are mean because they swoop down from the sky and eat animals and birds.

   (Hawks are helpful because they eat sick birds, rats, ground squirrels and other pests.)

2. What kind of wings does a hawk have?

__long pointed wings__

3. How does the hawk pick up its prey?

__It swoops down and grabs the prey in its beak and claws.__

4. What does "prey upon" mean?

__to kill other animals and eat them__

Page 76

Comprehension: Pet Crickets

Did you know that some people keep crickets as pets? These people always keep two crickets together. That way, the crickets do not get lonely! Crickets are kept in a flowerpot filled with dirt. The dirt helps the crickets feel at home. They are used to being outside. Over the flowerpot is a covering that lets air inside. It also keeps the crickets in! Some people use a small net; others use cheesecloth. They make sure there is room under the covering for crickets to hop!

Pet crickets like to eat bread and lettuce. They also like raw hamburger meat. Would you like to have a pet cricket?

Directions: Answer these questions about pet crickets.

1. Where do pet crickets live?

__in a flowerpot filled with dirt__

2. Why should you put dirt in with the crickets?

__It helps them feel at home.__

3. What is placed over the flowerpot?

__a covering that lets air inside__

4. Write three things pet crickets like to eat.

__bread, lettuce, raw hamburger meat__

Page 77

Comprehension: Our Solar System

There are nine planets in our solar system. All of them circle the Sun. The planet closest to the Sun is named Mercury. The Romans said Mercury was the messenger of the gods. The second planet from the Sun is named Venus. Venus shines the brightest. Venus was the Roman goddess of beauty. Earth is the third planet from the Sun. It is about the same size as Venus. After Earth is Mars, which is named after the Roman god of war. The other five planets are Jupiter, Saturn, Uranus, Neptune and Pluto. They, too, are named after Roman gods.

Directions: Answer these questions about our solar system.

1. How many planets are in our solar system?
   <u>nine planets</u>
2. What do the planets circle?
   <u>the Sun</u>
3. What are the planets named after?
   <u>Roman gods and goddesses</u>
4. Which planet is closest to the Sun?
   <u>Mercury</u>
5. Which planet is about the same size as Earth?
   <u>Venus</u>
6. Which planet comes after Earth in the solar system?
   <u>Mars</u>

Page 78

Comprehension: Moon

Our moon is not the only moon in the solar system. Some other planets have moons also. Saturn has 10 moons! Our moon is Earth's closest neighbor in the solar system. Sometimes our moon is 225,727 miles away. Other times, it is 252,002 miles away. Why? Because the Moon revolves around Earth. It does not go around Earth in a perfect circle. So, sometimes its path takes it further away from our planet.

When our astronauts visited the Moon, they found dusty plains, high mountains and huge craters. There is no air or water on the Moon. That is why life cannot exist there. The astronauts had to wear space suits to protect their skin from the bright Sun. They had to take their own air to breathe. They had to take their own food and water. The Moon was an interesting place to visit. Would you want to live there?

Directions: Answer these questions about the Moon.

1. Circle the main idea:

   <u>The Moon travels around Earth, and the astronauts visited the Moon.</u>

   Astronauts found that the Moon—Earth's closest neighbor—has no air or water and cannot support life.

2. Write three things our astronauts found on the Moon.
   1) <u>dusty plains</u> 2) <u>high mountains</u> 3) <u>huge craters</u>
3. Make a list of what to take on a trip to the Moon.
   <u>Answers will vary, but can include: space suits, food, water, and air.</u>

Page 79

Comprehension: Your Heart

Make your hand into a fist. Now look at it. That is about the size of your heart! Your heart is a strong pump. It works all the time. Right now it is beating about 90 times a minute. When you run, it beats about 150 times a minute.

Inside, your heart has four spaces. The two spaces on the top are called atria. This is where blood is pumped into the heart. The two spaces on the bottom are called ventricles. This is where blood is pumped out of the heart. The blood is pumped to every part of your body. How? Open and close your fist. See how it tightens and loosens? The heart muscle tightens and loosens, too. This is how it pumps blood.

Directions: Answer these questions about your heart.

1. How often does your heart work?
   <u>all the time</u>
2. How fast does it beat when you are sitting?
   <u>about 90 times a minute</u>
3. How fast does it beat when you are running?
   <u>about 150 times a minute</u>
4. How many spaces are inside your heart?   <u>four</u>
5. What are the heart's upper spaces called? What are the lower spaces called?
   <u>atria</u>   <u>ventricles</u>

Page 80

Making Inferences: Your Bones

Are you scared of skeletons? You shouldn't be. There is a skeleton inside of you! The skeleton is made up of all the bones in your body. These 206 bones give you your shape. They also protect your heart and everything else inside. Your bones come in many sizes. Some are short. Some are long. Some are rounded. Some are very tiny. The outside of your bones looks solid. Inside, they are filled with a soft material called marrow. This is what keeps your bones alive. Red blood cells and most white blood cells are made here. These cells help feed the body and fight disease.

Directions: Answer these questions about your bones.

1. Do you think your leg bone is short, long or rounded?
   <u>long</u>
2. Do you think the bones in your head are short, long or rounded?
   <u>rounded</u>
3. What is the size of the bones in your fingers?
   <u>small</u>
4. What is the "something soft" inside your bones?
   <u>marrow</u>
5. How many bones are in your skeleton?
   <u>206 bones</u>

Page 81

Comprehension: Beavers

The beaver is not only a great lumberjack. It can also swim quite well. Its special fur helps to keep it warm; its hind legs work like fins; its tail is used as a rudder to steer it through the water. The beaver can hold its breath under water for 15 minutes, and its special eyelids are transparent, so they work like goggles!

Even though the beaver is a very good swimmer and can stay under water for a long time, it does not live under water. When the beaver builds a dam it also builds a lodge. A lodge is a dome-shaped structure above water level in which the beaver lives. The beaver enters its lodge through underwater tunnels. The lodge provides a place for the beaver to rest, eat and raise young.

Directions: Answer these questions about the beaver.

1. What is the main idea of the first paragraph?
   <u>The beaver has many qualities that make it a very good swimmer.</u>
2. Which word in the first paragraph means "able to see through"?
   <u>transparent</u>
3. How long can the beaver hold its breath under water?
   <u>15 minutes</u>
4. How does a beaver enter his lodge?
   <u>through underwater tunnels</u>

Page 82

Making Inferences: Sheep

Sheep like to stay close together. They do not run off. They move together in a flock. They live on sheep ranches. Some sheep grow 20 pounds of fleece each year. After it is cut off, the fleece is called wool. Cutting off the wool is called "shearing." It does not hurt the sheep to be sheared. The wool is very warm and is used to make clothing.

Female sheep are called ewes ("yous"). Some types of ewes have only one baby each year. The baby is called a lamb. Other types of ewes have two or three lambs each year.

Directions: Answer these questions about sheep.

1. Why is sheep's behavior helpful to sheep ranchers?
   <u>Sheep like to stay close together.</u>
2. If you were a sheep farmer, would you rather own the kind of sheep that has one baby each year, or one that has two or three?
   <u>the kind that has two or three babies</u>
   Why?
   <u>because then you would have more sheep</u>
3. When it is still on the sheep, what is wool called?
   <u>fleece</u>
4. What is a group of sheep called?
   <u>flock</u>

Page 83

Comprehension: Rhinos

Rhinos are the second largest land animal. Only elephants are bigger.

Most people think rhinos are ugly. Their full name is "rhinoceros" (rhy-nos-ur-us). There are five kinds of rhinos—the square-lipped rhino, black rhino, great Indian rhino, Sumatran (sue-ma-trahn) rhino and Javan rhino.

Rhinos have a great sense of smell, which helps protect them. They can smell other animals far away. They don't eat them, though. Rhinos do not eat meat. They are vegetarians.

Directions: Answer these questions about rhinos.

1. What is the largest land animal?

   the elephant

2. What are the five kinds of rhinos?

   1) square-lipped rhino
   2) black rhino
   3) great Indian rhino
   4) Sumatran rhino
   5) Javan rhino

3. What is a "vegetarian"?

   Someone who does not eat meat, only plants.

Page 84

Comprehension: Rodents

You are surrounded by rodents (row-dents)! There are 1,500 different kinds of rodents. One of the most common rodents is the mouse. Rats, gophers (go-furs) and beavers are also rodents. So are squirrels and porcupines (pork-you-pines).

All rodents have long, sharp teeth. These sharp teeth are called incisors (in-size-ors). Rodents use these teeth to eat their food. They eat mostly seeds and vegetables. There is one type of rodent some children have as a pet. No, it is not a rat! It is the guinea (ginney) pig.

Directions: Answer these questions about rodents.

1. How many different kinds of rodents are there?

   1,500

2. Name seven kinds of rodents.

   1) mice
   2) rats
   3) gophers
   4) beavers
   5) squirrels
   6) porcupines
   7) guinea pigs

3. What are rodents' sharp teeth called?

   incisors

4. What rodent is sometimes a pet?

   guinea pig

Page 85

Drawing Conclusions

Drawing a conclusion means to use clues to make a final decision about something. To draw a conclusion, you must read carefully.

Directions: Read each story carefully. Use the clues given to draw a conclusion about the story.

The boy and girl took turns pushing the shopping cart. They went up and down the aisles. Each time they stopped the cart, they would look at things on the shelf and decide what they needed. Jody asked her older brother, "Will I need a box of 48 crayons in Mrs. Charles' class?"

"Yes, I think so," he answered. Then he turned to their mother and said, "I need some new notebooks. Can I get some?"

1. Where are they? at the store

2. What are they doing there? buying school supplies

3. How do you know? Write at least two clue words that helped you.

   Mrs. Charles's class, notebooks, box of 48 crayons

Eric and Randy held on tight. They looked around them and saw that they were not the only ones holding on. The car moved slowly upward. As they turned and looked over the side, they noticed that the people far below them seemed to be getting smaller and smaller. "Hey, Eric, did I tell you this is my first time on one of these?" asked Randy. As they started down the hill at a frightening speed, Randy screamed, "And it may be my last!"

1. Where are they? on a roller coaster

2. How do you know? Write at least two clue words that helped you.

   car moved slowly upward, down at frightening speed

Page 86

Drawing Conclusions: A Colorful Yard

Directions: Read the story, then answer the questions.

Mrs. Posy plants roses everywhere. She plants yellow roses near her front porch. She plants red roses near the back door. There are also pink roses and white roses in her yard. Every time the postal carrier comes to her house, he sneezes. "You should not plant so many flowers," he tells Mrs. Posy. Mrs. Posy just smiles.

1. What are Mrs. Posy's favorite flowers? roses

2. Why do you think the postal carrier tells Mrs. Posy, "You should not plant so many flowers"? He sneezes every time he comes near her house.

3. Why does Mrs. Posy smile? She thinks it's funny that her beautiful roses make the postal carrier sneeze.

Page 88

Alphabetical Order

Alphabetical order (or ABC order) is the order of letters in the alphabet. When putting words in alphabetical order, use the first letter of each word.

Directions: Number the words in each list from 1 to 5 in alphabetical order.

3 happy	5 zebra	2 banana
4 scared	1 gorilla	3 kiwi
5 worried	4 monkey	1 apple
1 amused	2 hyena	5 peach
2 excited	3 kangaroo	4 lemon

Page 89

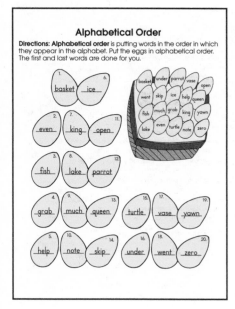

Alphabetical Order

Directions: Alphabetical order is putting words in the order in which they appear in the alphabet. Put the eggs in alphabetical order. The first and last words are done for you.

1. basket
2. even
3. fish
4. grab
5. help
6. ice
7. king
8. lake
9. much
10. note
11. open
12. parrot
13. queen
14. skip
15. turtle
16. under
17. vase
18. went
19. yawn
20. zero

Page 90

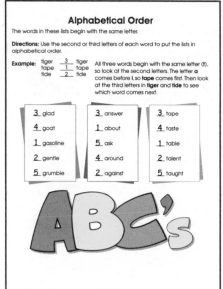

Alphabetical Order

The words in these lists begin with the same letter.

Directions: Use the second or third letters of each word to put the lists in alphabetical order.

Example: tiger _3_ tiger | All three words begin with the same letter (t), so look at the second letters. The letter **a** comes before **i**, so **tape** comes first. Then look at the third letters in **tiger** and **tide** to see which word comes next.
tape _1_ tape
tide _2_ tide

_3_ glad
_4_ goat
_1_ gasoline
_2_ gentle
_5_ grumble

_3_ answer
_1_ about
_5_ ask
_4_ around
_2_ against

_3_ tape
_4_ taste
_1_ table
_2_ talent
_5_ taught

Page 91

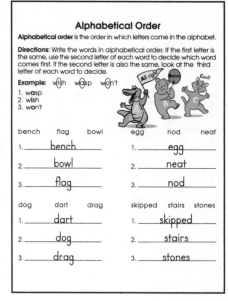

Alphabetical Order

Alphabetical order is the order in which letters come in the alphabet.

Directions: Write the words in alphabetical order. If the first letter is the same, use the second letter of each word to decide which word comes first. If the second letter is also the same, look at the third letter of each word to decide.

Example: wish wasp won't
1. **wa**sp
2. **wi**sh
3. **wo**n't

bench   flag   bowl
1. bench
2. bowl
3. flag

egg   nod   neat
1. egg
2. neat
3. nod

dog   dart   drag
1. dart
2. dog
3. drag

skipped   stairs   stones
1. skipped
2. stairs
3. stones

Page 92

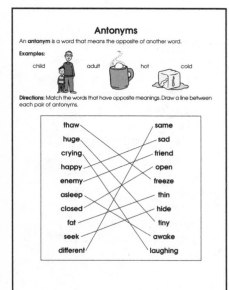

Antonyms

An **antonym** is a word that means the opposite of another word.

Examples:

child   adult   hot   cold

Directions: Match the words that have opposite meanings. Draw a line between each pair of antonyms.

thaw — freeze
huge — tiny
crying — laughing
happy — sad
enemy — friend
asleep — awake
closed — open
fat — thin
seek — hide
different — same

Page 93

Antonyms

Directions: Complete each sentence with an antonym pair from page 196. Some pairs will not be used.

Example: Usually we wear _different_ clothes, but today we are dressed the _same_.

1. A _child_ is allowed in the museum if he/she is with an _adult_.
2. Mom was _happy_ it rained since her garden was very dry, but I was _sad_ because I had to stay inside.
3. The _huge_ crowd of people tried to fit into the _tiny_ room.
4. The _crying_ baby was soon _laughing_ and playing in the crib.
5. We'll _freeze_ the meat for now, and Dad will _thaw_ it when we need it.
6. The windows were wide _open_, but the door was _closed_.

Now, write your own sentence using one of the antonym pairs.

Sentences will vary.

Page 94

Antonyms

Antonyms are words that are opposites.

Example: hairy   bald

Directions: Choose a word from the box to complete each sentence below.

| open | right | light | full | late | below |
| hard | clean | slow | quiet | old | nice |

Example:
My car was **dirty**, but now it's **clean**.

1. Sometimes my cat is naughty, and sometimes she's _nice_.
2. The sign said, "Closed," but the door was _open_.
3. Is the glass half empty or half _full_?
4. I bought new shoes, but I like my _old_ ones better.
5. Skating is easy for me, but _hard_ for my brother.
6. The sky is dark at night and _light_ during the day.
7. I like a noisy house, but my mother likes a _quiet_ one.
8. My friend says I'm wrong, but I say I'm _right_.
9. Jason is a fast runner, but Adam is a _slow_ runner.
10. We were supposed to be early, but we were _late_.

GRADE 3

Page 95

Antonyms

Directions: Write the antonym pairs from each sentence in the boxes.

Example: Many things are bought and sold at the market.

bought	sold

1. I thought I lost my dog, but someone found him.

lost	found

2. The teacher will ask questions for the students to answer.

ask	answer

3. Airplanes arrive and depart from the airport.

arrive	depart

4. The water in the pool was cold compared to the warm water in the whirlpool.

cold	warm

5. The tortoise was slow, but the hare was fast.

slow	fast

Page 96

Synonyms

Synonyms are words with nearly the same meaning.

Directions: Draw a line to match each word on the left with its synonym on the right.

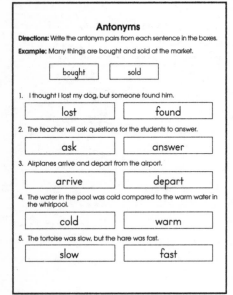

infant — baby
forest — woods
bucket — pail
hi — hello
bunny — rabbit
cheerful — happy
jacket — coat
alike — same
smile — grin
autumn — fall
little — small
thin — skinny
jump — hop
shirt — top
fix — repair

Page 97

Synonyms

Directions: Read each sentence. Choose a word from the box that has the same meaning as the bold word. Write the synonym on the line next to the sentence. The first one has been done for you.

skinniest	biggest	jacket	little	quickly	woods	joyful
grin	alike	trip	rabbit	fix	autumn	infant

1. The deer ran through the **forest**. _woods_
2. White mice are very **small** pets. _little_
3. Goldfish move **fast** in the water. _quickly_
4. The twins look exactly the **same**. _alike_
5. Trees lose their leaves in the **fall**. _autumn_
6. The blue whale is the **largest** animal on Earth. _biggest_
7. We will go to the ocean on our next **vacation**. _trip_
8. The **bunny** hopped through the tall grass. _rabbit_
9. The **baby** was crying because it was hungry. _infant_
10. Put on your **coat** before you go outside. _jacket_
11. Does that clown have a big **smile** on his face? _grin_
12. That is the **thinnest** man I have ever seen. _skinniest_
13. I will **repair** my bicycle as soon as I get home. _fix_
14. The children made **happy** sounds when they won. _joyful_

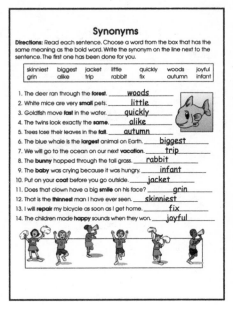

Page 98

Synonyms

Directions: Match the pairs of synonyms.

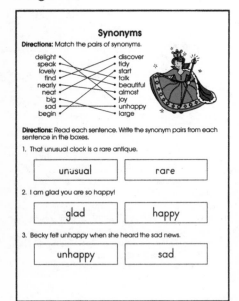

delight — discover
speak — tidy
lovely — start
find — talk
nearly — beautiful
neat — almost
big — joy
sad — unhappy
begin — large

Directions: Read each sentence. Write the synonym pairs from each sentence in the boxes.

1. That unusual clock is a rare antique.

unusual	rare

2. I am glad you are so happy!

glad	happy

3. Becky felt unhappy when she heard the sad news.

unhappy	sad

Page 99

Homophones

Homophones are words that sound the same but are spelled differently and have different meanings.

Example:

sew   sow   so

Directions: Read the sentences and write the correct word in the blanks.

Example:
blue	blew		She has **blue** eyes.
			The wind **blew** the barn down.

eye	I	He hurt his left _eye_ playing ball.
		_I_ like to learn new things.

see	sea	Can you _see_ the winning runner from here?
		He goes diving for pearls under the _sea_.

eight	ate	The baby _ate_ the banana.
		Jane was _eight_ years old last year.

one	won	Jill _won_ first prize at the science fair.
		I am the only _one_ in my family with red hair.

be	bee	Jenny cried when a _bee_ stung her.
		I have to _be_ in bed every night at eight o'clock.

two	to	too	My father likes _to_ play tennis.
			I like to play, _too_.
			It takes at least _two_ people to play.

Page 100

Homophones

Directions: Circle the correct word to complete each sentence. Then write the word on the line.

1. I am going to _write_ a letter to my grandmother. right (write)
2. Draw a circle around the _right_ answer. (right) write
3. Wait an _hour_ before going swimming. our (hour)
4. This is _our_ house. (our) hour
5. He got a _beet_ from his garden. beet (beet)
6. Our football team _beat_ that team. (beat) beet
7. Go to the store and _buy_ a loaf of bread. by (buy)
8. We will drive _by_ your house. (by) buy
9. It will be trouble if the dog _sees_ the cat. seas (sees)
10. They sailed the seven _seas_. (seas) sees
11. We have _two_ cars in the garage. to, too (two)
12. I am going _to_ the zoo today. (to) too, two
13. My little brother is going, _too_. to (too) two

Page 101

Homophones

Homophones are words that sound the same but have different spellings and meanings.

Directions: Complete each sentence using a word from the box.

| blew | night | blue | knight | hour | in | ant | inn |
| our | aunt | meet | too | two | to | meat | |

1. A red **ant** crawled up the wall.
2. It will be one **hour** before we can go back home.
3. Will you **meet** us later?
4. We plan to stay at an **inn** during our trip.
5. The king had a **knight** who fought bravely.
6. The wind **blew** so hard that I almost lost my hat.
7. His jacket was **blue**.
8. My **aunt** plans to visit us this week.
9. I will come **in** when it gets too cold outside.
10. It was late at **night** when we finally got there.
11. **Two** of us will go with you.
12. I will mail a note **to** someone at the bank.
13. Do you eat red **meat**?
14. We would like to join you, **too**.
15. Come over to see **our** new cat.

Page 102

Homophones

Directions: Circle the words that are not used correctly. Write the correct word above the circled word. Use the words in the box to help you. The first one has been done for you.

| road | see | one | be | so | I | brakes | piece | there |
| wait | not | some | hour | would | no | deer | you | heard |

Jake and his family were getting close to Grandpa's. It had taken them nearly an (our) to get (their) but Jake knew it was worth it. In his mind, he could already (sea) the pond and could almost feel the cool water. It had been (sew) hot this summer in the apartment.
"(Wood) (ewe) like a (peace) of my apple, Jake?" asked his big sister Clare.
"(Eye) can't eat any more."
"(Know) thank you," Jake replied. "I still have (sum) of my fruit left."
Suddenly, Dad slammed on the (brakes) "Did you see that (dear) on the (rode)?
I always (herd) that if you see (won), there might (bee) more."

"Good thinking, Dad. I'm glad you are a safe driver. We're (knot) very far from Grandpa's now. I can't (weight!)"

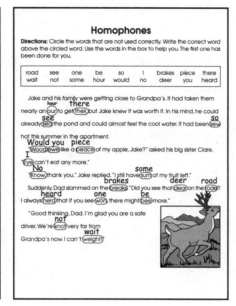

Page 103

Nouns

Nouns are words that tell the names of people, places or things.

Directions: Read the words below. Then write them in the correct column.

goat	Mrs. Jackson	girl
beach	tree	song
mouth	park	Jean Rivers
finger	flower	New York
Kevin Jones	Elm City	Frank Gates
Main Street	theater	skates
River Park	father	boy

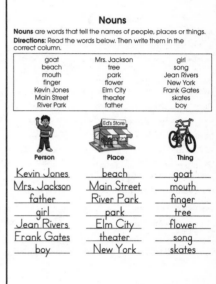

Person	Place	Thing
Kevin Jones	beach	goat
Mrs. Jackson	Main Street	mouth
father	River Park	finger
girl	park	tree
Jean Rivers	Elm City	flower
Frank Gates	theater	song
boy	New York	skates

Page 104

Common Nouns

Common nouns are nouns that name any member of a group of people, places or things, rather than specific people, places or things.

Directions: Read the sentences below and write the common noun found in each sentence.

Example: **socks** My socks do not match.

1. **bird** The bird could not fly.
2. **jelly beans** Ben likes to eat jelly beans.
3. **mother** I am going to meet my mother.
4. **lake** We will go swimming in the lake tomorrow.
5. **flowers** I hope the flowers will grow quickly.
6. **eggs** We colored eggs together.
7. **bicycle** It is easy to ride a bicycle.
8. **cousin** My cousin is very tall.
9. **boat** Ted and Jane went fishing in their boat.
10. **prize** They won a prize yesterday.
11. **ankle** She fell down and twisted her ankle.
12. **brother** My brother was born today.
13. **slide** She went down the slide.
14. **doctor** Ray went to the doctor today.

Page 105

Proper Nouns

Proper nouns are names of specific people, places or things. Proper nouns begin with a capital letter.

Directions: Read the sentences below and circle the proper nouns found in each sentence.

Example: (Aunt Frances) gave me a puppy for my birthday.

1. We lived on (Jackson Street) before we moved to our new house.
2. (Angela's) birthday party is tomorrow night.
3. We drove through (Cheyenne, Wyoming) on our way home.
4. (Dr. Charles) always gives me a treat for not crying.
5. (George Washington) was our first president.
6. Our class took a field trip to the (Johnson Flower Farm.)
7. (Uncle Jack) lives in (New York City.)
8. (Amy) and (Elizabeth) are best friends.
9. We buy doughnuts at the (Grayson Bakery.)
10. My favorite movie is (E.T.)
11. We flew to (Miami, Florida) in a plane.
12. We go to (Riverfront Stadium) to watch the baseball games.
13. (Mr. Fields) is a wonderful music teacher.
14. My best friend is (Tom Dunlap.)

Page 106

Proper Nouns

Directions: Rewrite each sentence, capitalizing the proper nouns.

1. mike's birthday is in september.

Mike's birthday is in September.

2. aunt katie lives in detroit, michigan.

Aunt Katie lives in Detroit, Michigan.

3. in july, we went to canada.

In July, we went to Canada.

4. kathy jones moved to utah in january.

Kathy Jones moved to Utah in January.

5. My favorite holiday is valentine's day in february.

My favorite holiday is Valentine's Day in February.

6. On friday, mr. polzin gave the smith family a tour.

On Friday, Mr. Polzin gave the Smith family a tour.

7. saturday, uncle cliff and I will go to the mall of america in minnesota.

Saturday, Uncle Cliff and I will go to the Mall of America in Minnesota.

Page 107

Plural Nouns

A **plural** is more than one person, place or thing. We usually add an **s** to show that a noun names more than one. If a noun ends in **x**, **ch**, **sh** or **s**, we add an **es** to the word.

Example: pizza   pizzas

Directions: Write the plural of the words below.

Example: dog + s = dogs

cat   cats
boot   boots
house   houses

Example: peach + es = peaches

lunch   lunches
bunch   bunches
punch   punches

Example: ax + es = axes

fox   foxes
tax   taxes
box   boxes

Example: glass + es = glasses

mess   messes
guess   guesses
class   classes

Example: dish + es = dishes

bush   bushes
ash   ashes
brush   brushes

walrus

walruses

Page 108

Plural Nouns

To write the plural forms of words ending in **y**, we change the **y** to **ie** and add **s**.

Example: pony   ponies

Directions: Write the plural of each noun on the lines below.

berry   berries
cherry   cherries
bunny   bunnies
penny   pennies
family   families
candy   candies
party   parties

Now, write a story using some of the words that end in **y**. Remember to use capital letters and periods.

_____

Answers will vary.

_____

Page 109

Plural Nouns

Directions: Write the plural of each noun to complete the sentences below. Remember to change the **y** to **ie** before you add **s**!

1. I am going to two birthday ___parties___ this week.
(party)

2. Sandy picked some ___cherries___ for Mom's pie.
(cherry)

3. At the store, we saw lots of ___bunnies___.
(bunny)

4. My change at the candy store was three ___pennies___.
(penny)

5. All the ___ladies___ baked cookies for the bake sale.
(lady)

6. Thanksgiving is a special time for ___families___ to gather together.
(family)

7. Boston and New York are very large ___cities___.
(city)

Page 110

Plural Nouns

Directions: The **singular form** of a word shows one person, place or thing. Write the singular form of each noun on the lines below.

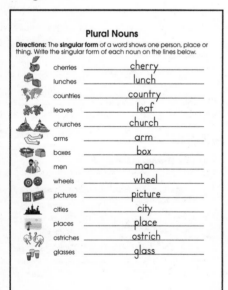

cherries _____ cherry
lunches _____ lunch
countries _____ country
leaves _____ leaf
churches _____ church
arms _____ arm
boxes _____ box
men _____ man
wheels _____ wheel
pictures _____ picture
cities _____ city
places _____ place
ostriches _____ ostrich
glasses _____ glass

Page 111

Possessive Nouns

Possessive nouns tell who or what is the owner of something. With singular nouns, we use an apostrophe **before** the **s**. With plural nouns, we use an apostrophe **after** the **s**.
Example:
singular: one elephant
The **elephant's** dance was wonderful.
plural: more than one elephant
The **elephants'** dance was wonderful.
Directions: Put the apostrophe in the correct place in each bold word. Then write the word in the blank.

1. The **lion's** cage was big. ___lion's or lions'___
2. The **bears'** costumes were purple. ___bears'___
3. One **boy's** laughter was very loud. ___boy's___
4. The **trainer's** dogs were dancing about. ___trainer's or trainers'___
5. The **man's** popcorn was tasty and good. ___man's___
6. **Mark's** cotton candy was delicious. ___Mark's___
7. A little **girl's** balloon burst in the air. ___girl's___
8. The big **clown's** tricks were very funny. ___clown's or clowns'___
9. **Laura's** sister clapped for the clowns. ___Laura's___
10. The **woman's** money was lost in the crowd. ___woman's___
11. **Kelly's** mother picked her up early. ___Kelly's___

Page 112

Possessive Nouns

Directions: Circle the correct possessive noun in each sentence and write it in the blank.

Example: One ___girl's___ mother is a teacher.
(girl's)   girls'

1. The ___cat's___ tail is long.
(cat's)   cats'

2. One ___boy's___ baseball bat is aluminum.
(boy's)   boys'

3. The ___waitresses'___ aprons are white.
(waitresses')   waitress's

4. My ___grandmother's___ apple pie is the best!
(grandmother's)   grandmothers'

5. My five ___brothers'___ uniforms are dirty.
brother's   (brothers')

6. The ___child's___ doll is pretty.
(child's)   childs'

7. These ___dogs'___ collars are different colors.
dog's   (dogs')

8. The ___cow's___ tail is short.
(cow's)   cows'

Page 113

Pronouns

Pronouns are words that are used in place of nouns.
Examples: he, she, it, they, him, them, her, him

Directions: Read each sentence. Write the pronoun that takes the place of each noun.

Example:
The **monkey** dropped the banana. _It_

1. **Dad** washed the car last night. _He_
2. **Mary and David** took a walk in the park. _They_
3. **Peggy** spent the night at her grandmother's house. _She_
4. The baseball **players** lost their game. _they_
5. **Mike Van Meter** is a great soccer player. _He_
6. The **parrot** can say five different words. _It_
7. **Megan** wrote a story in class today. _She_
8. They gave a party for **Teresa**. _her_
9. Everyone in the class was happy for **Ted**. _him_
10. The children petted the **giraffe**. _it_
11. Linda put the **kittens** near the warm stove. _them_
12. **Gina** made a chocolate cake for my birthday. _She_
13. **Pete and Matt** played baseball on the same team. _They_
14. Give the books to **Herbie**. _him_

Page 114

Pronouns

Singular Pronouns	Plural Pronouns
I me my mine	we us our ours
you your yours	you your yours
he she it her	they them their theirs
hers his its him	

Directions: Underline the pronouns in each sentence.

1. Mom told <u>us</u> to wash <u>our</u> hands.
2. Did <u>you</u> go to the store?
3. <u>We</u> should buy <u>him</u> a present.
4. <u>I</u> called <u>you</u> about <u>their</u> party.
5. <u>Our</u> house had damage on <u>its</u> roof.
6. <u>They</u> want to give <u>you</u> a prize at <u>our</u> party.
7. <u>My</u> cat ate <u>her</u> sandwich.
8. <u>Your</u> coat looks like <u>his</u> coat.

Page 115

Possessive Pronouns

Possessive pronouns show ownership.
Example: his hat, **her** shoes, **our** dog
We can use these pronouns before a noun:
my, our, you, his, her, its, their
Example: his bike.
We can use these pronouns on their own:
mine, yours, ours, his, hers, theirs, its
Example: That is mine.
Directions: Write each sentence again, using a pronoun instead of the words in bold letters. Be sure to use capitals and periods.
Example:
My **dog's** bowl is brown. **Its** bowl is brown.

1. That is **Lisa's** book. _That is her book._
2. This is **my pencil**. _This is mine._
3. This hat is **your hat**. _This hat is yours._
4. Fifi is **Kevin's** cat. _Fifi is his cat._
5. That beautiful house is **our home**. _That beautiful house is ours._
6. **The gerbil's** cage is too small. _Its cage is too small._

Page 116

Abbreviations

An **abbreviation** is the shortened form of a word. Most abbreviations begin with a capital letter and end with a period.

Mr.	Mister	St.	Street
Mrs.	Missus	Ave.	Avenue
Dr.	Doctor	Blvd.	Boulevard
A.M.	before noon	Rd.	Road
P.M.	after noon		

Days of the week: Sun. Mon. Tues. Wed. Thurs. Fri. Sat.
Months of the year: Jan. Feb. Mar. Apr. Aug. Sept. Oct. Nov. Dec.

Directions: Write the abbreviations for each word.

street	St.	doctor	Dr.	Tuesday	Tues.
road	Rd.	mister	Mr.	avenue	Ave.
missus	Mrs.	October	Oct.	Friday	Fri.
before noon	A.M.	March	Mar.	August	Aug.

Directions: Write each sentence using abbreviations.
1. On Monday at 9:00 before noon Mister Jones had a meeting.
On Mon. at 9:00 A.M., Mr. Jones had a meeting.
2. In December Doctor Carlson saw Missus Zuckerman.
In Dec., Dr. Carlson saw Mrs. Zuckerman.
3. One Tuesday in August Mister Wood went to the park.
One Tues. in Aug., Mr. Wood went to the park.

Page 117

Adjectives

Adjectives are words that tell more about nouns, such as a **happy** child, a **cold** day or a **hard** problem. Adjectives can tell how many (**one** airplane) or which one (**those** shoes).
Directions: The nouns are in bold letters. Circle the adjectives that describe the nouns.
Example: Some people have (unusual)**pets**.

1. Some people keep(wild)**animals**, like lions and bears.
2. (These)**pets** need special care.
3. (These)**animals** want to be free when they get older.
4. Even(small)**animals** can be difficult if they are wild.
5. Raccoons and squirrels are not(tame)**pets**.
6. Never touch a(wild)**animal** that may be sick.

Complete the story below by writing in your own adjectives. Use your imagination.

My Cat

My cat is a very _____ animal. She has _____
and _____ fur. Her _____ ball.
She has _____ Answers will vary. _____ tail.
She has a _____ face and _____ whiskers.
I think she is the _____ cat in the world!

Page 118

Adjectives and Nouns

Directions: Underline the nouns in each sentence below. Then draw an arrow from each adjective to the noun it describes.
Example:
A <u>platypus</u> is a furry <u>animal</u> that lives in <u>Australia</u>.

1. This <u>animal</u> likes to swim.
2. The <u>nose</u> looks like a duck's <u>bill</u>.
3. It has a broad <u>tail</u> like a <u>beaver</u>.
4. <u>Platypuses</u> are great <u>swimmers</u>.
5. They have webbed <u>feet</u> which help them swim.
6. Their flat <u>tails</u> also help them move through the <u>water</u>.
7. The <u>platypus</u> is an unusual <u>mammal</u> because it lays <u>eggs</u>.
8. The <u>eggs</u> look like reptile <u>eggs</u>.
9. <u>Platypuses</u> can lay three <u>eggs</u> at a time.
10. These <u>babies</u> do not leave their <u>mothers</u> for one <u>year</u>.
11. This <u>animal</u> spends most of its <u>time</u> hunting near <u>streams</u>.

Page 119

Adjectives

A chart of adjectives can also be used to help describe nouns.

Directions: Look at the pictures. Complete each chart.

Example:

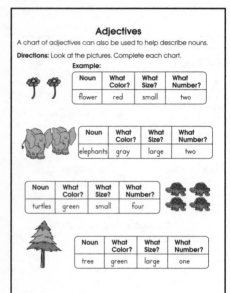

Noun	What Color?	What Size?	What Number?
flower	red	small	two

Noun	What Color?	What Size?	What Number?
elephants	gray	large	two

Noun	What Color?	What Size?	What Number?
turtles	green	small	four

Noun	What Color?	What Size?	What Number?
tree	green	large	one

Page 120

Prefixes

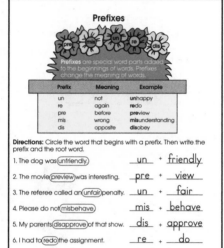

Prefixes are special word parts added to the beginnings of words. Prefixes change the meaning of words.

Prefix	Meaning	Example
un	not	unhappy
re	again	redo
pre	before	preview
mis	wrong	misunderstanding
dis	opposite	disobey

Directions: Circle the word that begins with a prefix. Then write the prefix and the root word.

1. The dog was (unfriendly). un + friendly
2. The movie (preview) was interesting. pre + view
3. The referee called an (unfair) penalty. un + fair
4. Please do not (misbehave). mis + behave
5. My parents (disapprove) of that show. dis + approve
6. I had to (redo) the assignment. re + do

Page 121

Suffixes

Suffixes are word parts added to the ends of words. Suffixes change the meaning of words.

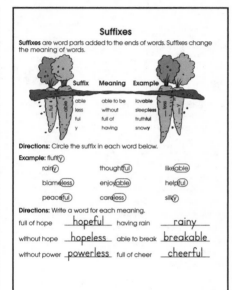

Suffix	Meaning	Example
able	able to be	lovable
less	without	sleepless
ful	full of	truthful
y	having	snowy

Directions: Circle the suffix in each word below.

Example: fluff(y)

rain(y)	thought(ful)	like(able)
blame(less)	enjoy(able)	help(ful)
peace(ful)	care(less)	silk(y)

Directions: Write a word for each meaning.

full of hope	hopeful	having rain	rainy
without hope	hopeless	able to break	breakable
without power	powerless	full of cheer	cheerful

Page 122

Verbs

A **verb** is the action word in a sentence, the word that tells what something does or that something exists. **Examples: run, jump, skip.**

Directions: Draw a box around the verb in each sentence below.

1. Spiders [spin] webs of silk.
2. A spider [waits] in the center of the web for its meals.
3. A spider [sinks] its sharp fangs into insects.
4. Spiders [eat] many insects.
5. Spiders [make] their nests with silk.
6. Female spiders [wrap] silk around their eggs to [protect] them.

Directions: Choose the correct verb from the box and write it in the sentences below.

hides	swims	eats	grabs	hurt

1. A crab spider __hides__ deep inside a flower where it cannot be seen.
2. The crab spider __grabs__ insects when they land on the flower.
3. The wolf spider is good because it __eats__ wasps.
4. The water spider __swims__ under water.
5. Most spiders will not __hurt__ people.

Page 123

Verbs

When a verb tells what one person or thing is doing now, it usually ends in s. **Example:** She **sings**.

When a verb is used with **you, I** or **we,** we do not add an s.

Example: I **sing.**

Directions: Write the correct verb in each sentence.

Example:

I __write__ a newspaper about our street. **writes, write**

1. My sister __helps__ me sometimes. **helps, help**
2. She __draws__ the pictures. **draw, draws**
3. We __deliver__ them together. **delivers, deliver**
4. I __tell__ the news about all the people. **tell, tells**
5. Mr. Macon __grows__ the most beautiful flowers. **grow, grows**
6. Mrs. Jones __talks__ to her plants. **talks, talk**
7. Kevin Turner __lets__ his dog loose everyday. **lets, let**
8. Little Mikey Smith __gets__ lost once a week. **get, gets**
9. You may __think__ I live on an interesting street. **thinks, think**
10. We __say__ it's the best street in town. **say, says**

Page 124

Helping Verbs

A **helping verb** is a word used with an action verb.

Examples: may, shall, and **are**

Directions: Write a helping verb from the box with each action verb.

can	could	must	will
may	would	should	do
shall	did	does	am
had	have	has	
are	were	is	
be	being	been	

Example: Answers will vary but may include:

Tomorrow, I __may__ play soccer.

1. Mom __may__ buy my new soccer shoes tonight.
2. Yesterday, my old soccer shoes __were__ ripped by the cat.
3. I __am__ going to ask my brother to go to the game.
4. He usually __does__ not like soccer.
5. But, he __will__ go with me because I am his sister.
6. He __has__ promised to watch the entire soccer game.
7. He has __been__ helping me with my homework.
8. I __can__ spell a lot better because of his help.
9. Maybe I __could__ finish the semester at the top of my class.

Page 125

Past-Tense Verbs

The **past tense** of a verb tells about something that has already happened. We add a **d** or an **ed** to most verbs to show that something has already happened.

Directions: Use the verb from the first sentence to complete the second sentence.

Example:
Please **walk** the dog. I already __walked__ her.
1. The flowers look good. They __looked__ better yesterday.
2. Please accept my gift. I __accepted__ it for my sister.
3. I wonder who will win. I __wondered__ about it all night.
4. He will saw the wood. He __sawed__ some last week.
5. Fold the paper neatly. She __folded__ her paper.
6. Let's cook outside tonight. We __cooked__ outside last night.
7. Do not block the way. They __blocked__ the entire street.
8. Form the clay this way. He __formed__ it into a ball.
9. Follow my car. We __followed__ them down the street.
10. Glue the pages like this. She __glued__ the flowers on.

Page 126

Present-Tense Verbs

The **present tense** of a verb tells about something that is happening now, happens often or is about to happen. These verbs can be written two ways: The bird sings. The bird is sing**ing**.

Directions: Write each sentence again, using the verb **is** and writing the **ing** form of the verb.

Example: He cooks the cheeseburgers.
__He is cooking the cheeseburgers.__
1. Sharon dances to that song.
__Sharon is dancing to that song.__
2. Frank washed the car.
__Frank is washing the car.__
3. Mr. Benson smiles at me.
__Mr. Benson is smiling at me.__

Write a verb for the sentences below that tells something that is happening now. Be sure to use the verb **is** and the **ing** form of the verb.

Example: The big, brown dog __is barking__
1. The little baby _____
2. Most nine-year-olds _____
3. The monster on television _____

Answers will vary.

Page 127

Future-Tense Verbs

The **future tense** of a verb tells about something that has not happened yet but will happen in the future. **Will** or **shall** are usually used with future tense.

Directions: Change the verb tense in each sentence to future tense.

Example: She cooks dinner.
__She will cook dinner.__
1. He plays baseball.
__He will play baseball.__
2. She walks to school.
__She will walk to school.__
3. Bobby talks to the teacher.
__Bobby will talk to the teacher.__
4. I remember to vote.
__I will remember to vote.__
5. Jack mows the lawn every week.
__Jack will mow the lawn every week.__
6. We go on vacation soon.
__We will go on vacation soon.__

Page 128

Irregular Verbs

Irregular verbs are verbs that do not change from the present tense to the past tense in the regular way with **d** or **ed**.
Example: sing, sang
Directions: Read the sentence and underline the verbs. Choose the past-tense form from the box and write it next to the sentence.

blow — blew	fly — flew
come — came	give — gave
take — took	wear — wore
make — made	sing — sang
grow — grew	

Example:
Dad will make a cake tonight. __made__
1. I will probably grow another inch this year. __grew__
2. I will blow out the candles. __blew__
3. Everyone will give me presents. __gave__
4. I will wear my favorite red shirt. __wore__
5. My cousins will come from out of town. __came__
6. It will take them four hours. __took__
7. My Aunt Betty will fly in from Cleveland. __flew__
8. She will sing me a song when she gets here. __sang__

Page 129

Irregular Verbs

Directions: Circle the verb that completes each sentence.

1. Scientists will try to (find, found) the cure.
2. Eric (brings, (brought)) his lunch to school yesterday.
3. Everyday, Betsy ((sings), sang) all the way home.
4. Jason (breaks, (broke)) the vase last night.
5. The ice had (freezes, (frozen)) in the tray.
6. Mitzi has (swims, (swum)) in that pool before.
7. Now I ((choose), chose) to exercise daily.
8. The teacher has (rings, (rung)) the bell.
9. The boss (speaks, (spoke)) to us yesterday.
10. She (says, (said)) it twice already.

Page 130

Irregular Verbs

The verb **be** is different from all other verbs. The present-tense forms of **be** are **am**, **is** and **are**. The past-tense forms of **be** are **was** and **were**. The verb **to be** is written in the following ways:

singular: I am, you are, he is, she is, it is
plural: we are, you are, they are

Directions: Choose the correct form of **be** from the words in the box and write it in each sentence.

are	am	is	was	were

Example: Answers will vary, but may include:
I __am__ feeling good at this moment.
1. My sister __is__ a good singer.
2. You __are__ going to the store with me.
3. Sandy __was__ at the movies last week.
4. Rick and Tom __are__ best friends.
5. He __is__ happy about the surprise.
6. The cat __is__ hungry.
7. I __am__ going to the ball game.
8. They __are__ silly.
9. I __am__ glad to help my mother.

Page 131

Linking Verbs

Linking verbs connect the noun to a descriptive word. Linking verbs are often forms of the verb **be**.

Directions: The linking verb is underlined in each sentence. Circle the two words that are being connected.

Example: The (cat) is (fat.)

1. My favorite (food) is (pizza.)

2. The (car) was (red.)

3. (I) am (tired.)

4. (Books) are (fun!)

5. The (garden) is (beautiful.)

6. (Pears) taste (juicy.)

7. The (airplane) looks (large.)

8. (Rabbits) are (furry.)

Page 132

Adverbs

Adverbs are words that describe verbs. They tell where, how or when.

Directions: Circle the adverb in each of the following sentences.

Example: The doctor worked (carefully.)

1. The skater moved (gracefully) across the ice.

2. Their call was returned (quickly.)

3. We (easily) learned the new words.

4. He did the work (perfectly.)

5. She lost her purse (somewhere.)

Directions: Complete the sentences below by writing your own adverbs in the blanks.

Example: The bees worked ____busily____.

1. The dog barked _____

2. The baby smiled _____

3. She wrote her name ____

4. The horse ran _____

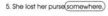
Answers may vary.

Page 133

Adverbs

Directions: Read each sentence. Then answer the questions on the lines below.

Example: Charles ate hungrily.

who? __Charles__
what? __ate__   how? __hungrily__

1. She dances slowly.
who? __She__
what? __dances__   how? __slowly__

2. The girl spoke carefully.
who? __girl__
what? __spoke__   how? __carefully__

3. My brother ran quickly.
who? __brother__
what? __ran__   how? __quickly__

4. Jean walks home often.
who? __Jean__
what? __walks__   when? __often__

5. The children played there.
who? __children__
what? __played__   where? __there__

Page 134

Prepositions

Prepositions show relationships between the noun or pronoun and another noun in the sentence. The preposition comes before that noun.

Example: The book is on the table.

Common Prepositions				
above	behind	by	near	over
across	below	in	off	through
around	beside	inside	on	under

Directions: Circle the prepositions in each sentence.

1. The dog ran fast (around) the house.

2. The plates (in) the cupboard were clean.

3. Put the card (inside) the envelope.

4. The towel (on) the sink was wet.

5. I planted flowers (in) my garden.

6. My kite flew high (above) the trees.

7. The chair (near) the counter was sticky.

8. (Under) the ground, worms lived (in) their homes.

9. I put the bow (around) the box.

10. (Beside) the pond, there was a playground.

Page 135

Articles

Articles are words used before nouns. **A**, **an** and **the** are articles. We use **a** before words that begin with a consonant. We use **an** before words that begin with a vowel.

Example: a peach   an apple

Directions: Write **a** or **an** in the sentences below.

Example: My bike had ___a___ flat tire.

1. They brought ___a___ goat to the farm.

2. My mom wears ___an___ old pair of shoes to mow the lawn.

3. We had ___a___ party for my grandfather.

4. Everybody had ___an___ ice-cream cone after the game.

5. We bought ___a___ picnic table for our backyard.

6. We saw ___a___ lion sleeping in the shade.

7. It was ___an___ evening to be remembered.

8. He brought ___a___ blanket to the game.

9. ___An___ exit sign was above the door.

10. They went to ___an___ orchard to pick apples.

11. He ate ___an___ orange for lunch.

Page 136

Commas

Commas are used to separate words in a series of three or more.
Example: My favorite fruits are apples, bananas and oranges.

Directions: Put commas where they are needed in each sentence.

1. Please buy milk, eggs, bread and cheese.

2. I need a folder, paper and pencils for school.

3. Some good pets are cats, dogs, gerbils, fish and rabbits.

4. Aaron, Mike and Matt went to the baseball game.

5. Major forms of transportation are planes, trains and automobiles.

Page 137

Commas

We use commas to separate the day from the year.
Example: May 13, 1950

Directions: Write the dates in the blanks. Put the
commas in and capitalize the name of each month.

Example:

Jack and Dave were born on february 22 1982.
February 22, 1982

1. My father's birthday is may 19 1948.
May 19, 1948

2. My sister was fourteen on december 13 1994.
December 13, 1994

3. Lauren's seventh birthday was on november 30 1998.
November 30, 1998

4. october 13 1996 was the last day I saw my lost cat.
October 13, 1996

5. On april 17 1997, we saw the Grand Canyon.
April 17, 1997

6. Our vacation lasted from april 2 1998 to april 26 1998.
April 2, 1998   April 26, 1998

7. Molly's baby sister was born on august 14 1991.
August 14, 1991

8. My mother was born on june 22 1959.
June 22, 1959

Page 138

Capitalization

The names of **people**, **places** and **pets**, the **days of the week**, the
months of the year and **holidays** begin with a capital letter.

Directions: Read the words in the box. Write the words in the correct
column with capital letters at the beginning of each word.

ron polsky	tuesday	march	april
presidents' day	saturday	woofy	october
blackie	portland, oregon	corning, new york	molly yoder
valentine's day	fluffy	harold edwards	arbor day
bozeman, montana	sunday		

People	Places	Pets
Ron Polsky	Bozeman, Montana	Blackie
Harold Edwards	Portland, Oregon	Fluffy
Molly Yoder	Corning, New York	Woofy

Days	Months	Holidays
Tuesday	March	Valentine's Day
Saturday	April	Presidents' Day
Sunday	October	Arbor Day

Page 139

Parts of Speech

Nouns, pronouns, verbs, adjectives, adverbs and prepositions are
all **parts of speech**.

Directions: Label the words in each sentence with the correct part
of speech.

Example: The cat is fat.
article / noun / verb / adjective

1. My cow walks in the barn.
pronoun / noun / verb / preposition / article / noun

2. Red flowers grow in the garden.
adjective / noun / verb / preposition / article / noun

3. The large dog was excited.
article / adjective / noun / verb / adjective

Page 140

Parts of Speech

Directions: Ask someone to give you nouns, verbs, adjectives and
pronouns where shown. Write them in the blanks. Read the story to
your friend when you finish.

The _____ (adjective) Adventure

I went for a _____ (noun) . I found a really big _____ (noun)

It was so _____ (adjective) that I _____ (verb) all the

way home. I put it in my _____ (noun) my amazement, it

began to _____ (verb) took it to my

_____ (place) . I sh_____ _____ (plural noun)

I decided _____ it in a box and wrap it up with

_____ (adjective) paper. I gave it to _____ (person) for a

present. When _____ (pronoun) opened it, _____ (pronoun)

_____ (past-tense verb) . _____ (pronoun) shouted, "Thank you!

This is the best _____ (noun) I've ever had!"

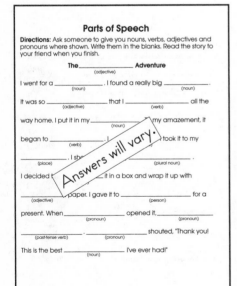
Answers will vary.

Page 141

Parts of Speech

Directions: Write the part of speech of each underlined word.

NOUN PRONOUN VERB ADJECTIVE ADVERB PREPOSITION

① ②
There are many different kinds of animals. Some animals live in the
③
wild. Some animals live in the zoo. And still others live in homes. The animals
④
that live in homes are called pets.

There are many types of pets. Some pets without fur are fish, turtles,
⑤ ⑥
snakes and hermit crabs. Trained birds can fly around your house. Some
⑦
furry animals are cats, dogs, rabbits, ferrets, gerbils or hamsters. Some animals
⑧ ⑨
can successfully learn tricks that you teach them. Whatever your favorite
⑩
animal is, animals can be special friends!

1. verb   4. verb
2. adjective   5. preposition   7. adjective   9. pronoun
3. noun   6. pronoun   8. adverb   10. adjective

Page 142

And and But

We can use **and** or **but** to make one longer sentence from two
short ones.

Directions: Use **and** or **but** to make two short
sentences into a longer, more interesting one.
Write the new sentence on the line below
the two short sentences.

Example:

The skunk has black fur. The skunk has a white stripe.

The skunk has black fur and a white stripe.

1. The skunk has a small head. The skunk has small ears.
The skunk has a small head and small ears.

2. The skunk has short legs. Skunks can move quickly.
The skunk has short legs but can move easily.

3. Skunks sleep in hollow trees. Skunks sleep underground.
Skunks sleep in hollow trees and underground.

4. Skunks are chased by animals. Skunks do not run away.
Skunks are chased by animals but do not run away.

5. Skunks sleep during the day. Skunks hunt at night.
Skunks sleep during the day and hunt at night.

Page 143

Subjects

A **subject** tells who or what the sentence is about.

Directions: Underline the subject in the following sentences.

Example:
<u>The zebra</u> is a large animal.

1. <u>Zebras</u> live in Africa.

2. <u>Zebras</u> are related to horses.

3. <u>Horses</u> have longer hair than zebras.

4. <u>Zebras</u> are good runners.

5. <u>Their feet</u> are protected by their hooves.

6. <u>Some animals</u> live in groups.

7. <u>These groups</u> are called herds.

8. <u>Zebras</u> live in herds with other grazing animals.

9. <u>Grazing animals</u> eat mostly grass.

10. <u>They</u> usually eat three times a day.

11. <u>They</u> often travel to water holes.

Page 144

Simple Subjects

A **simple subject** is the main noun or pronoun in the complete subject.

Directions: Draw a line between the subject and the predicate. Circle the simple subject.

Example: The black (bear) lives in the zoo.

1. (Penguins) look like they wear tuxedos.

2. The (seal) enjoys raw fish.

3. The (monkeys) like to swing on bars.

4. The beautiful (peacock) has colorful feathers.

5. (Bats) like dark places.

6. Some (snakes) eat small rodents.

7. The orange and brown (giraffes) have long necks.

8. The baby (zebra) is close to his mother.

Page 145

Compound Subjects

Compound subjects are two or more nouns that have the same predicate.

Directions: Combine the subjects to create one sentence with a compound subject.

Example: Jill can swing
Whitney can swing.
Luke can swing.
Jill, Whitney and Luke can swing.

1. Roses grow in the garden. Tulips grow in the garden.

<u>Roses and tulips grow in the garden.</u>

2. Apples are fruit. Oranges are fruit. Bananas are fruit.

<u>Apples, oranges and bananas are fruit.</u>

3. Bears live in the zoo. Monkeys live in the zoo.

<u>Bears and monkeys live in the zoo.</u>

4. Jackets keep us warm. Sweaters keep us warm.

<u>Jackets and sweaters keep us warm.</u>

Page 146

Compound Subjects

Directions: Underline the simple subjects in each compound subject.

Example: <u>Dogs</u> and <u>cats</u> are good pets.

1. <u>Blueberries</u> and <u>strawberries</u> are fruit.

2. <u>Jesse</u>, <u>Jake</u> and <u>Hannah</u> like school.

3. <u>Cows</u>, <u>pigs</u> and <u>sheep</u> live on a farm.

4. <u>Boys</u> and <u>girls</u> ride the bus.

5. <u>My family</u> and <u>I</u> took a trip to Duluth.

6. <u>Fruits</u> and <u>vegetables</u> are good for you.

7. <u>Katarina</u>, <u>Lexi</u> and <u>Mandi</u> like to go swimming.

8. <u>Petunias</u>, <u>impatiens</u>, <u>snapdragons</u> and <u>geraniums</u> are all flowers.

9. <u>Coffee</u>, <u>tea</u> and <u>milk</u> are beverages.

10. <u>Dave</u>, <u>Karla</u> and <u>Tami</u> worked on the project together.

Page 147

Predicates

A **predicate** tells what the subject is doing, has done or will do.

Directions: Underline the predicate in the following sentences.

Example: Woodpeckers <u>live in trees.</u>

1. They <u>hunt for insects in the trees.</u>

2. Woodpeckers <u>have strong beaks.</u>

3. They <u>can peck through the bark.</u>

4. The pecking sound <u>can be heard from far away.</u>

Directions: Circle the groups of words that can be predicates.

(have long tongues)   (pick up insects)
hole in bark   sticky substance
(help it to climb trees)   tree bark

Now, choose the correct predicates from above to finish these sentences.

1. Woodpeckers <u>have long tongues</u>

2. They use their tongues to <u>pick up insects</u>

3. Its strong feet <u>help it to climb trees</u>

Page 148

Simple Predicates

A **simple predicate** is the main verb or verbs in the complete predicate.

Directions: Draw a line between the complete subject and the complete predicate. Circle the simple predicate.

Example: The ripe apples (fell) to the ground.

1. The farmer (scattered) feed for the chickens.

2. The horses (galloped) wildly around the corral.

3. The baby chicks (were staying) warm by the light.

4. The tractor (was baling) hay.

5. The silo (was) full of grain.

6. The cows (were being) milked.

7. The milk truck (drove) up to the barn.

8. The rooster (woke) everyone up.

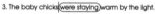

Page 149

Compound Predicates

Compound predicates have two or more verbs that have the same subject.

Directions: Combine the predicates to create one sentence with a compound predicate.

Example: We went to the zoo.
We watched the monkeys.
We went to the zoo and watched the monkeys.

1. Students read their books. Students do their work.

Students read their books and do their work.

2. Dogs can bark loudly. Dogs can do tricks.

Dogs can bark loudly and do tricks.

3. The football player caught the ball. The football player ran.

The football player caught the ball and ran.

4. My dad sawed wood. My dad stacked wood.

My dad sawed and stacked wood.

5. My teddy bear is soft. My teddy bear likes to be hugged.

My teddy bear is soft and likes to be hugged.

Page 150

Compound Predicates

Directions: Underline the simple predicates (verbs) in each predicate.

Example: The fans <u>clapped</u> and <u>cheered</u> at the game.

1. The coach <u>talks</u> and <u>encourages</u> the team.

2. The cheerleaders <u>jump</u> and <u>yell</u>.

3. The basketball players <u>dribble</u> and <u>shoot</u> the ball.

4. The basketball <u>bounces</u> and <u>hits</u> the backboard.

5. The ball <u>rolls</u> around the rim and <u>goes</u> into the basket.

6. Everyone <u>leaps</u> up and <u>cheers</u>.

7. The team <u>scores</u> and <u>wins</u>!

Page 151

Subjects and Predicates

Directions: Write the words for the subject to answer the **who** or **what** questions. Write the words for the predicate to answer the **does, did, is** or **has** questions.

Example:

My friend has two pairs of sunglasses.   who? My friend
has? has two pairs of sunglasses.

1. John's dog went to school with him.   what? John's dog
   did? went to school with him.

2. The Eskimo traveled by dog sled.   who? The Eskimo
   did? traveled by dog sled.

3. Alex slept in his treehouse last night.   who? Alex
   did? slept in his treehouse last night

4. Cherry pie is my favorite kind of pie.   what? Cherry pie
   is? is my favorite kind of pie.

5. The mail carrier brings the mail to the door.   who? The mail carrier
   does? brings the mail to the door.

6. We have more than enough bricks to build the wall.   who? We
   has? have more than enough bricks to build the wall.

7. The bird has a worm in its beak.   what? The bird
   has? has a worm in its beak.

Page 152

Subjects and Predicates

Directions: Draw one line under the subjects and two lines under the predicates in the sentences below.

1. <u>My mom</u> <u>likes to plant flowers</u>.

2. <u>Our neighbors</u> <u>walk their dog</u>.

3. <u>Our car</u> <u>needs gas</u>.

4. <u>The children</u> <u>play house</u>.

5. <u>Movies and popcorn</u> <u>go well together</u>.

6. <u>Peanut butter and jelly</u> <u>is my favorite kind of sandwich</u>.

7. <u>Bill, Sue and Nancy</u> <u>ride to the park</u>.

8. <u>We</u> <u>use pencils, markers and pens to write on paper</u>.

9. <u>Trees and shrubs</u> <u>need special care</u>.

Page 153

Sentences and Non-Sentences

A **sentence** tells a complete idea.

Directions: Circle the groups of words that tell a complete idea.

1. (Sharks are fierce hunters.)
2. Afraid of sharks.
3. (The great white shark will attack people.)
4. (Other kinds will not.)
5. (Sharks have an outer row of teeth for grabbing food.)
6. (When the outer teeth fall out, another row of teeth moves up.)
7. Keep the ocean clean by eating dead animals.
8. Not a single bone in its body.
9. Cartilage.
10. Made of the same material as the tip of your nose.
11. (Unlike other fish, sharks cannot float.)
12. In motion constantly.
13. Even while sleeping.

Page 154

Statements and Questions

Statements are sentences that tell about something. Statements begin with a capital letter and end with a period. **Questions** are sentences that ask about something. Questions begin with a capital letter and end with a question mark.

Directions: Rewrite the sentences using capital letters and either a period or a question mark.

Example: walruses live in the Arctic

Walruses live in the Arctic.

1. are walruses large sea mammals or fish

Are walruses large sea mammals or fish?

2. they spend most of their time in the water and on ice

They spend most of their time in the water and on ice.

3. are floating sheets of ice called ice floes

Are floating sheets of ice called ice floes?

4. are walruses related to seals

Are walruses related to seals?

5. their skin is thick, wrinkled and almost hairless

Their skin is thick, wrinkled and almost hairless.

Page 155

Statements and Questions

Directions: Change the statements into questions and the questions into statements.

Example: Jane is happy.   Is Jane happy?
Were you late?   You were late.

1. The rainbow was brightly colored.
   Is the rainbow brightly colored?

2. Was the sun coming out?
   The sun was coming out.

3. The dog is doing tricks.
   Is the dog doing tricks?

4. Have you washed the dishes today?
   You have washed the dishes today.

5. Kurt was the circus ringmaster.
   Was Kurt the circus ringmaster?

6. Were you planning on going to the library?
   You were planning on going to the library.

Page 156

Exclamations

Exclamation points are used for sentences that express strong feelings. These sentences can have one or two words or be very long.

Example: Wait! or **Don't forget to call!**

Directions: Add an exclamation point at the end of sentences that express strong feelings. Add a period at the end of the statements.

1. My parents and I were watching television.
2. The snow began falling around noon.
3. Wow!
4. The snow was really coming down!
5. We turned the television off and looked out the window.
6. The snow looked like a white blanket.
7. How beautiful!
8. We decided to put on our coats and go outside.
9. Hurry!
10. Get your sled.
11. All the people on the street came out to see the snow.
12. How wonderful!
13. The children began making a snowman.
14. What a great day!

Page 157

Contractions

Contractions are shortened forms of two words. We use apostrophes to show where letters are missing.

Example: It is = it's

Directions: Write the words that are used in each contraction.

we're __we__ + __are__   they'll __they__ + __will__
you'll __you__ + __will__   aren't __are__ + __not__
I'm __I__ + __am__   isn't __is__ + __not__

Directions: Write the contraction for the two words shown.

you have __you've__   have not __haven't__
had not __hadn't__   we will __we'll__
they are __they're__   he is __he's__
she had __she'd__   it will __it'll__
I am __I'm__   is not __isn't__

Page 158

Apostrophes

Apostrophes are used to show ownership by placing an **s** at the end of a single person, place or thing.

Example: Mary's cat

Directions: Write the apostrophes in the contractions below.

Example: We shouldn't be going to their house so late at night.

1. We didn't think that the ice cream would melt so fast.
2. They're never around when we're ready to go.
3. Didn't you need to make a phone call?
4. Who's going to help you paint the bicycle red?

Directions: Add an apostrophe and an **s** to the words to show ownership of a person, place or thing.

Example: Jill's bike is broken.

1. That is Holly's flower garden.
2. Mark's new skates are black and green.
3. Mom threw away Dad's old shoes.
4. Buster's food dish was lost in the snowstorm.

Page 159

Quotation Marks

Quotation marks are punctuation marks that tell what is said by a person. Quotation marks go before the first word and after the punctuation of a direct quote. The first word of a direct quote begins with a capital letter.

Example: Katie said, "Never go in the water without a friend."

Directions: Put quotation marks around the correct words in the sentences below.

Example: "Wait for me, please," said Laura.

1. "John, would you like to visit a jungle?" asked his uncle.
2. The police officer said, "Don't worry, we'll help you."
3. James shouted, "Hit a home run!"
4. My friend Carol said, "I really don't like cheeseburgers."

Directions: Write your own quotations by answering the questions below. Be sure to put quotation marks around your words.

1. What would you say if you saw a din...

2. What would your... if your hair turned purple?

Answers will vary.

Page 160

Quotation Marks

Directions: Put quotation marks around the correct words in the sentences below.

1. Can we go for a bike ride? asked Katrina.
   "Can we go for a bike ride?" asked Katrina.

2. Yes, said Mom.
   "Yes," said Mom.

3. Let's go to the park, said Mike.
   "Let's go to the park," said Mike.

4. Great idea! said Mom.
   "Great idea!" said Mom.

5. How long until we get there? asked Katrina.
   "How long until we get there?" asked Katrina.

6. Soon, said Mike.
   "Soon," said Mike.

7. Here we are! exclaimed Mom.
   "Here we are!" exclaimed Mom.

Page 161

Parts of a Paragraph

A **paragraph** is a group of sentences that all tell about the same thing. Most paragraphs have three parts: a **beginning**, a **middle** and an **end**.

Directions: Write **beginning**, **middle** or **end** next to each sentence in the scrambled paragraphs below. There can be more than one middle sentence.

Example:

__middle__ We took the tire off the car.

__beginning__ On the way to Aunt Louise's, we had a flat tire.

__middle__ We patched the hole in the tire.

__end__ We put the tire on and started driving again.

__middle__ I took all the ingredients out of the cupboard.

__beginning__ One morning, I decided to bake a pumpkin pie.

__end__ I forgot to add the pumpkin!

__middle__ I mixed the ingredients together, but something was missing.

__middle__ The sun was very hot and our throats were dry.

__end__ We finally decided to turn back.

__beginning__ We started our hike very early in the morning.

__middle__ It kept getting hotter as we walked.

Page 162

Topic Sentences

A **topic sentence** is usually the first sentence in a paragraph. It tells what the story will be about.

Directions: Read the following sentences. Circle the topic sentence that should go first in the paragraph that follows.

[Rainbows have seven colors.]

There's a pot of gold.

I like rainbows.

The colors are red, orange, yellow, green, blue, indigo and violet. Red forms the outer edge, with violet on the inside of the rainbow.

He cut down a cherry tree.

His wife was named Martha.

[George Washington was a good president.]

He helped our country get started. He chose intelligent leaders to help him run the country.

[Mark Twain was a great author.]

Mark Twain was unhappy sometimes.

Mark Twain was born in Missouri.

One of his most famous books is *Huckleberry Finn*. He wrote many other great books.

Page 163

Middle Sentences

Middle sentences support the topic sentence. They tell more about it.

Directions: Underline the middle sentences that support each topic sentence below.

Topic Sentence:

Penguins are birds that cannot fly.

Pelicans can spear fish with their sharp bills.
Many penguins waddle or hop about on land.
Even though they cannot fly, they are excellent swimmers.
Pelicans keep their food in a pouch.

Topic Sentence:

Volleyball is a team sport in which the players hit the ball over the net.

There are two teams with six players on each team.
My friend John would rather play tennis with Lisa.
Players can use their heads or their hands.
I broke my hand once playing handball.

Topic Sentence:

Pikes Peak is the most famous of all the Rocky Mountains.

Some mountains have more trees than other mountains.
Many people like to climb to the top.
Many people like to ski and camp there, too.
The weather is colder at the top of most mountains.

Page 164

Ending Sentences

Ending sentences are sentences that tie the story together.

Directions: Choose the correct ending sentence for each story from the sentences below. Write it at the end of the paragraph.

A new pair of shoes!
All the corn on the cob I could eat!
A new eraser!

Corn on the Cob

Corn on the cob used to be my favorite food. That is, until I lost my four front teeth. For one whole year, I had to sit and watch everyone else eat my favorite food without me. Mom gave me creamed corn, but it just wasn't the same. When my teeth finally came in, Dad said he had a surprise for me. I thought I was going to get a bike or a new C.D. player or something. I was just as happy to get what I did.

__All the corn on the cob I could eat!__

I would like to take a train ride every year.
Trains move faster than I thought they would.
She had brought her new gerbil along for the ride.

A Train Ride

When our family took its first train ride, my sister brought along a big box. She would not tell anyone what she had in it. In the middle of the trip, we heard a sound coming from the box. "Okay, Jan, now you have to open the box," said Mom. When she opened the box we were surprised.

__She had brought her new gerbil along for the ride.__

Page 166

Vocabulary: Beginning and Ending Sounds

Directions: Use the words in the box to answer the questions below.

ax	mix
beach	church
class	kiss
brush	crash

Which word:

begins with the same sound as **breakfast** and ends with the same sound as **fish**? __brush__

begins with the same sound as **children** and ends with the same sound as **catch**? __church__

begins and ends with the same sound as **cuts**? __kiss__

sounds like **acts**? __ax__

begins with the same sound as **coconut** and ends with the same sound as **splash**? __crash__

rhymes with **tricks**? __mix__

has **each** in it? __beach__

Page 167

Vocabulary: Sentences

Directions: Use a word from the box to complete each sentence. Use each word only once.

| ax | mix | beach | church | class | kiss | brush | crash |

1. Those two cars are going to __crash__.
2. He chopped the wood with an __ax__.
3. Grandma gave me a __kiss__ on my cheek.
4. Before you go, __brush__ your hair.
5. How many students are in your __class__ at school?
6. The waves bring sand to the __beach__.
7. To make orange, you __mix__ yellow and red.
8. On Sunday, we always go to __church__.

Page 168

Vocabulary: Plurals

A word that names one thing is **singular**, like **house**. A word that names more than one thing is **plural**, like **houses**.
To make a word plural, we usually add **s**.
Examples: one book — two book**s**   one tree — four tree**s**

To make plural words that end in **s, ss, x, sh** and **ch**, we add **es**.
Examples: one fox — two fox**es**   one bush — three bush**es**

Directions: Write the word that is missing from each pair below. Add **s** or **es** to make the plural words. The first one is done for you.

Singular	Plural
table	tables
beach	beaches
class	classes
ax	axes
brush	brushes
crash	crashes

Page 169

Vocabulary: Spelling

Directions: Circle the word in each sentence which is not spelled correctly. Then write the word correctly.

1. How many clases are in your school? __classes__
2. Our town has six chirches. __churches__
3. Have you been to Maryland's beechs? __beaches__
4. Water mixs with dirt to make mud. __mixes__
5. We need two axs for this tree. __axes__
6. That car has been in three crashs. __crashes__
7. She gave the baby lots of kises. __kisses__
8. I lost both of my brushs at school. __brushes__

Page 170

Vocabulary: Nouns and Verbs

A **noun** names a person, place or thing. A **verb** tells what something does or what something is. Some words can be a noun one time and a verb another time.

Directions: Complete each pair of sentences with a word from the box. The word will be a noun in the first sentence and a verb in the second sentence.

| mix | kiss | brush | crash |

1. Did your dog ever give you a __kiss__ (noun)?
   I have a cold, so I can't __kiss__ (verb) you today.
2. I brought my comb and my __brush__ (noun).
   I will __brush__ (verb) the leaves off your coat.
3. Was anyone hurt in the __crash__ (noun)?
   If you aren't careful, you will __crash__ (verb) into me.
4. We bought a cake __mix__ (noun) at the store.
   I will __mix__ (verb) the eggs together.

Page 171

Vocabulary: Nouns and Verbs

Directions: Write the correct word in each sentence. Use each word once. Write **N** above the words that are used as nouns (people, places and things). Write **V** above the words that are used as verbs (what something does or what something is).

Example:
I need a __drink__ (N). I will __drink__ (V) milk.

| mix | beach | church | class | kiss | brush | crash |

1. It's hot today, so let's go to the __beach__ (N).
2. The __church__ (N) was crowded.
3. I can't find my paint __brush__ (N).
4. Will you __kiss__ (V) my finger and make it stop hurting?
5. I will __mix__ (V) the red and yellow paint to get orange.
6. The teacher asked our __class__ (N) to get in line.
7. If you move that bottom can, the rest will __crash__ (V) to the floor.

Page 172

Vocabulary: Sentences

Every sentence must have two things: a **noun** that tells who or what is doing something and a **verb** that tells what the noun is doing.

Directions: Add a **noun** or a **verb** to complete each sentence. Be sure to begin your sentences with capital letters and end them with periods.

Example: reads after school (needs a noun)

Brandy reads after school.

1. brushes her dog every day
2. at the beach, we
3. ki...
4. ... class
5. stopped with a crash

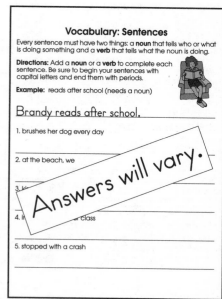
Answers will vary.

Page 173

Vocabulary

Directions: Find the picture that matches each sentence below. Then complete each sentence with the word under the picture.

list

search

spill

toast

pound

load

1. I will __search__ until I find it.

2. Be careful you don't __spill__ the paint.

3. Is that __load__ too heavy for you?

4. They made __toast__ for breakfast.

5. Please go to the store and buy a __pound__ of butter.

6. Is my name on the __list__?

Page 174

Vocabulary

Directions: Find the picture that matches each sentence below. Then complete the sentence with the word under the picture.

hug

plan

clap

stir

drag

grab

1. She will __plan__ where to go on her trip.

2. __Drag__ that big box over here, please.

3. My little brother always tries to __grab__ my toys.

4. May I help you __stir__ the soup?

5. I like to __hug__ my dog because he is so soft.

6. After she played, everyone started to __clap__.

Page 175

Vocabulary: Beginning and Ending Sounds

Directions: Write the words from the box that begin or end with the same sound as the pictures.

| stir | clap | drag | hug | plan | grab |

1. Which word **begins** with the same sound as each picture?

2. Which word (or words) **ends** with the same sound as each picture?

clap	stir
hug	clap
grab	plan
drag	grab
stir	drag
plan	hug

Page 176

Vocabulary: Explaining Sentences

Directions: Complete each sentence, explaining why each event might have happened.

She hugged me because _____

He didn't want to play with us because _____

We planned to go to the _____

We _____ loudly because _____

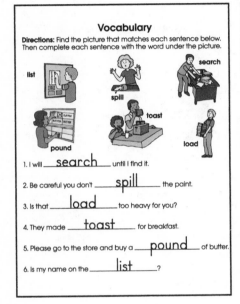

Answers will vary.

Page 177

Vocabulary: Verbs

Directions: Write the verb that answers each question. Write a sentence using that verb.

| stir | clap | drag | hug | plan | grab |

Which verb means to put your arms around someone?

__hug__

Answers will vary.

Which verb means to mix something with a spoon?

__stir__

Answers will vary.

Which verb means to pull something along the ground?

__drag__

Answers will vary.

Which verb means to take something suddenly?

__grab__

Answers will vary.

Page 178

Vocabulary: Past-Tense Verbs

The past tense of a verb tells that something already happened. To tell about something that already happened, add **ed** to most verbs. If the verb already ends in **e**, just add **d**.

Examples:

We enter**ed** the contest last week.
I fold**ed** the paper wrong.
He add**ed** two boxes to the pile.
We tast**ed** the cupcakes.
They decid**ed** quickly.
She shar**ed** her cupcake.

Directions: Use the verb from the first sentence to complete the second sentence. Add **d** or **ed** to show that something already happened.

Example:

My mom looks fine today. Yesterday, she __looked__ tired.

1. You enter through the middle door.
   We __entered__ that way last week.

2. Please add this for me. I already __added__ it twice.

3. Will you share your cookie with me?
   I __shared__ my apple with you yesterday.

4. It's your turn to fold the clothes. I __folded__ them yesterday.

5. May I taste another one? I already __tasted__ one.

6. You need to decide. We __decided__ this morning.

Page 179

Vocabulary: Past-Tense Verbs

When you write about something that already happened, you add **ed** to most verbs. For some verbs that have a short vowel and end in one consonant, you double the consonant before adding **ed.**

Examples:

He hug**ged** his pillow.   The dog grab**bed** the stick.
She stir**red** the carrots.   We plan**ned** to go tomorrow.
They clap**ped** for me.   They drag**ged** their bags on the ground.

Directions: Use the verb from the first sentence to complete the second sentence. Change the verb in the second part to the past tense. Double the consonant and add **ed.**

Example:

We skip to school. Yesterday, we __skipped__ the whole way.

1. It's not nice to grab things.
   When you __grabbed__ my cookie, I felt angry.

2. Did anyone hug you today? Dad __hugged__ me this morning.

3. We plan our vacations every year. Last year, we __planned__ to go to the beach.

4. Is it my turn to stir the pot? You __stirred__ it last time.

5. Let's clap for Andy, just like we __clapped__ for Amy.

6. My sister used to drag her blanket everywhere.
   Once, she __dragged__ it to the store.

Page 180

Vocabulary: Past-Tense Verbs

When you write about something that already happened, you add **ed** to most verbs. Here is another way to write about something in the past tense.

Examples: The dog walked.   The dog was walking.
             The cats played.   The cats were playing.

Directions: Write each sentence again, writing the verb a different way.

Example: The baby pounded the pans.

The baby was pounding the pans.

1. Gary loaded the car by himself.

Gary was loading the car by himself.

2. They searched for a long time.

They were searching for a long time.

3. The water spilled over the edge.

The water was spilling over the edge.

4. Dad toasted the rolls.

Dad was toasting the rolls.

Page 181

Vocabulary: Past-Tense Verbs

Directions: Write sentences that tell about each picture using the words **is, are, was** and **were.** Use words from the box as either nouns or verbs.

pound	spill	toast	list	load	search

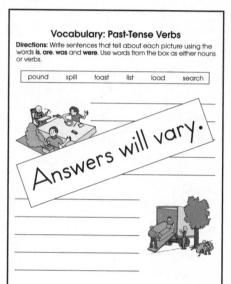

Answers will vary.

Page 182

Vocabulary: Present-Tense Verbs

When something is happening right now, it is in the **present tense.** There are two ways to write verbs in the present tense:

Examples: The dog **walks.**   The cats **play.**
             The dog **is walking.**   The cats **are playing.**

Directions: Write each sentence again, writing the verb a different way.

Example:

He lists the numbers.

He is listing the numbers.

1. She is pounding the nail.

She pounds the nail.

2. My brother toasts the bread.

He is toasting the bread.

3. They search for the robber.

They are searching for the robber.

4. The teacher lists the pages.

The teacher is listing the pages.

5. They are spilling the water.

They spill the water.

6. Ken and Amy load the packages.

They are loading the packages.

Page 183

Vocabulary: Sentences

Directions: Write a word from the box to complete each sentence. Use each word only once.

glue	enter	share	add	decide	fold

1. I know how to __add__ 3 and 4.

2. Which book did you __decide__ to read?

3. Go in the door that says "__Enter__".

4. I will __glue__ a yellow circle for the sun onto my picture.

5. I help __fold__ the clothes after they are washed.

6. She will __share__ her banana with me.

Page 184

Vocabulary

Directions: Follow the directions below.

glue	enter	share	add	decide	fold

1. Add letters to these words to make words from the box.

old __fold__   are __share__

2. Write the two words from the box that begin with vowels.

__enter__   __add__

3. Change one letter of each word to make a word from the box.

food __fold__   clue __glue__

4. Change two letters of this word to make a word from the box.

beside __decide__

Page 185

Vocabulary: Statements

A **statement** is a sentence that tells something.

Directions: Use the words in the box to complete the statements below. Write the words on the lines.

glue	decide	add
share	enter	fold

1. It took ten minutes for Kayla to ___add___ the numbers.

2. Ben wants to ___share___ his cookies with me.

3. "I can't ___decide___ which color to choose," said Rocky.

4. ___Glue___ can be used to make things stick together.

5. "This is how you ___fold___ your paper in half," said Mrs. Green.

6. The opposite of **leave** is ___enter___.

Write your own statement on the line.

Answers will vary.

Page 186

Vocabulary: Questions

Questions are asking sentences. They begin with a capital letter and end with a question mark. Many questions begin with the words **who, what, why, when, where** and **how.** Write six questions using the question words below. Make sure to end each question with a question mark.

1. Who _____

2. What _____

Answers will vary.

4. W_____

5. Where _____

6. How _____

Page 187

Vocabulary: Commands

A **command** is a sentence that tells someone to do something.

Directions: Use the words in the box to complete the commands below. Write the words on the lines.

glue	decide	add	share	enter	fold

1. ___Add___ a cup of flour to the cake batter.

2. ___Decide___ how much paper you will need to write your story.

3. Please ___glue___ the picture of the apple onto the paper.

4. ___Enter___ through this door and leave through the other door.

5. Please ___fold___ the letter and put it into an envelope.

6. ___Share___ your toys with your sister.

Write your own command on the lines.

Answers will vary.

Page 188

Vocabulary: Directions

A **direction** is a sentence written as a command.

Directions: Write the missing directions for these pictures. Begin each direction with one of the verbs below.

glue	enter	share	add	decide	fold

How To Make a Peanut Butter and Jelly Sandwich:

1. Spread peanut butter on bread.

2. _____

3. Cut th___

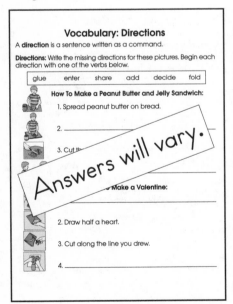
Answers will vary.

___ Make a Valentine:

2. Draw half a heart.

3. Cut along the line you drew.

4. _____

Page 189

Kinds of Sentences

A **statement** is a sentence that tells something.
A **question** is a sentence that asks something.
A **command** is a sentence that tells someone to do something.
Commands begin with a verb or **please.** They usually end with a period. The noun is **you** but does not need to be part of the sentence.
Example: "Come here, please." means "**You** come here, please."
Examples of commands: Stand next to me.
　　　　　　　　　　　　Please give me some paper.

Directions: Write **S** in front of the statements, **Q** in front of the questions and **C** in front of the commands. End each sentence with a period or a question mark.
Example:

　C___ Stop and look before you cross the street.
　Q___ 1. Did you do your math homework?
　S___ 2. I think I lost my math book.
　Q___ 3. Will you help me find it?
　S___ 4. I looked everywhere.
　C___ 5. Please open your math books to page three.
　Q___ 6. Did you look under your desk?
　S___ 7. I looked, but it's not there.
　Q___ 8. Who can add seven and four?
　C___ 9. Come up and write the answer on the board.
　Q___ 10. Chris, where is your math book?
　S___ 11. I don't know for sure.
　C___ 12. Please share a book with a friend.

Page 190

Kinds of Sentences

Remember: a **statement** tells something, a **question** asks something and a **command** tells someone to do something.

Directions: On each line, write a statement, question or command. Use a word from the box in each sentence.

glue	share	decide
enter	add	fold

Example:
Question:
Can he add anything else?

1. Statement: _____

2. Quest___

Answers will vary.

3. _____

4. Statement: _____

5. Question: _____

Page 191

Kinds of Sentences

Directions: Use the group of words below to write three sentences: a **statement**, a **question** and a **command**.

| add | can | these | he | quickly | numbers |

Example:

Statement:

He can add these numbers quickly.

Question:

Can he can add these numbers quickly?

Command:

Add these numbers quickly.

| fold | here | should |

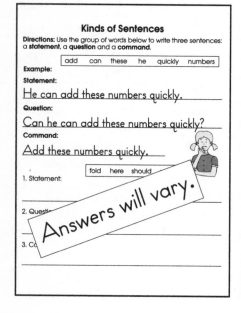

1. Statement:

2. Questio~~n~~

3. C~~ommand~~

Answers will vary.

Page 192

Vocabulary: Completing a Story

Directions: Use verbs to complete the story below. The verbs that tell about things that happened in the past will end in **ed**.

Answers may vary.

Last week, Amy and I ___entered___ a contest. We were supposed to make a card to give to a child in a hospital. First, we ___folded___ a big sheet of white paper in half to make the card. Then we ___decided___ to draw a rainbow on the front. Amy started coloring the rainbow all by herself. "Wait!" I said. "We both ___entered___ the contest. Let me help!" "Okay," Amy said. "Let's ___share___ . You ___add___ a color, and then I'll ___add___ a color." It was more fun when we ___shared___ . When we finished making the rainbow, we ___decided___ to ___add___ a sun to the picture. I cut one out of yellow paper. Then Amy ___glued___ it just above the rainbow. Well, our card didn't win the contest, but it did make a little boy with a broken leg smile. Amy and I felt so happy! We ___decided___ to go right home and make some more cards!

Page 193

Homophones

Homophones are words that sound the same but are spelled differently and have different meanings.

Directions: Use the homophones in the box to answer the riddles below.

| main | meat | peace | dear | to |
| mane | meet | piece | deer | too |

1. Which word has the word **pie** in it? — piece
2. Which word rhymes with **ear** and is an animal? — deer
3. Which word rhymes with **shoe** and means **also**? — too
4. Which word has the word **eat** in it and is something you might eat? — meat
5. Which word has the same letters as the word **read** but in a different order? — dear
6. Which word rhymes with **train** and is something on a pony? — mane
7. Which word, if it began with a capital letter, might be the name of an important street? — main
8. Which word sounds like a number but has only two letters? — to
9. Which word rhymes with and is a synonym for **greet**? — meet
10. Which word rhymes with the last syllable in **police** and can mean quiet? — peace

Page 194

Homophones: Sentences

Directions: Write a word from the box to complete each sentence.

| main | meat | peace | dear | two |
| mane | meet | piece | deer | too |

1. The horse had a long, beautiful ___mane___ .

   The ___main___ idea of the paragraph was boats.

2. Let's ___meet___ at my house to do our homework.

   The lion was fed ___meat___ at mealtime.

3. We had ___two___ kittens.

   Mike has a red bike. Tom does, ___too___ .

4. The ___deer___ ran in front of the car.

   I begin my letters with " ___Dear___ Mom."

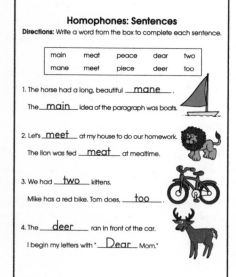

Page 195

Homophones: Spelling

Directions: Circle the word in each sentence which is not spelled correctly. Then write the word correctly.

1. Please (meat) me at the park. — meet

2. I would like a (peace) of pie. — piece

3. There were (too) cookies left. — two

4. The horse's (main) needed to be brushed. — mane

5. We saw a (dear) in the forest. — deer

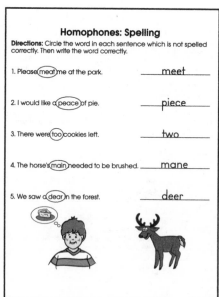

Page 196

Homophones: Rhymes

Directions: Use homophones to create two-lined rhymes.

Example: I found it a **pain**
To comb the horse's **mane**!

1. _____

2. _____

3. _____

Answers will vary.

Page 197

Short Vowels

Short vowel patterns usually have a single vowel followed by a consonant sound.

Short a is the sound you hear in the word **can**.
Short e is the sound you hear in the word **men**.
Short i is the sound you hear in the word **pig**.
Short o is the sound you hear in the word **pot**.
Short u is the sound you hear in the word **truck**.

fast	stop
spin	track
wish	lunch
bread	block

Directions: Use the words in the box to answer the questions below.

Which word:

begins with the same sound as **blast** and ends with the same sound as **look**? __block__

rhymes with **stack**? __track__

begins with the same sound as **phone** and ends with the same sound as **lost**? __fast__

has the same vowel sound as **hen**? __bread__

rhymes with **crunch**? __lunch__

begins with the same sound as **spot** and ends with the same sound as **can**? __spin__

begins with the same sound as **win** and ends with the same sound as **crush**? __wish__

has the word **top** in it? __stop__

Page 198

Short Vowels: Sentences

Directions: Use the words in the box to complete each sentence.

| fast | wish | truck | bread | sun |
| best | stop | track | lunch | block |

Race cars can go very __fast__.

Carol packs a __lunch__ for Ted before school.

Throw a penny in the well and make a __wish__.

The __truck__ had a flat tire.

My favorite kind of __bread__ is whole wheat.

Page 199

Short Vowels: Spelling

Directions: Circle the word in each sentence which is not spelled correctly. Then write the word correctly.

1. Be sure to (stopp) at the red light. __stop__

2. The train goes down the (trak). __track__

3. Please put the (bred) in the toaster. __bread__

4. I need another (blok) to finish. __block__

5. The (beasst) player won a trophy. __best__

6. Blow out the candles and make a (wiish). __wish__

7. The (truk) blew its horn. __truck__

Page 200

Long Vowels

Long vowels are the letters **a, e, i, o** and **u** which say the letter name sound.

Long a is the sound you hear in **cane**.
Long e is the sound you hear in **green**.
Long i is the sound you hear in **pie**.
Long o is the sound you hear in **bowl**.
Long u is the sound you hear in **cube**.

lame	goal
pain	few
street	fright
nose	gray
bike	fuse

Directions: Use the words in the box to answer the questions below.

1. Add one letter to each of these words to make words from the box.

ray __gray__ use __fuse__ right __fright__

2. Change one letter from each word to make a word from the box.

pail __pain__ goat __goal__
late __lame__ bite __bike__

3. Write the word from the box that . . .

has the long e sound. __street__
rhymes with **you**. __few__
is a homophone for **knows**. __nose__

Page 201

Long Vowels: Sentences

Directions: Use the words in the box to complete each sentence.

| lame | goal | pain | few | bike |
| street | fright | nose | gray | fuse |

1. Look both ways before crossing the __street__.

2. My __bike__ had a flat tire.

3. Our walk through the haunted house gave us such a __fright__.

4. I kicked the soccer ball and scored a __goal__.

5. The __gray__ clouds mean rain is coming.

6. Cover your __nose__ when you sneeze.

7. We blew a __fuse__ at my house last night.

Page 202

Long Vowels

Directions: Use long vowel words from the box to answer the clues below. Write the letters of the words on the lines.

| few | bike | dime | goal | fuse | lame | street | nose | fright | pain |

1. f r i g h t (rhymes with **night**)
2. s t r e e t (could be Main or Maple)
3. f e w (synonym for **a couple**)
4. l a m e (rhymes with **tame**)
5. b i k e (can be ridden on a trail)
6. p a i n (homophone for **pane**)
7. d i m e (ten of these make a dollar)
8. g o a l (changing one letter of this word makes **goat**)
9. f u s e (has the word **use** in it)
10. n o s e (homophone for **knows**)

Now, read the letters in the boxes from top to bottom to find out what kind of a job you did! __tremendous__

Page 203

Adjectives

Directions: Use the words in the box to answer the questions below. Use each word only once.

polite	careless	neat	shy	selfish	thoughtful

1. Someone who is quiet and needs some time to make new friends is __shy__.

2. A person who says "please" and "thank you" is __polite__.

3. Someone who always puts all the toys away is __neat__.

4. A person who won't share with others is being __selfish__.

5. A person who leaves a bike out all night is being __careless__.

6. Someone who thinks of others is __thoughtful__.

Page 204

Adjectives

Directions: Use the adjectives in the box to answer the questions below.

polite	careless	neat	shy	selfish	thoughtful

1. Change a letter in each word to make an adjective.

near __neat__

why __shy__

2. Write the word that rhymes with each of these.

fell dish __selfish__

not full __thoughtful__

hair mess __careless__

3. Find these words in the adjectives. Write the adjective.

at __neat__

are __careless__

it __polite__

Page 205

Adjectives: Spelling

Directions: Circle the word in each sentence which is not spelled correctly. Then write the word correctly.

1. John isn't (shelfish) at all. __selfish__

2. He (sharred) his lunch with me today. __shared__

3. I was (careles) and forgot to bring mine. __careless__

4. My father says if I (planed) better, that wouldn't happen all the time. __planned__

5. John is kind of quiet, and I used to think he was (shie). __shy__

6. Now, I know he is really (thotful). __thoughtful__

7. He's also very (polyte) and always asks before he borrows anything. __polite__

8. He would never just reach over and (grabb) something he wanted. __grab__

9. I'm glad John (desided) to be my friend. __decided__

Page 206

Adjectives: Explaining Sentences

Directions: Use a word from the box to tell about a person in each picture below. Then write a sentence that explains why you chose that word.

polite	neat	careless	shy	selfish	thoughtful

Sample answers given.

The word I picked: __shy__

I think so because . . .

__the girl is standing alone and looks sad.__

The word I picked: __thoughtful__

I think so because . . .

__it is thoughtful to give someone flowers.__

The word I picked: __selfish__

I think so because . . .

__the boy is not sharing his cookies.__

Page 207

Adjectives

Directions: Look at each picture. Then add adjectives to the sentences. Use colors, numbers, words from the box and any other words you need to describe each picture.

polite	neat	careless
shy	selfish	thoughtful

Example:

The boy shared his pencil.

__The polite boy shared his red pencil.__

The girl dropped her coat.

The boy p...

The boy put books away.

Answers will vary.

Page 208

C, K, CK Words: Spelling

Directions: Write the words from the box that answer the questions.

crowd	keeper	cost	pack	kangaroo	thick

1. Which words spell the **k** sound with a **k**?

__keeper__   __kangaroo__

2. Which words spell the **k** sound with a **c**?

__crowd__   __cost__

3. Which words spell the **k** sound with **ck**?

__pack__   __thick__

4. Circle the letters that spell **k** in these words:

(c)oo(k)   bla(ck)   (c)ool   (k)ite

(c)ake   po(ck)et   po(k)e

5. Which words from the box rhyme with each of these?

tossed __cost__   deeper __keeper__

proud __crowd__   all in blue __kangaroo__

Page 209

C, K, CK Words: Sentences

The **k** sound can be spelled with a **c, k** or **ck** after a short vowel sound.

Directions: Use the words from the box to complete the sentences. Use each word only once.

crowd	keeper
cost	pack
kangaroo	thick

1. On sunny days, there is always a __crowd__ of people at the zoo.

2. It doesn't __cost__ much to get into the zoo.

3. We always get hungry, so we __pack__ a picnic lunch.

4. We like to watch the __kangaroo__.

5. Its __thick__ tail helps it jump and walk.

6. The __keeper__ always makes sure the cages are clean.

Page 210

C, K, CK Words: Sentences

Remember: every sentence must have a noun that tells who or what is doing something and a verb that tells what the noun is doing.

Directions: Parts of each sentence below are missing. Rewrite each sentence, adding a noun or a verb, periods and capital letters.

Example:
read a book every day (needs a noun)

__Leon reads a book every day.__

1. packed a lunch

2. the crowd at the beach

3. cost

Answers will vary.

4. kan___ ___eir babies

5. was too thick to chew

Page 212

Addition

Directions: Add.
Example:

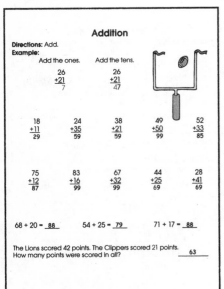

Add the ones.	Add the tens.
26 +21 = 7	26 +21 = 47

| 18 +11 = 29 | 24 +35 = 59 | 38 +21 = 59 | 49 +50 = 99 | 52 +33 = 85 |

| 75 +12 = 87 | 83 +16 = 99 | 67 +32 = 99 | 44 +25 = 69 | 28 +41 = 69 |

68 + 20 = __88__   54 + 25 = __79__   71 + 17 = __88__

The Lions scored 42 points. The Clippers scored 21 points. How many points were scored in all?   __63__

Page 213

Subtraction

Subtraction means "taking away" or subtracting one number from another to find the difference. For example, 10 - 3 = 7.

Directions: Subtract.
Example:

Subtract the ones.	Subtract the tens.
39 -24 = 5	39 -24 = 15

| 48 -35 = 13 | 95 -22 = 73 | 87 -16 = 71 | 55 -43 = 12 |

| 37 -14 = 23 | 69 -57 = 12 | 44 -23 = 21 | 99 -78 = 21 |

66 - 44 = __22__   57 - 33 = __24__

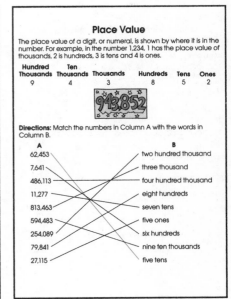

The yellow car traveled 87 miles per hour. The orange car traveled 66 miles per hour. How much faster was the yellow car traveling?   __21 m.p.h.__

Page 214

Place Value

The place value of a digit, or numeral, is shown by where it is in the number. For example, in the number 1,234, 1 has the place value of thousands, 2 is hundreds, 3 is tens and 4 is ones.

Hundred Thousands	Ten Thousands	Thousands	Hundreds	Tens	Ones
9	4	3	8	5	2

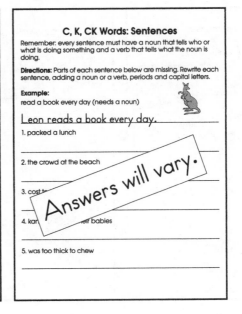

Directions: Match the numbers in Column A with the words in Column B.

A	B
62,453	two hundred thousand
7,641	three thousand
486,113	four hundred thousand
11,277	eight hundreds
813,463	seven tens
594,483	five ones
254,089	six hundreds
79,841	nine ten thousands
27,115	five tens

Addition: Regrouping

Addition means "putting together" or adding two or more numbers to find the sum. For example, 3 + 5 = 8. To regroup is to use ten ones to form one ten, ten tens to form one 100 and so on.

Directions: Add using regrouping.

Example:

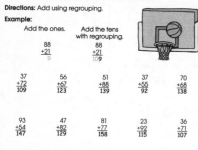

Add the ones.

88
+21
9

Add the tens with regrouping.

88
+21
109

37	56	51	37	70
+72	+67	+88	+55	+68
109	123	139	92	138

93	47	81	23	36
+54	+82	+77	+92	+71
147	129	158	115	107

92 + 13 = __105__   73 + 83 = __156__   54 + 61 = __115__

The Blues scored 63 points. The Reds scored 44 points. How many points were scored in all? __107__

Subtraction: Regrouping

Subtraction means "taking away" or subtracting one number from another to find the difference. For example, 10 - 3 = 7. To regroup is to use one ten to form ten ones, one 100 to form ten tens and so on.

Directions: Study the example. Subtract using regrouping.

Example:

32	=	2 tens	+	12 ones
-13	=	1 ten	+	3 ones
19	=	1 ten	+	9 ones

33	86	92	71
-28	-59	-37	-48
5	27	55	23

63	45	31	55
-47	-18	-22	-39
16	27	9	16

82 - 69 = __13__   73 - 36 = __37__

The Yankees won 85 games. The Cubs won 69 games. How many more games did the Yankees win? __16__

Addition and Subtraction: Regrouping

Addition means "putting together" or adding two or more numbers to find the sum. Subtraction means "taking away" or subtracting one number from another to find the difference. To regroup is to use one ten to form ten ones, one 100 to form ten tens and so on.

Directions: Add or subtract. Regroup when needed.

92	58	63	77
-47	+26	+18	-38
45	84	81	39

27	31	56	67
-17	+42	-29	+33
10	73	27	100

72	87	93	54
+19	-58	-89	+27
91	29	4	81

The soccer team scored 83 goals this year. The soccer team scored 68 goals last year. How many goals did they score in all? __151__

How many more goals did they score this year than last year? __15__

Addition: Regrouping

Directions: Study the example. Add using regrouping.

Examples:

Add the ones. Regroup.

1
156
+267
3

6
+7
13

Add the tens. Regroup.

1   11
5   156
+6 +267
12 23

Add the hundreds.

1
156
+267
423

29	81	52	49	
46	78	67	37	162
+12	+33	+23	+19	+349
87	192	142	105	511

273	655	783	385	428
+198	+297	+148	+169	+122
471	952	931	554	550

Sally went bowling. She had scores of 115, 129 and 103. What was her total score for three games? __347__

Addition: Regrouping

Directions: Add using regrouping. Then use the code to discover the name of a United States president.

348	642	386	184	578
+752	+277	+787	+875	+874
1,100	919	1,173	1,059	1,452

653	653	946	393	199
+768	+359	+239	+257	+843
1,421	1,012	1,185	650	1,042

721
+679
1,400

G W A S H I N G T O N

1012	1173	1059	1421	919	650	1452	1042	1100	1400	1185
N	A	S	I	W	T	H	O	G	N	G

Addition: Regrouping

Directions: Study the example. Add using regrouping.

Example:

Steps:
5,356   1. Add the ones.
+3,976   2. Regroup the tens. Add the tens.
9,332   3. Regroup the hundreds. Add the hundreds.
         4. Add the thousands.

6,849	1,846	9,221
+3,276	+8,384	+6,769
10,125	10,230	15,990

2,758	5,299	7,932
+3,663	+8,764	+6,879
6,421	14,063	14,811

A plane flew 1,838 miles on the first day. It flew 2,347 miles on the second day. How many miles did it fly in all? __4,185__

Page 221

Addition: Mental Math

Directions: Try to do these addition problems in your head without using paper and pencil.

7 +4 11	6 +3 9	8 +1 9	10 + 2 12	2 +9 11	6 +6 12
10 +20 30	40 +20 60	80 +100 180	60 +30 90	50 +70 120	100 + 40 140
350 +150 500	300 +500 800	400 +800 1,200	450 + 10 460	680 +100 780	900 + 70 970
1,000 + 200 1,200	4,000 400 + 30 4,430	300 200 + 80 580	8,000 500 + 60 8,560	9,800 + 150 9,950	7,000 300 + 30 7,330

Page 222

Subtraction: Regrouping

Directions: Regrouping for subtraction is the opposite of regrouping for addition. Study the example. Subtract using regrouping. Then use the code to color the flowers.

Example:

647
-453
194

Steps:
1. Subtract ones.
2. Subtract tens. Five tens cannot be subtracted from 4 tens.
3. Regroup tens by regrouping 6 hundreds (5 hundreds + 10 tens).
4. Add the 10 tens to the four tens.
5. Subtract 5 tens from 14 tens.
6. Subtract the hundreds.

If the answer has:
1 one, color it red;
8 ones, color it pink;
5 ones, color it yellow.

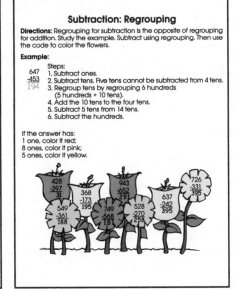

428
-397
31

368
-173
195

943
-652
291

726
-331
395

549
-361
188

749
-568
181

528
-270
258

637
-242
395

Page 223

Subtraction: Regrouping

Directions: Study the example. Follow the steps. Subtract using regrouping.

Example:

634
-455
179

Steps:
1. Subtract ones. You cannot subtract five ones from 4 ones.
2. Regroup ones by regrouping 3 tens to 2 tens + 10 ones.
3. Subtract 5 ones from 14 ones.
4. Regroup tens by regrouping hundreds (5 hundreds + 10 tens).
5. Subtract 5 tens from 12 tens.
6. Subtract hundreds.

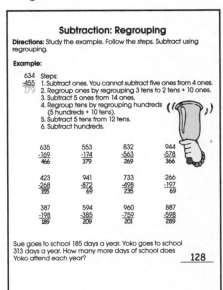

635 -169 466	553 -174 379	832 -563 269	944 -578 366
423 -268 155	941 -872 69	733 -498 235	266 -197 69
387 -198 189	594 -385 209	960 -759 201	887 -598 289

Sue goes to school 185 days a year. Yoko goes to school 313 days a year. How many more days of school does Yoko attend each year? **128**

Page 224

Subtraction: Regrouping

Directions: Study the example. Follow the steps. Subtract using regrouping. If you have to regroup to subtract ones and there are no tens, you must regroup twice.

Example:

300
-182
118

Steps:
1. Subtract ones. You cannot subtract 2 ones from 0 ones.
2. Regroup. No tens. Regroup hundreds (2 hundreds + 10 tens).
3. Regroup tens (9 tens + 10 ones).
4. Subtract 2 ones from ten ones.
5. Subtract 8 tens from 9 tens.
6. Subtract 1 hundred from 2 hundreds.

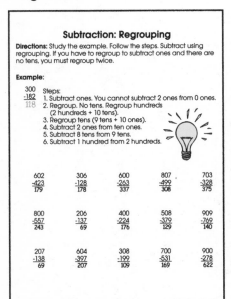

602 -423 179	306 -128 178	600 -263 337	807 -499 308	703 -328 375
800 -557 243	206 -137 69	400 -224 176	508 -379 129	909 -769 140
207 -138 69	604 -397 207	308 -199 109	700 -531 169	900 -278 622

Page 225

Subtraction: Regrouping

Directions: Subtract. Regroup when necessary. The first one is done for you.

7,354 -5,295 2,059	4,214 -3,185 1,029	8,437 -5,338 3,099	6,837 -4,318 2,519
5,735 -3,826 1,909	1,036 - 947 89	6,735 -6,646 89	3,841 -1,953 1,888

Columbus discovered America in 1492. The pilgrims landed in America in 1620. How many years difference was there between these two events?

1620
-1492
128 years

Page 226

Subtraction: Mental Math

Directions: Try to do these subtraction problems in your head without using paper and pencil.

9 -3 6	12 - 6 6	7 -6 1	5 -1 4	15 - 5 10	2 -0 2
40 -20 20	90 - 80 10	100 - 50 50	20 -20 0	60 -10 50	70 - 40 30
450 -250 200	500 - 300 200	250 - 20 230	690 -100 590	320 - 20 300	900 -600 300
1,000 - 400 600	8,000 - 500 7,500	7,000 - 900 6,100	4,000 -2,000 2,000	9,500 -4,000 5,500	5,000 -2,000 3,000

Page 227

Review

Directions: Add or subtract using regrouping.

28	82	33	67
56	49	75	94
+93	+51	+128	+248
177	182	236	409

683	756	818	956
-495	+139	-387	+267
188	895	431	1,223

1,588	4,675	8,732	2,938
- 989	-2,976	-5,664	+3,459
599	1,699	3,068	6,397

N.Y. TO MIAMI
N.Y. TO L.A.

To drive from New York City to Los Angeles is 2,832 miles. To drive from New York City to Miami is 1,327 miles. How much farther is it to drive from New York City to Los Angeles than from New York City to Miami?

2,832
-1,327
1,505

Page 228

Rounding: The Nearest Ten

If the ones number is 5 or greater, "round up" to the nearest 10. If the ones number is 4 or less, the tens number stays the same and the ones number becomes a zero.

Examples: 15 round up to 20   23 round down to 20   47 round up to 50

7	10	58	60
12	10	81	80
33	30	94	90
27	30	44	40
73	70	88	90
25	30	66	70
39	40	70	70

Page 229

Rounding: The Nearest Hundred

If the tens number is 5 or greater, "round up" to the nearest hundred. If the tens number is 4 or less, the hundreds number remains the same.

REMEMBER... Look at the number directly to the right of the place you are rounding to.

Example:

230 round down to 200   470 round up to 500

150 round up to 200   732 round down to 700

456	500	120	100
340	300	923	900
867	900	550	600
686	700	231	200
770	800	492	500

Page 230

Front-End Estimation

Front-end estimation is useful when you don't need to know the exact amount, but a close answer will do.

When we use front-end estimation, we use only the first number, and then add the numbers together to get the estimate.

Example:

153	→	100	apples
226	→	200	oranges
+341	→	+300	bananas
720		600	
actual		estimate	

You can even do this mentally!

Directions: Estimate the sum of these numbers.

456	→	400	910	→	900	686	→	600
121	→	100	280	→	200	307	→	300
+438	→	+400	+320	→	+300	+711	→	+700
		900			1,400			1,600

Page 231

Multiplication

Multiplication is a short way to find the sum of adding the same number a certain amount of times. For example, we write 7 x 4 = 28 instead of 7 + 7 + 7 + 7 = 28.

Directions: Study the example. Multiply.

Example:

There are two groups of seashells. There are 3 seashells in each group. How many seashells are there in all?   2 x 3 = 6

4 + 4 = 8
2 x 4 = 8

3 + 3 + 3 = 9
3 x 3 = 9

2	3	4	6	7
x3	x5	x3	x2	x3
6	15	12	12	21

5	6	4	7	8
x2	x3	x2	x2	x3
10	18	8	14	24

5	9	8	6	9
x5	x4	x5	x6	x3
25	36	40	36	27

Page 232

Multiplication

Directions: Multiply.

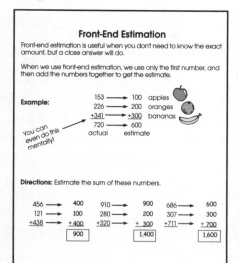

3	4	3
x5	x6	x8
15	24	24

5	4	5
x5	x8	x4
25	32	20

6	3	2	7	9
x7	x9	x8	x6	x4
42	27	16	42	36

6	5	7	5	8
x8	x6	x7	x3	x9
48	30	49	15	72

A river boat makes 3 trips a day every day. How many trips does it make in a week?   21

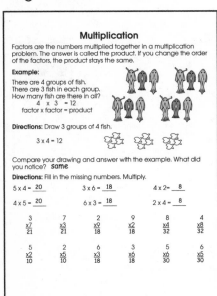

Page 233

Multiplication

Factors are the numbers multiplied together in a multiplication problem. The answer is called the product. If you change the order of the factors, the product stays the same.

Example:

There are 4 groups of fish.
There are 3 fish in each group.
How many fish are there in all?
$4 \times 3 = 12$
factor x factor = product

Directions: Draw 3 groups of 4 fish.

$3 \times 4 = 12$

Compare your drawing and answer with the example. What did you notice? **same**

Directions: Fill in the missing numbers. Multiply.

$5 \times 4 = \underline{20}$ $3 \times 6 = \underline{18}$ $4 \times 2 = \underline{8}$

$4 \times 5 = \underline{20}$ $6 \times 3 = \underline{18}$ $2 \times 4 = \underline{8}$

3	7	2	3	8	4
x7	x3	x9	x2	x4	x8
21	21	18	18	32	32

5	2	6	3	5	6
x2	x5	x3	x6	x6	x5
10	10	18	18	30	30

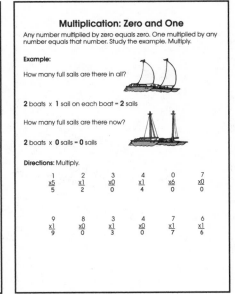

Page 234

Multiplication: Zero and One

Any number multiplied by zero equals zero. One multiplied by any number equals that number. Study the example. Multiply.

Example:

How many full sails are there in all?

2 boats x **1** sail on each boat = **2** sails

How many full sails are there now?

2 boats x **0** sails = **0** sails

Directions: Multiply.

1	2	3	4	0	7
x5	x1	x0	x1	x6	x0
5	2	0	4	0	0

9	8	3	4	7	6
x1	x0	x1	x0	x1	x1
9	0	3	0	7	6

Page 235

Multiplication

Directions: Time yourself as you multiply. How quickly can you complete this page?

3	8	1	1	3	0
x2	x7	x0	x6	x4	x4
6	56	0	6	12	0

4	4	2	9	9	5
x1	x4	x5	x3	x9	x3
4	16	10	27	81	15

0	2	9	8	7	4
x8	x6	x6	x5	x3	x2
0	12	54	40	21	8

3	2	4	1	0	3
x5	x0	x6	x3	x0	x3
15	0	24	3	0	9

Page 236

Multiplication Table

Directions: Complete the multiplication table. Use it to practice your multiplication facts.

X	0	1	2	3	4	5	6	7	8	9	10
0	0	0	0	0	0	0	0	0	0	0	0
1	0	1	2	3	4	5	6	7	8	9	10
2	0	2	4	6	8	10	12	14	16	18	20
3	0	3	6	9	12	15	18	21	24	27	30
4	0	4	8	12	16	20	24	28	32	36	40
5	0	5	10	15	20	25	30	35	40	45	50
6	0	6	12	18	24	30	36	42	48	54	60
7	0	7	14	21	28	35	42	49	56	63	70
8	0	8	16	24	32	40	48	56	64	72	80
9	0	9	18	27	36	45	54	63	72	81	90
10	0	10	20	30	40	50	60	70	80	90	100

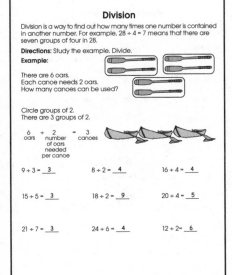

Page 237

Division

Division is a way to find out how many times one number is contained in another number. For example, $28 \div 4 = 7$ means that there are seven groups of four in 28.

Directions: Study the example. Divide.

Example:

There are 6 oars.
Each canoe needs 2 oars.
How many canoes can be used?

Circle groups of 2.
There are 3 groups of 2.

$\underset{\text{oars}}{6} + \underset{\substack{\text{number}\\\text{of oars}\\\text{needed}\\\text{per canoe}}}{2} = \underset{\text{canoes}}{3}$

$9 \div 3 = \underline{3}$ $8 \div 2 = \underline{4}$ $16 \div 4 = \underline{4}$

$15 \div 5 = \underline{3}$ $18 \div 2 = \underline{9}$ $20 \div 4 = \underline{5}$

$21 \div 7 = \underline{3}$ $24 \div 6 = \underline{4}$ $12 \div 2 = \underline{6}$

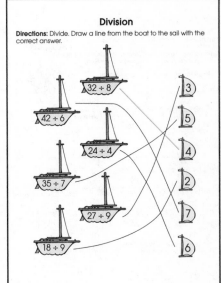

Page 238

Division

Directions: Divide. Draw a line from the boat to the sail with the correct answer.

$32 \div 8$ $\quad$ 3
$42 \div 6$ $\quad$ 5
$24 \div 4$ $\quad$ 4
$35 \div 7$ $\quad$ 2
$27 \div 9$ $\quad$ 7
$18 \div 9$ $\quad$ 6

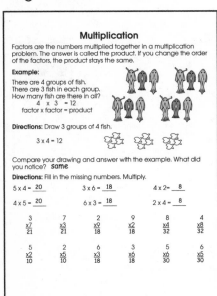

Page 239

Order of Operations

When you solve a problem that involves more than one operation, this is the order to follow:

    ( )   Parentheses first
    x   Multiplication
    ÷   Division
    +   Addition
    –   Subtraction

Example:
2 + (3 x 5) - 2 = 15
2 + 15 - 2 = 15
17 - 2 = 15

Directions: Solve the problems using the correct order of operations.

(5 - 3) ÷ 4 x 7 = __30__
  2   28

1 + 2 x 3 + 4 = __11__
    6

6 x 3 - 1 = __17__
    18

(8 ÷ 2) x 4 = __16__
    4

9 ÷ 3 x 3 + 0 = __1__
    9

5 - 2 x 1 + 2 = __1__
    2

Page 240

Order of Operations

Directions: Use +, –, x and ÷ to complete the problems so the number sentence is true.

Example: 4 _+_ 2 _–_ 1 = 5

(8 _÷_ 2) _+_ 4 = 8

(1 _+_ 2) _÷_ 3 = 1

9 _+_ 3 _–_ 9 = 3

(7 _–_ 5) _x_ 1 = 2

8 _x_ 5 _+_ 4 = 10

5 _–_ 4 _+_ 1 = 1

REMEMBER...
USE THE ORDER OF OPERATIONS

Page 241

Review

Directions: Multiply or divide. Fill in the blanks with the missing numbers or x or ÷ signs. The first one is done for you.

5 x 4 = 20   6 x 8 = __48__   7 x __2__ = 14

3 _x_ 6 = 18   7 x 2 = __14__   __8__ x 3 = 24

6 _÷_ 2 = 3   24 ÷ 6 = __4__   6 x 5 = __30__

25 _÷_ 5 = 5   49 ÷ 7 = __7__   8 x __4__ = 32

3 _x_ 8 = 24   18 ÷ 3 = __6__   9 x 5 = __45__

12 _÷_ 3 = 4   9 x 8 = __72__   6 x __6__ = 36

Page 242

Division

Division is a way to find out how many times one number is contained in another number. The ÷ sign means "divided by." Another way to divide is to use ⌐. The dividend is the larger number that is divided by the smaller number, or divisor. The answer of a division problem is called the quotient.

Directions: Study the example. Divide.

Example:

    20 ÷ 4 = 5
dividend divisor quotient

quotient
   5
4⟌20
divisor⟋dividend

35 ÷ 7 = __5__   5
7⟌35

42 ÷ 6 = __7__   7
6⟌42

 6
2⟌12

 6
3⟌18

 9
4⟌36

 10
5⟌50

 4
6⟌24

 3
7⟌21

 4
8⟌32

 3
9⟌27

36 ÷ 6 = __6__ 28 ÷ 4 = __7__ 15 ÷ 5 = __3__ 12 ÷ 2 = __6__

A tree farm has 36 trees. There are 4 rows of trees.
How many trees are there in each row? __9__

Page 243

Division: Zero and One

Directions: Study the rules of division and the examples. Divide, then write the number of the rule you used to solve each problem.

Examples:

Rule 1: 5
1⟌5   Any number divided by 1 is that number.

Rule 2: 1
5⟌5   Any number except 0 divided by itself is 1.

Rule 3: 0
7⟌0   Zero divided by any number is zero.

Rule 4: 0⟌7   You cannot divide by zero.

 6
1⟌6 Rule __1__   4 ÷ 1 = __4__ Rule __1__

 1
7⟌7 Rule __2__   9 ÷ 9 = __1__ Rule __2__

 0
9⟌0 Rule __3__   7 ÷ 1 = __7__ Rule __1__

 4
1⟌4 Rule __1__   6 ÷ 0 = __—__ Rule __4__

ZERO ONE

Page 244

Division: Remainders

Division is a way to find out how many times one number is contained in another number. For example, 28 ÷ 4 = 7 means that there are seven groups of four in 28. The dividend is the larger number that is divided by the smaller number, or divisor. The quotient is the answer in a division problem. The remainder is the amount left over. The remainder is always less than the divisor.

Directions: Study the example. Find each quotient and remainder.

Example:
There are 11 dog biscuits.
Put them in groups of 3.
There are 2 left over.

  3
3⟌11
 -9
  2 remainder

 3 r 2
3⟌11

Remember: The remainder must be less than the **divisor!**

 4 r1
3⟌13

 4 r1
4⟌17

 5 r2
6⟌32

 5 r1
5⟌26

9 ÷ 4 = __2 r1__ 12 ÷ 5 = __2 r2__ 26 ÷ 4 = __6 r2__ 49 ÷ 9 = __5 r4__

The pet store has 7 cats.
Two cats go in each cage. How many cats are left over? __1__

Page 245

Divisibility Rules

A number is divisible... by 2 if the last digit is 0 or even (2, 4, 6, 8).
by 3 if the sum of all digits is divisible by 3.
by 4 if the last two digits are divisible by 4.
by 5 if the last digit is a 0 or 5.
by 10 if the last digit is 0.

Example: 250 is divisible by _2, 5, 10_

Directions: Tell what numbers each of these numbers is divisible by.

3,732 _2, 3, 4_   439 _—_

50 _2, 5, 10_   444 _2, 3, 4_

7,960 _2, 4, 5, 10_   8,212 _2, 4_

104,924 _2, 4_   2,345 _5_

Page 246

Factor Trees

Factors are the smaller numbers multiplied together to make a larger number. Factor trees are one way to find all the factors of a number.

Example:

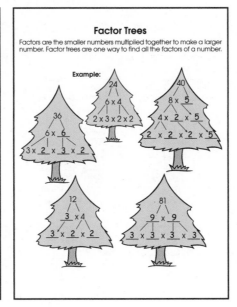

Page 247

Percentages

A percentage is the amount of a number out of 100. This is the percent sign: %

Directions: Fill in the blanks.

Example: 70% = $\frac{70}{100}$ _40_ % = $\frac{40}{100}$

30% = $\frac{30}{100}$ 10% = $\frac{10}{100}$

90% = $\frac{90}{100}$ 40% = $\frac{40}{100}$

70% = $\frac{70}{100}$ 80% = $\frac{80}{100}$

_20_ % = $\frac{20}{100}$ _60_ % = $\frac{60}{100}$

_30_ % = $\frac{30}{100}$ _10_ % = $\frac{10}{100}$

_50_ % = $\frac{50}{100}$ _90_ % = $\frac{90}{100}$

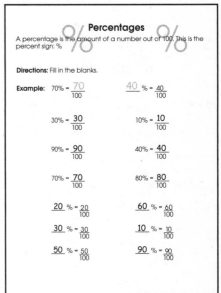

Page 248

Fractions

A fraction is a number that names part of a whole, such as $\frac{1}{2}$ or $\frac{1}{3}$.

Directions: Write the fraction that tells what part of each figure is colored. The first one is done for you.

Example:
2 parts shaded
5 parts in the whole figure

$\frac{1}{3}$ $\frac{1}{2}$ $\frac{3}{4}$

$\frac{5}{9}$ $\frac{2}{4}$ $\frac{3}{6}$

$\frac{1}{4}$ $\frac{4}{8}$ $\frac{3}{6}$

Page 249

Fractions: Equivalent

Fractions that name the same part of a whole are equivalent fractions.

Example:

$\frac{1}{2} = \frac{2}{4}$

Directions: Fill in the numbers to complete the equivalent fractions.

$\frac{1}{4} = \frac{2}{8}$ $\frac{2}{3} = \frac{4}{6}$

$\frac{1}{6} = \frac{2}{12}$ $\frac{2}{3} = \frac{4}{6}$

$\frac{1}{3} = \frac{4}{12}$ $\frac{1}{5} = \frac{3}{15}$ $\frac{1}{4} = \frac{2}{8}$

$\frac{1}{2} = \frac{3}{6}$ $\frac{2}{3} = \frac{6}{9}$ $\frac{2}{6} = \frac{6}{18}$

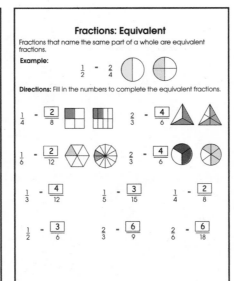

Page 250

Fractions: Division

A fraction is a number that names part of an object. It can also name part of a group.

Directions: Study the example. Divide by the bottom number of the fraction to find the answers.

Example:
There are 6 cheerleaders.
$\frac{1}{3}$ of the cheerleaders are boys.
How many cheerleaders are boys?

6 cheerleaders ÷ 2 groups = 3 boys

$\frac{1}{2}$ of 6 = 3 $\frac{1}{2}$ of 8 = _4_

$\frac{1}{2}$ of 10 = _5_ $\frac{1}{3}$ of 9 = _3_ $\frac{1}{5}$ of 10 = _2_

$\frac{1}{4}$ of 12 = _3_ $\frac{1}{8}$ of 32 = _4_ $\frac{1}{3}$ of 27 = _9_

$\frac{1}{5}$ of 30 = _6_ $\frac{1}{2}$ of 14 = _7_ $\frac{1}{9}$ of 18 = _2_

$\frac{1}{6}$ of 24 = _4_ $\frac{1}{3}$ of 18 = _6_ $\frac{1}{10}$ of 50 = _5_

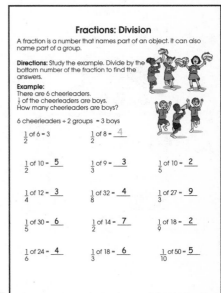

Page 251

Fractions: Comparing

Directions: Circle the fraction in each pair that is larger.

Example:

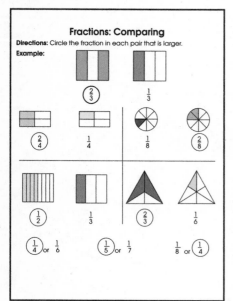

Page 252

Decimals

A decimal is a number with one or more numbers to the right of a decimal point. A decimal point is a dot placed between the ones place and the tens place of a number, such as 2.5.

Example:

$\frac{3}{10}$ can be written as .3   They are both read as three-tenths.

Directions: Write the answer as a decimal for the shaded parts.

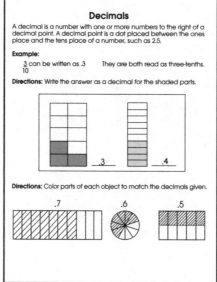

.3   .4

Directions: Color parts of each object to match the decimals given.

.7   .6   .5

Page 253

Decimals

A decimal is a number with one or more numbers to the right of a decimal point, such as 6.5 or 2.25. Equivalent means numbers that are equal.

Directions: Draw a line between the equivalent numbers.

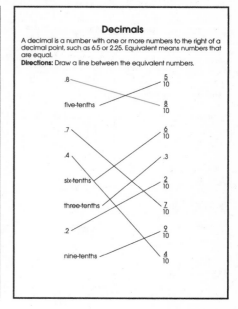

.8 — $\frac{5}{10}$
five-tenths — $\frac{8}{10}$
.7 — $\frac{6}{10}$
.4 — .3
six-tenths — $\frac{2}{10}$
three-tenths — $\frac{7}{10}$
.2 — $\frac{9}{10}$
nine-tenths — $\frac{4}{10}$

Page 254

Decimals Greater Than 1

Directions: Write the decimal for the part that is shaded.

Example: $2\frac{4}{10}$

Write: 2.4   Read: two and four-tenths

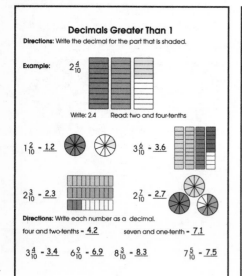

$1\frac{2}{10}$ - **1.2** $3\frac{6}{10}$ - **3.6**

$2\frac{3}{10}$ - **2.3** $2\frac{7}{10}$ - **2.7**

Directions: Write each number as a decimal.

four and two-tenths = **4.2**   seven and one-tenth = **7.1**

$3\frac{4}{10}$ - **3.4** $6\frac{9}{10}$ - **6.9** $8\frac{3}{10}$ - **8.3** $7\frac{5}{10}$ - **7.5**

Page 255

Decimals: Addition and Subtraction

Decimals are added and subtracted in the same way as other numbers. Simply carry down the decimal point to your answer.

Directions: Add or subtract.

Examples:

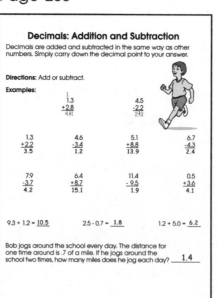

```
  1
 1.3          4.5
+2.8         -2.2
 4.1          2.3
```

```
 1.3      4.6      5.1      6.7
+2.2     -3.4     +8.8     -4.3
 3.5      1.2     13.9      2.4
```

```
 7.9      6.4     11.4      0.5
-3.7     +8.7     - 9.5     +3.6
 4.2     15.1      1.9      4.1
```

9.3 + 1.2 = **10.5**   2.5 - 0.7 = **1.8**   1.2 + 5.0 = **6.2**

Bob jogs around the school every day. The distance for one time around is .7 of a mile. If he jogs around the school two times, how many miles does he jog each day?   **1.4**

Page 256

Patterns

Directions: Write the one that would come next in each pattern.

0 2 0 4 0 6   **0**

1 3 5 7 9 11   **13**

5 10 20 40 80   **160**

▽ □ ▷ □ ▽ □   ▷

◇ □ ▽ ◇ □ ▽   ◇

○ ○ ● ● ○ ○   ●

1 A 2 B 3 C   **4**

A B C 1 2 3   **D**

Page 257

Pattern Maze
Directions: Follow the pattern: ● ■ ▲ ☆ to get through the maze.

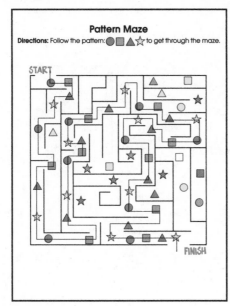

Page 258

Geometry
Geometry is the branch of mathematics that has to do with points, lines and shapes.

cube   rectangular prism   cone   cylinder   sphere

Directions: Use the code to color the picture.

Color:
cubes — blue
rectangular prisms — red
cones — green
cylinders — yellow
spheres —orange

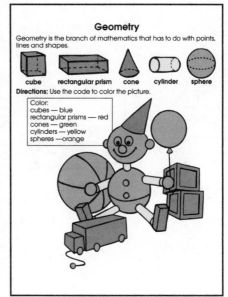

Page 259

Tangram
Directions: Cut out the tangram below. Use the shapes to make a cat, a chicken, a boat and a large triangle.

Page 261

Geometric Coloring
Directions: Color the geometric shapes in the box below.

Page 262

Geometry: Lines Segments, Rays, Angles
Geometry is the branch of mathematics that has to do with points, lines and shapes.

A **line** goes on and on in both directions. It has no end points.

Line CD

A **segment** is part of a line. It has two end points.

Segment AB

A **ray** has a line segment with only one end point. It goes on and on in the other direction.

Ray EF

An **angle** has two rays with the same end point.

Angle BAC

Directions: Write the name for each figure.

line   ray   segment

line   angle   line

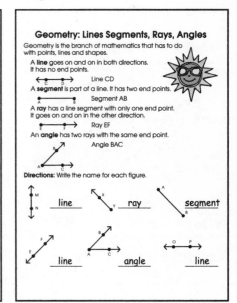

Page 267

Geometry: Perimeter

The perimeter is the distance around an object. Find the perimeter by adding the lengths of all the sides.

Directions: Find the perimeter for each object (ft. = feet).

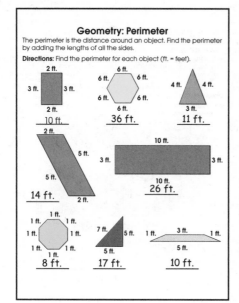

2 ft.
3 ft. 3 ft.
2 ft.
__10 ft.__

6 ft.
6 ft. 6 ft.
6 ft. 6 ft.
6 ft.
__36 ft.__

4 ft. 4 ft.
3 ft.
__11 ft.__

2 ft.
5 ft.
5 ft.
__14 ft.__
2 ft.

10 ft.
3 ft. 3 ft.
10 ft.
__26 ft.__

1 ft.
1 ft. 1 ft.
1 ft. 1 ft.
1 ft. 1 ft.
1 ft.
__8 ft.__

7 ft. 5 ft.
5 ft.
__17 ft.__

1 ft. 3 ft. 1 ft.
5 ft.
__10 ft.__

Page 268

Flower Power

Directions: Count the flowers and answer the questions.

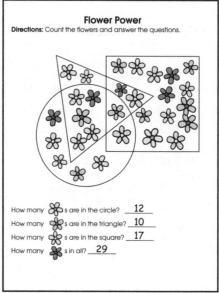

How many ❀s are in the circle? __12__

How many ❀s are in the triangle? __10__

How many ❀s are in the square? __17__

How many ❀s in all? __29__

Page 269

Map Skills: Scale

A **map scale** shows how far one place is from another. This map scale shows that 1 inch on this page equals 1 mile at the real location.

Directions: Use a ruler and the map scale to find out how far it is from Ann's house to other places. Round to the nearest inch.

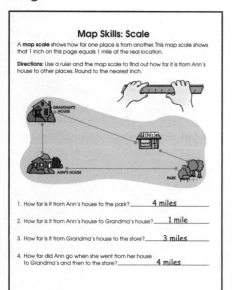

1. How far is it from Ann's house to the park? __4 miles__

2. How far is it from Ann's house to Grandma's house? __1 mile__

3. How far is it from Grandma's house to the store? __3 miles__

4. How far did Ann go when she went from her house to Grandma's and then to the store? __4 miles__

Page 270

Map Skills: Scale

Directions: Use a ruler and the map scale to measure the map and answer the questions. Round to the nearest inch.

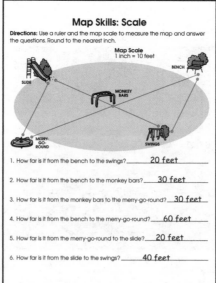

Map Scale
1 inch = 10 feet

1. How far is it from the bench to the swings? __20 feet__

2. How far is it from the bench to the monkey bars? __30 feet__

3. How far is it from the monkey bars to the merry-go-round? __30 feet__

4. How far is it from the bench to the merry-go-round? __60 feet__

5. How far is it from the merry-go-round to the slide? __20 feet__

6. How far is it from the slide to the swings? __40 feet__

Page 271

Graphs

A graph is a drawing that shows information about numbers.

Directions: Color the picture. Then tell how many there are of each object by completing the graph.

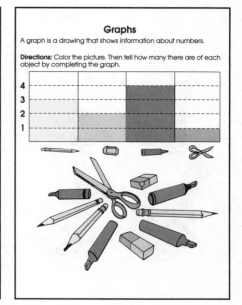

Page 272

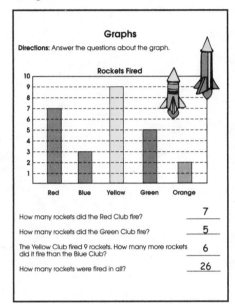

Graphs

Directions: Answer the questions about the graph.

Rockets Fired

How many rockets did the Red Club fire? **7**

How many rockets did the Green Club fire? **5**

The Yellow Club fired 9 rockets. How many more rockets did it fire than the Blue Club? **6**

How many rockets were fired in all? **26**

Page 273

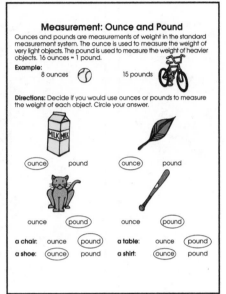

Measurement: Ounce and Pound

Ounces and pounds are measurements of weight in the standard measurement system. The ounce is used to measure the weight of very light objects. The pound is used to measure the weight of heavier objects. 16 ounces = 1 pound.

Example:
8 ounces   15 pounds

Directions: Decide if you would use ounces or pounds to measure the weight of each object. Circle your answer.

(ounce)   pound   (ounce)   pound

ounce   (pound)   ounce   (pound)

a chair: ounce   (pound)   **a table:** ounce   (pound)

a shoe: (ounce)   pound   **a shirt:** (ounce)   pound

Page 274

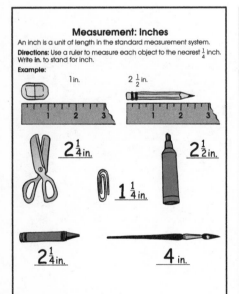

Measurement: Inches

An inch is a unit of length in the standard measurement system.

Directions: Use a ruler to measure each object to the nearest $\frac{1}{4}$ inch. Write **in.** to stand for inch.

Example:
1 in. $2\frac{1}{2}$ in.

$2\frac{1}{4}$ in. $2\frac{1}{2}$ in.

$1\frac{1}{4}$ in.

$2\frac{1}{4}$ in.   4 in.

Page 275

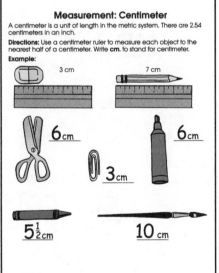

Measurement: Centimeter

A centimeter is a unit of length in the metric system. There are 2.54 centimeters in an inch.

Directions: Use a centimeter ruler to measure each object to the nearest half of a centimeter. Write **cm.** to stand for centimeter.

Example:
3 cm   7 cm

6 cm   6 cm

3 cm

$5\frac{1}{2}$ cm   10 cm

Page 276

Measurement: Foot, Yard, Mile

Directions: Decide whether you would use foot, yard or mile to measure each object.

1 foot = 12 inches
1 yard = 36 inches or 3 feet
1 mile = 1,760 yards

length of a river **miles**

height of a tree **yard or foot**

width of a room **foot**

length of a football field **yard**

height of a door **foot**

length of a dress **foot**

length of a race **yard or mile**

height of a basketball hoop **foot**

width of a window **foot**

distance a plane travels **mile**

Directions: Solve the problem.

Tara races Tom in the 100-yard dash. Tara finishes 10 yards in front of Tom. How many feet did Tara finish in front of Tom? **30 ft.**

Page 277

Measurement: Meter and Kilometer

Meters and kilometers are units of length in the metric system. A meter is equal to 39.37 inches. A kilometer is equal to about $\frac{5}{8}$ of a mile.

Directions: Decide whether you would use meter or kilometer to measure each object.

1 meter = 100 centimeters
1 kilometer = 1,000 meters

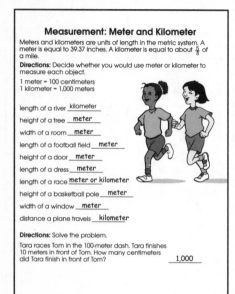

length of a river __kilometer__

height of a tree __meter__

width of a room __meter__

length of a football field __meter__

height of a door __meter__

length of a dress __meter__

length of a race __meter or kilometer__

height of a basketball pole __meter__

width of a window __meter__

distance a plane travels __kilometer__

Directions: Solve the problem.

Tara races Tom in the 100-meter dash. Tara finishes 10 meters in front of Tom. How many centimeters did Tara finish in front of Tom? __1,000__

Page 278

Coordinates

Directions: Locate the points on the grid and color in each box.

What animal did you form? __Answers will vary.__

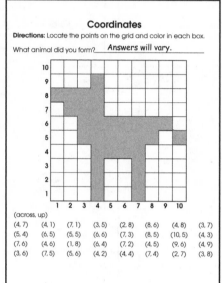

(across, up)

(4, 7)	(4, 1)	(7, 1)	(3, 5)	(2, 8)	(8, 6)	(4, 8)	(3, 7)
(5, 4)	(6, 5)	(5, 5)	(6, 6)	(7, 3)	(8, 5)	(10, 5)	(4, 3)
(7, 6)	(4, 6)	(1, 8)	(6, 4)	(7, 2)	(4, 5)	(9, 6)	(4, 9)
(3, 6)	(7, 5)	(5, 6)	(4, 2)	(4, 4)	(7, 4)	(2, 7)	(3, 8)

Page 279

Roman Numerals

Another way to write numbers is to use Roman numerals.

I	1	VII	7
II	2	VIII	8
III	3	IX	9
IV	4	X	10
V	5	XI	11
VI	6	XII	12

Directions: Fill in the Roman numerals on the watch.

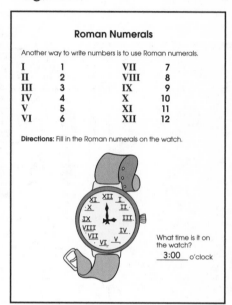

What time is it on the watch?

__3:00__ o'clock

Page 280

Roman Numerals

I	1	VII	7
II	2	VIII	8
III	3	IX	9
IV	4	X	10
V	5	XI	11
VI	6	XII	12

Directions: Write the number.

V __5__   VII __7__

X __10__   IX __9__

II __2__   XII __12__

Directions: Write the Roman numeral.

4 __IV__   5 __V__

10 __X__   8 __VIII__

6 __VI__   3 __III__

Page 281

Time: Hour, Half-Hour, Quarter-Hour, 5 Min. Intervals

Directions: Write the time shown on each clock.

Example:

7:15   7:00

8:35   9:00   10:15

4:15   2:00   11:45

1:30   7:10   3:45

Page 282

Time: a.m. and p.m.

In telling time, the hours between 12:00 midnight and 12:00 noon are a.m. hours. The hours between 12:00 noon and 12:00 midnight are p.m. hours.

Directions: Draw a line between the times that are the same.

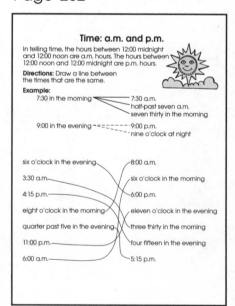

Example:

7:30 in the morning — 7:30 a.m.
— half-past seven a.m.
— seven thirty in the morning

9:00 in the evening — 9:00 p.m.
— nine o'clock at night

six o'clock in the evening — 8:00 a.m.

3:30 a.m. — six o'clock in the morning

4:15 p.m. — 6:00 p.m.

eight o'clock in the morning — eleven o'clock in the evening

quarter past five in the evening — three thirty in the morning

11:00 p.m. — four fifteen in the evening

6:00 a.m. — 5:15 p.m.

Page 283

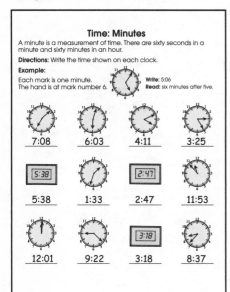

Time: Minutes

A minute is a measurement of time. There are sixty seconds in a minute and sixty minutes in an hour.

Directions: Write the time shown on each clock.

Example:

Each mark is one minute.
The hand is at mark number 6.

Write: 5:06
Read: six minutes after five.

7:08   6:03   4:11   3:25

5:38   1:33   2:47   11:53

12:01   9:22   3:18   8:37

Page 284

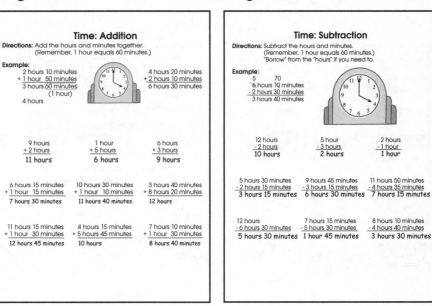

Time: Addition

Directions: Add the hours and minutes together.
(Remember, 1 hour equals 60 minutes.)

Example:

2 hours 10 minutes
+ 1 hour 50 minutes
3 hours 60 minutes
(1 hour)
4 hours

4 hours 20 minutes
+ 2 hours 10 minutes
6 hours 30 minutes

9 hours
+ 2 hours
11 hours

1 hour
+ 5 hours
6 hours

6 hours
+ 3 hours
9 hours

6 hours 15 minutes
+ 1 hour 15 minutes
7 hours 30 minutes

10 hours 30 minutes
+ 1 hour 10 minutes
11 hours 40 minutes

3 hours 40 minutes
+ 8 hours 20 minutes
12 hours

11 hours 15 minutes
+ 1 hour 30 minutes
12 hours 45 minutes

4 hours 15 minutes
+ 5 hours 45 minutes
10 hours

7 hours 10 minutes
+ 1 hour 30 minutes
8 hours 40 minutes

Page 285

Time: Subtraction

Directions: Subtract the hours and minutes.
(Remember, 1 hour equals 60 minutes.)
"Borrow" from the "hours" if you need to.

Example:

5   70
6 hours 10 minutes
- 2 hours 30 minutes
3 hours 40 minutes

12 hours
- 2 hours
10 hours

5 hour
- 3 hours
2 hours

2 hours
- 1 hour
1 hour

5 hours 30 minutes
- 2 hours 15 minutes
3 hours 15 minutes

9 hours 45 minutes
- 3 hours 15 minutes
6 hours 30 minutes

11 hours 50 minutes
- 4 hours 35 minutes
7 hours 15 minutes

12 hours
- 6 hours 30 minutes
5 hours 30 minutes

7 hours 15 minutes
- 5 hours 30 minutes
1 hour 45 minutes

8 hours 10 minutes
- 4 hours 40 minutes
3 hours 30 minutes

Page 286

Money: Coins and Dollars

penny = 1¢ or $.01
nickel = 5¢ or $.05
dime = 10¢ or $.10
quarter = 25¢ or $.25
half-dollar = 50¢ or $.50
dollar = 100¢ or $1.00

Directions: Write the amount for each group of money shown. Use a dollar sign and decimal point. The first one is done for you.

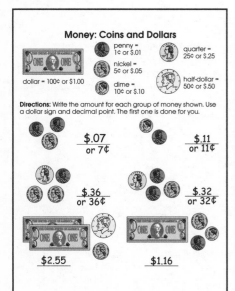

$.07 or 7¢

$.11 or 11¢

$.36 or 36¢

$.32 or 32¢

$2.55

$1.16

Page 287

Money: Five-Dollar Bill and Ten-Dollar Bill

Directions: Write the amount for each group of money shown. Use a dollar sign and decimal point. The first one is done for you.

Five-dollar bill = 5 one dollar bills

Ten-dollar bill = 2 five-dollar bills or 10 one-dollar bills

$15.00

$6.00

$6.35

$16.31

7 one-dollar bills, 2 quarters $7.50

2 five-dollar bills, 3 one-dollar bills, half-dollar $13.50

3 ten-dollar bills, 1 five-dollar bill, 3 quarters $35.75

Page 288

Money: Counting Change

Directions: Subtract the money using decimals to show how much change a person would receive in each of the following.

Example:
Bill had 3 dollars.
He bought a baseball for $2.83.
How much change did he receive?

$3.00
-$2.83
$ .17

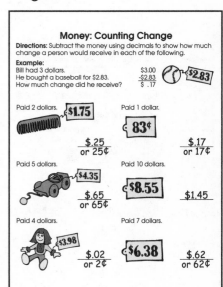

Paid 2 dollars. $1.75

$.25 or 25¢

Paid 1 dollar. 83¢

$.17 or 17¢

Paid 5 dollars. $4.35

$.65 or 65¢

Paid 10 dollars. $8.55

$1.45

Paid 4 dollars. $3.98

$.02 or 2¢

Paid 7 dollars. $6.38

$.62 or 62¢

Page 289

Money: Comparing

Directions: Compare the amount of money in the left column with the price of the object in the right column. Is the amount of money in the left column enough to purchase the object in the right column? Circle yes or no.

Example:

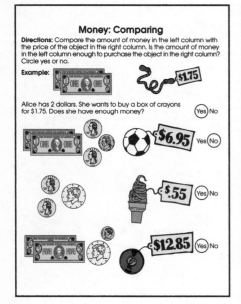

Alice has 2 dollars. She wants to buy a box of crayons for $1.75. Does she have enough money? (Yes) No

$6.95 Yes (No)

$.55 (Yes) No

$12.85 (Yes) No

Page 290

Review

Directions: Complete each clock to show the time written below it.

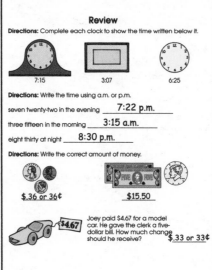

7:15   3:07   6:25

Directions: Write the time using a.m. or p.m.

seven twenty-two in the evening __7:22 p.m.__

three fifteen in the morning __3:15 a.m.__

eight thirty at night __8:30 p.m.__

Directions: Write the correct amount of money.

$.36 or 36¢ $15.50

$4.67 — Joey paid $4.67 for a model car. He gave the clerk a five-dollar bill. How much change should he receive? __$.33 or 33¢__

Page 291

Review

Directions: Read and solve each of the problems.

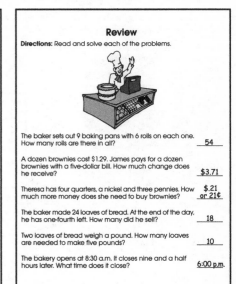

The baker sets out 9 baking pans with 6 rolls on each one. How many rolls are there in all? __54__

A dozen brownies cost $1.29. James pays for a dozen brownies with a five-dollar bill. How much change does he receive? __$3.71__

Theresa has four quarters, a nickel and three pennies. How much more money does she need to buy brownies? __$.21 or 21¢__

The baker made 24 loaves of bread. At the end of the day, he has one-fourth left. How many did he sell? __18__

Two loaves of bread weigh a pound. How many loaves are needed to make five pounds? __10__

The bakery opens at 8:30 a.m. It closes nine and a half hours later. What time does it close? __6:00 p.m.__

Page 292

Review
Place Value

Directions: Write the number's value in each place: **678,421**.

__1__ ones   __6__ hundred thousands
__8__ thousands   __4__ hundreds
__2__ tens   __7__ ten thousands

Addition and Subtraction

Directions: Add or subtract. Remember to regroup, if you need to.

88	46	75	93	76
− 19	+ 39	+ 24	− 68	− 59
69	85	99	25	17

		84	97	
683	855	49	54	9,731
− 496	+ 138	+ 62	+ 361	− 4,664
187	993	195	512	5,067

Rounding

Directions: Round to the nearest 10, 100 or 1,000.

72 __70__   49 __50__   31 __30__   66 __70__
151 __200__   296 __300__   917 __900__   621 __600__

Page 293

Multiplication and Division

3	3	9	9	7
× 6	× 8	× 8	× 5	× 2
18	24	72	45	14

5)25 = **5**   2)6 = **3**   3)18 = **6**   8)24 = **3**   7)49 = **7**

Fractions

$\frac{1}{3}$ of 12 = __4__ $\frac{1}{7}$ of 28 = __4__ $\frac{1}{9}$ of 45 = __5__

Directions: Color parts to match the fractions given.

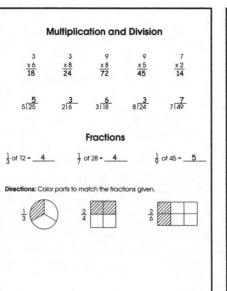

$\frac{1}{3}$ $\frac{2}{4}$ $\frac{2}{6}$

Page 294

Decimals

Directions: Write the decimal for each fraction.

$\frac{4}{10}$ = __.4__ $3\frac{3}{10}$ = __3.3__ $\frac{9}{10}$ = __.9__ $21\frac{3}{10}$ = __21.3__

Directions: Add or Subtract.

8.2 + 1.1 = __9.3__   3.6 − 1.8 = __1.8__   3.9 + 2.6 = __6.5__

Geometry

Directions: Write the name for each figure.

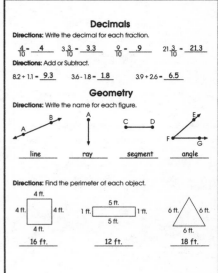

line   ray   segment   angle

Directions: Find the perimeter of each object.

4 ft square (4 ft, 4 ft, 4 ft, 4 ft): __16 ft.__

5 ft rectangle (1 ft, 5 ft): __12 ft.__

6 ft triangle (6 ft, 6 ft, 6 ft): __18 ft.__

Page 295

Graphing

Directions: Answer the questions.

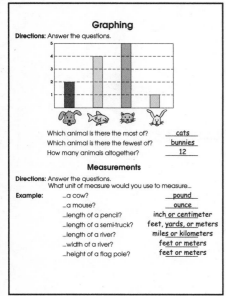

Which animal is there the most of?	cats
Which animal is there the fewest of?	bunnies
How many animals altogether?	12

Measurements

Directions: Answer the questions.
What unit of measure would you use to measure...

Example:

...a cow?	pound
...a mouse?	ounce
...length of a pencil?	inch or centimeter
...length of a semi-truck?	feet, yards, or meters
...length of a river?	miles or kilometers
...width of a river?	feet or meters
...height of a flag pole?	feet or meters

Page 296

Time

Directions: Complete each clock to show the time written below it.

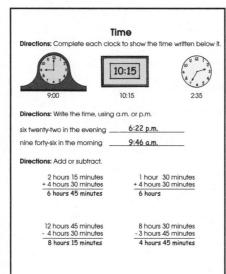

9:00   10:15   2:35

Directions: Write the time, using a.m. or p.m.

six twenty-two in the evening	6:22 p.m.
nine forty-six in the morning	9:46 a.m.

Directions: Add or subtract.

```
  2 hours 15 minutes        1 hour  30 minutes
+ 4 hours 30 minutes      + 4 hours 30 minutes
  6 hours 45 minutes        6 hours

 12 hours 45 minutes        8 hours 30 minutes
-  4 hours 30 minutes      - 3 hours 45 minutes
  8 hours 15 minutes        4 hours 45 minutes
```

Page 297

Problem-Solving: Addition, Subtraction

Directions: Read and solve each problem. The first one is done for you.

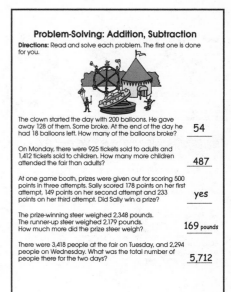

The clown started the day with 200 balloons. He gave away 128 of them. Some broke. At the end of the day he had 18 balloons left. How many of the balloons broke?	54
On Monday, there were 925 tickets sold to adults and 1,412 tickets sold to children. How many more children attended the fair than adults?	487
At one game booth, prizes were given out for scoring 500 points in three attempts. Sally scored 178 points on her first attempt, 149 points on her second attempt and 233 points on her third attempt. Did Sally win a prize?	yes
The prize-winning steer weighed 2,348 pounds. The runner-up steer weighed 2,179 pounds. How much more did the prize steer weigh?	169 pounds
There were 3,418 people at the fair on Tuesday, and 2,294 people on Wednesday. What was the total number of people there for the two days?	5,712

Page 298

Problem-Solving: Multiplication, Division

Directions: Read and solve each problem.

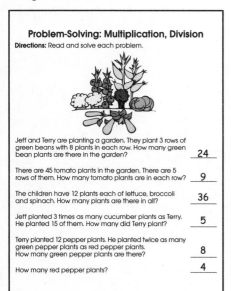

Jeff and Terry are planting a garden. They plant 3 rows of green beans with 8 plants in each row. How many green bean plants are there in the garden?	24
There are 45 tomato plants in the garden. There are 5 rows of them. How many tomato plants are in each row?	9
The children have 12 plants each of lettuce, broccoli and spinach. How many plants are there in all?	36
Jeff planted 3 times as many cucumber plants as Terry. He planted 15 of them. How many did Terry plant?	5
Terry planted 12 pepper plants. He planted twice as many green pepper plants as red pepper plants. How many green pepper plants are there?	8
How many red pepper plants?	4

Page 299

Problem-Solving: Fractions, Decimals

A fraction is a number that names part of a whole, such as $\frac{1}{2}$ or $\frac{1}{3}$.

Directions: Read and solve each problem.

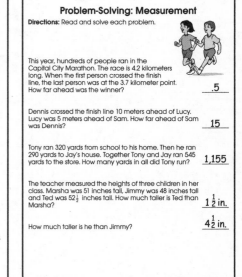

There are 20 large animals on the Browns' farm. Two-fifths are horses, two-fifths are cows and the rest are pigs. Are there more pigs or cows on the farm?	cows
Farmer Brown had 40 eggs to sell. He sold half of them in the morning. In the afternoon, he sold half of what was left. How many eggs did Farmer Brown have at the end of the day?	10
There is a fence running around seven-tenths of the farm. How much of the farm does not have a fence around it? Write the amount as a decimal.	.3
The Browns have 10 chickens. Two are roosters and the rest are hens. Write a decimal for the number that are roosters and for the number that are hens.	.2 roosters .8 hens
Mrs. Brown spends three-fourths of her day working outside and the rest working inside. Does she spend more time inside or outside?	outside

Page 300

Problem-Solving: Measurement

Directions: Read and solve each problem.

This year, hundreds of people ran in the Capital City Marathon. The race is 4.2 kilometers long. When the first person crossed the finish line, the last person was at the 3.7 kilometer point. How far ahead was the winner?	.5
Dennis crossed the finish line 10 meters ahead of Lucy. Lucy was 5 meters ahead of Sam. How far ahead of Sam was Dennis?	15
Tony ran 320 yards from school to his home. Then he ran 290 yards to Jay's house. Together Tony and Jay ran 545 yards to the store. How many yards in all did Tony run?	1,155
The teacher measured the heights of three children in her class. Marsha was 51 inches tall, Jimmy was 48 inches tall and Ted was 52½ inches tall. How much taller is Ted than Marsha?	1½ in.
How much taller is he than Jimmy?	4½ in.

Page 301

Problem-Solving

Directions: Read and solve each problem.

Ralph has $8.75. He buys a teddy bear and a puzzle.
How much money does he have left? $2.17

Kelly wants to buy a teddy bear and a ball. She has $7.25. $.19
How much more money does she need?   or 19¢

Kim paid a five-dollar bill, two one-dollar bills, two quarters,
one dime and eight pennies for a book.
How much did it cost? $7.68

Michelle leaves for school at 7:45 a.m.
It takes her 20 minutes to get there.
On the clock, draw the time that she
arrives at school.

Frank takes piano lessons every
Saturday morning at 11:30.
The lesson lasts for an hour and
15 minutes. On the clock, draw
the time his piano lesson ends.
Is it a.m. or p.m.?
Circle the correct answer.

Directions: Cut out the squares below. Match them to the pictures that are missing these letter-sound combinations.

ai	ea	ee
ie	ou	oo
aw	ow	oa

p__nt	l__f	sh__p
p__	h__se	b__ts
p__	sn___	b__t

Directions: Cut out the squares below. Match them to the pictures that are missing these letter-sound combinations.

mb	au	ph
dge	stle	ight
ew	spl	kn

co___	s__cer	dol__in
bri___	whi_____	n_____
scr__	___ash	__ock

Credits

Lürzer's Archive
**200 Best Ad Photographers
worldwide 20**
ISBN 978-3-902393-90-6

Cover page:
🄾 Jonathan Knowles
✎ Lauren Catten
✏ Jaina Minton
🄲 Getty Images

Customer Happiness: Cora Bundur
cb@luerzersarchive.com

Administration/Editorial Office:
Lürzer GmbH, Keinergasse 29
1030 Vienna, Austria,
phone: (43) 1 715 24 24
submission@luerzersarchive.com

Printers:
AV•ASTORIA Druckzentrum GmbH
Faradaygasse 6
1030 Vienna, Austria
www.av-astoria.at
www.stadtdruckereiwien.at

Publisher & Editor-in-chief:
Michael Weinzettl
CEO: Christian Lürzer
Managing Editor: Christian Hrdlicka
Associate Editor: Natalia Michalak
Art Director: Christine Thierry
Database Assistant: Ovidiu Cristea

Sales Representatives:
Kate Brown, Claudia Coffman,
Diana Dragomir, Sheila King,
Carina Wicke
Sales Assistant:
Cora Bundur

**How to use your Archive –
Guide to symbols:**
🅆 Client
🄰 Advertising Agency
👁 Creative Director
✎ Art Director
✎ Copywriter
🄾 Photographer
✎ Modelmaker
🄲 Illustrator
✏ Digital Artist
✉ Post Production
🄲 Illustrator
🀤 Stylist & Makeup Artist
🝙 Food Stylist

**Contents © 2020 by Lürzer GmbH,
Vienna. FN222125t.**

Submission of work to Lürzer's
Int'l Archive and books of the 200
Best series constitutes representation
that the submitter has the authority to
grant and grants Lürzer's Int'l Archive
the right and permission to reproduce,
edit and comment editorially on all or
any part of the submission in Archive's
editorial section. Lürzer's Archive
assumes no responsibility to return
unsolicited material, and reserves
the right to accept or reject any
advertising material for any reason.

All editorial material reproduced in a
Lürzer's Archive book are categorized
by product, e.g. "Animals."
Product groups are shown alphabeti-
cally. Every editorial page is crossrefer-
enced with an Archive number, the first
two digits indicating the year in which
the special was published, and the
second three digits being continu-
ous page numbers for that particular
product group. For example, 200bph
20.001 under "Animals" indicates
the Volume published in 2020, and
page 1 of that product group.

Distributors:
Argentina: La Paragrafica, tool@paragrafica.com.ar
Australia: Speedimpex, sales@speedimpex.com.au
Brazil: Livraria Freebook Ltda., maria@freebook.com.br;
Casa Ono Com. e Imp. Ltda., casaono@uol.com.br;
Open Books, romeu@openbooks.com.br
Bulgaria: Signcafe, tanya_lefterova@signcafe.bg
Canada: Keng Seng Enterprises Inc., canada@kengseng.com
Chile: Desingbooks Chile, desingbookschile@hotmail.com
Colombia: Foto Colombia, stamayo@fotocolombia.com; Publigra-
phic Ediciones, publigraphic2003@yahoo.com
Costa Rica: BAUM S.A., baumsa@racsa.co.cr
Czech Republic: ADC Czech Republic, info@adc-czech.cz
Denmark: Creas, lis@creas.com
El Salvador: Publicidad Comercial, La Libertad,
urodriguez@pcomercial.com
Finland: Suomalainen Kirjakauppa,
tom.nordstrom@suomalainenkk.fi
Georgia: Parnasus Books, info@parnasi.ge
Germany: Lürzer's Archive, office@luerzersarchive.com,
LuerzersArchive.com/shop
Ghana: Chini Africa, archive.africa@chinionline.com
Hong Kong: Keng Seng Trading & Co. Ltd.,
lawrence@kengseng.com
Hungary: Librotrade Kft., periodicals@librotrade.hu;
Kreativ, vandora@kreativ.hu
India: SBD, sbds@bol.net.in
Indonesia: Basheer Graphic Books, abdul@basheergraphic.com
Iran: Vijeh Nashr, info@vijehnashr.com
Israel: DraftFCB, ehasson@draftfcb.co.il
Italy: Eliesette, eliesette@eliesette.com;
RED, info@redonline.it
Japan: Nippon IPS Co. Ltd., dip_inquiry@nippan-ips.co.jp
Korea: Yi Sam Sa, yss23k@kornet.net
Latvia: Valters un Rapa, santa@valtersunrapa.lv
Lebanon: Levant International, t.balmain@levantgroup.com
Malaysia: The Other Bookstore, hajaothebookstore@yahoo.com
Mexico: Rolando de la Piedra, hosrapb@prodigy.net.mx
Netherlands/Belgium: Bruil & Van de Staaij, info@bruil.info
Nigeria: Chini Africa, archive.africa@chinionline.com
Norway: Luth & Co/Font Shop, info@luth.no
Pakistan: Liberty Books, info@libertybooks.com
Panama: Latin Magazine Group, csmith@publicist.com
Peru: Librería Mediatica, isabel@arcadiamediatica.com
Poland: VFP Communications, piotr.lukowski@media.com.pl
Portugal: Marka Lda., apoio.clientes@marka.pt;
belmiro@mail.telepac.pt; Magkiosk lda., email@magkiosk.com
Romania: Prior Books, ion.arzoiu@prior.ro
Singapore: Basheer Graphic Books, abdul@basheergraphic.com;
Page One, pageone@singnet.com.sg
Slovakia: Dual Production s.r.o., la@dual.sk; Archive F.K., pred-
plathe@predplatne.net
South Africa: Pulpbooks, janita@pulpbooks.co.za;
Chini Africa, archive.africa@chinionline.com
Spain: Bibliopolis Libros, bibliopolisilibros@hotmail.com; Graphic-
book, risto@graphicbook.com; Promotora De Prensa, evelaz-
quez@promopress.es
Sri Lanka: Leo Burnett Solutions Inc.,
swarna_goonetilleke@leoburnett.lk
Sweden: Svenska Interpress, info@interpress.se
Taiwan: Far Go Chen Co. Ltd., fargo899@ms35.hinet.net
Thailand: Aluta European Press represented by FPS,
f.p.s.gmbH@t-online.de
Turkey: Alternatif, alternatif@grafiktaplan.com
**United Arab Emirates / Bahrein / Ku-wait / Oman /
Saudi Arabia / Qatar:** MBR Bookshop LLC, ason@emirates.net.ae
United Kingdom / Ireland: Kate Brown, kb@luerzersarchive.com;
Central Books, sasha@centralbooks.com
Uruguay: Graffiti S.R.L., graffiti@fastlink.com.uy
United States: Lürzer's Archive Inc.,
custsvc_archive@fulcoinc.com
Venezuela: Circulo de Creativos: circulocreativovzla@gmail.com
All other countries: Bruil & Van de Staaij, info@bruil.info

For further contact details visit:
LuerzersArchive.us/static/contact/site/distributors